At Loose in the Puckerbrush

Carving out a Homestead in Vermont

Robert Machin

LIBRARY OF CONGRESS

CATALOGING-IN-PUBLICATION DATA

Machin, Robert

At Loose in the Puckerbrush / Robert Machin

Cover Photograph by Ben Machin

ISBN 978-1-936711-60-4

10 9 8 7 6 5 4 3 2 1

Railroad Street Press
394 Railroad St., Suite 2
St. Johnsbury, VT 05819

Dedication

To those living the life and those who aspire to.

Thanks to Michael Sacca, Chris Doyle, Joann Waltermire, Maya Machin, Kate McKenney & John Douglas

Contents

Intro: Can you get here from there?

There is a famous line that every Vermonter hopes to be able to use someday on the smiling inhabitants of a car with out–of-state plates stopping by as he works on his fence along one of the dirt roads among many in the rabbit warrens of dirt roads off the highways, and they roll down the windows and ask please can't you tell us how to get to some place X, and he would reply lugubriously "You can't get there from here" without cracking a smile but inwardly gleeful at the opportunity to recite the magic line. I was able to be the fall-guy in one such scene back when I was a recent arrival and therefore an easy target. I was talking with a little old man who lived by himself at the top of a hill in a little old house along a narrow road which seemed to wander off through the woods beyond and I asked him "Where does this road go?" I noticed the immediate sparkle in his eye and the amusement in his face as he could scarcely believe his luck at being presented the chance to reply – "It ain't going nowheah. Its staying right theah" He then commenced to laugh outright, so happy was he to be given this once-in-a-lifetime opportunity.

The road may be staying right there but the journeys go on and this is the story of a journey into back-to-the-land and through homesteading beyond onto a small piece of land in back-country Vermont with the goal of trying to get there from here even without much of a map. It is also the story of that piece of land, its history, its character and its varied inhabitants; animal, vegetable and mineral. We will wander into tales agricultural, horticultural, silvicultural and get intimate with fire, water and dirt. The story and the journey have their roots in the 1960's and early 70's when it seemed that the whole world was young, idealistic and fed up with the status quo. The U.S. government was hopelessly evil, the corporate world was corrupt, 'busyness' was a waste of a life and the only real truths were art, music, free love and the earth. The only way out of the stink and corruption was 'back to the land'. The profit motive was out and share the wealth was in. The 'Whole Earth Catalogue' became the bible and Helen and Scott Nearing the prophets of the movement. Agricultural communes sprouted around the globe and marijuana smoke became the holy sacrament. Now, that was our generation -Jo graduated college in 66 and I in 68 – but I was no hippie and neither was she. She was a full-time nurse and I was in the US Army along with a lot of other guys who didn't want to be there. I did my time and was lucky enough to stay out of the horror show that was Vietnam but I wasn't immune to the fervor or the smoke that was in the air and I read the Nearing's book and I 'inhaled' my share. I also had put in a lot of time in and around indigenous and peasant cultures in Latin America while in the army and after. I was a suburban boy, the product of "one of the best educations in the world", and there I was encountering people, illiterate and earth bound, who were way smarter, more savvy and worldly wise than I. I learned plenty from those people about simple man-powered and animal powered agriculture and about all sorts of things I didn't yet know like the history of the U.S. government messing around in Latin America, so, by the time Jo and I got together in 73, I was primed to try homesteading.

'Homesteading' – what exactly are we talking about when we say that? Well, there is no exactly about it but let's see if we can come up with some kind of definition for the sake of discussion. I've been living it forever so by now the term is taken for granted but I realize that for many people it doesn't ring true in today's world. It's too nineteenth century; too western; too "Little House on the Prairie". But, for lack of a better term, homesteading is what the majority of farmers around the world is still doing today. They are dedicated to a wee piece of land that they alone are responsible for in order to feed, clothe and house themselves and their family. It is farming for a living, not for a profit. It's growing your own, making your own, building your own and figuring your own. It's about raising kids away from the shlock. It's by hand and at home. It's living outside the money economy as much as you can get away with. It's about staying out from under fluorescent lights and away from computers. Its farming without tractors and machine power – too expensive of money and time – spare parts, new tires, diesel fuel, endless hours coaxing and cursing – that's a pact with the devil. It's just you depending on yourself. The joy of it is the tremendous challenge you face. Both physical and mental, the challenges are something to get up for every day. Can you figure it and then can you do it? If you have access to plenty of money and/or you plan to earn plenty farming (that is possible!), then why not invest in all the machines and let them do the work? We were not subject to either one of those conditions so we were committed to hand and foot power, animal power and as little buying and selling as we could get by with. The definition of homesteading might be stretched to include living in a commune with like-minded people but we've seen in the past what eventually happens in those situations. Where there is a group, there is politics and where there is politics, there is discord. That was not for us.

Once you have decided to homestead, where do you do it? And what kind of place are you looking for? Once the human race took to farming many millennia ago, they have farmed everywhere and anywhere except on the ice and in the desert. And to this day, uncountable millions are still doing it on a homestead level wherever they find themselves. So I suppose that means that you could homestead just about anywhere. However, given that we have a choice, some places are much more appealing than others. To begin with, I would eliminate any site that depends on irrigation. Consistent and abundant rainfall is a great blessing and I consider it to be the number one priority. Anything below 30"is suspect. Reasonable soil is number two. Granted, you could start with zero fertility and over time, turn it into prime garden soil, but you would rather not begin in a peat bog, or an alkali flat, or a clay field or with rock ledge just below the surface. It would also be helpful to have open meadows available for hay making and pasture. The property should neither be too big nor too small. Too small, that's obvious, you're not going to get what you need. Too big, not so obvious, but can you afford to buy it and continue to pay the taxes and although it must be satisfying to be a land baron, that is not our goal here. Climate choice is a more subjective decision. How hot do you like it? How much winter do you want? Personally I consider the northern winter and cool summer a homestead advantage. Many vegetables, like most greens, don't thrive in high heat and many insect pests are held back by freezing winters. Another consideration would be the availability of trees for construction material and firewood. Another would be the presence of wild harvests, be they fruit, nuts, berries, mushrooms or maple syrup. Another would be microclimate – in the north, you would rather face south and you don't want to be stuck in a 'frost pocket' – that means that a mild side hill would be beneficial, allowing the cold air to drain away during those questionable nights in the spring and fall. And finally, though certainly not exclusively, it would nice to be part of a community with agricultural roots and open minds.

That said, we came to Vermont to begin with not because we considered any of the above factors but because Jo had family connections here. We rented a few places to start – all farm houses – before we started to look for the "right" piece of land on which to homestead. It turned out that Vermont was ideal for us just as it was for the Nearings before they moved to Maine to escape the encroaching tourist tides. They were unlucky in that the surf was rolling in close by their location but the topography of Vermont is such that there are uncountable hidden nooks and pockets all over the state where people have farmed recently or 100 years ago. Even when the 'leaf peepers' are meandering the state in October, you are not likely to run into any off the paved roads. And there are hundreds of miles of dirt roads and trails which come off the highways in the valleys and ruminate their way through forest and field up and over passing homes tucked away everywhere but hardly ever in sight of each other. There are some wide open spaces in the state but these are basically confined to the major valleys to the east and west but even coming out of those, you start to elevate rapidly. Vermont is a mountain state, an Appalachian state, and because of this, historically the farms have tended to be small – the land divided into homestead sized plots which makes it easier for someone looking for just that.

When we decided that Vermont would do and began seriously to search out a place, land prices were not that extravagant. They were on their way up from the depths of the late 50's when the depopulation of the hill country reached its nadir. I met a man who had bought up thousands of acres in the surrounding region for $5 an acre when nobody wanted it. Another man had sold his family farm just over the ridge from us and moved down into Chelsea village because he thought that there was no future out there. They weren't even ploughing the roads and during mud time, you couldn't go anywhere for weeks. The family farmhouse was well built and in good shape when this same $5 man bought it and then hired the ex-owner who had turned to carpentry, to shape it up. Nobody anticipated, except maybe Mr. $5, the explosion of interest in living on the hills and in the back country of Vermont that was occasioned by two factors. First, the building of the interstate highways and second, the influx of the hippies and the back-to-the-landers. I suppose there was also a third factor and that was the ever increasing wealth that was accumulating in the nation after the war and recovery years. Life in the beautiful Vermont landscape was more attractive if you could make a quick trip to Boston or New York whenever, and if you could afford to grade an all-weather driveway to your chosen hilltop. But it really was the 'hippie' factor that created a revolution in the state, the after effects of which are now defining features of life here. The evidence can be most readily seen in the present day politics of Vermont. Historically Vermont voted strictly Republican right down the line but since the 70's, it has voted more Democratic until now it is considered the most "liberal" state in the union. Granted, that style of historical Republicanism would at this writing be considered actually liberal in comparison to today's, but the point is that the back-to-the-landers started something that led to the continuing influx of free-swinging personalities with new ideas and plans to create 'organic' agricultural products. As a result, in our time here, Vermont has become a fermenting hot-bed of delicious niche products renowned for their healthfulness.

Besides the general requirements necessary for a homestead spot, there were a couple of specifics that we insisted on. One was a spring located uphill from a house site and the other was a potential sugar bush – a stand of maples that could be tapped for syrup production. If you were going to homestead in Vermont, almost by definition, you should be making maple syrup. That was one sure way of making a little cash and of course, providing yourself with sugar. And spring water – that was a number one priority. We didn't want anything to do with drilling a well, especially in a place where water is ubiquitous and abundant. We also wanted to avoid electric pumps and pressure tanks. My goal was a direct line between the spring and the spigot powered by gravity. Gravity flow systems are not uncommon in Vermont. The topography favors the method and historically the dairy farms in the valleys have all been located where there is water enough for 30 cows coming down from the hillside above the barn. Most of these farms were located before the advent of electricity but the idea is still good – if the electricity goes down, the water still flows.

O.K. Did we find the perfect homestead site, and were we lucky enough or persistent to the point that we found a place that met all the requirements? What was the place like that became Gingerbrook farm? Perfect might exist somewhere but perfection we did not find, however we have made a life here and it has suited us just fine. What is not perfect we will get to in due course but let's set the scene first. Most of the towns in Vermont were located in the river valleys and that's where, in the bottom land, the first arrived European settlers laid out their farms. The subsequent land hunters followed the water out of the valleys and that's where the roads are, often on top of ancient Indian trails. Where the streams divide, so do the roads, leading to smaller and narrower valleys until the water sources and the road either stops there or trucks on up and over the height of land into another watershed. Our homestead lies in one of those tiny valleys that cradles the source of one of the

tributaries of one of the streams that flows to the White River which flows into the Connecticut River and down to the Atlantic. In fact, the actual brook that we named the Gingerbrook because of the wild ginger which we discovered growing along its banks, sources out of several springs on our land and becomes the tributary of the tributary. The valley is less than a mile wide from ridge to ridge and only a quarter mile flat at

View from the Gingerbrook Bridge

the bottom, and from the confluence at the entrance to the dead - end of the road is one mile and to the wetland and beaver paradise which is the source of the stream, is a mile and a half. The valley runs almost exactly north - south like the topography throughout the state. Traveling east – west in Vermont is almost always an uphill-downhill challenge and the only sideways route out of our valley is on a four wheel drive lane going west which forms our northern boundary. The height of land at the head of the valley is very close to a three-way divide which sheds the rainfall not only south to the White River, but north to the Winooski, Lake Champlain, the St. Lawrence and out to the Atlantic and also east to the Waits river and the Connecticut to the Atlantic. The road up the valley lies on the west side of the stream and the homestead is on the west side of the road, starting about ½ mile up from the confluence. There is very little flat land anywhere in this narrow valley and what we have of it is a two acre strip no more than 100ft wide right along the road. The rest of the piece tilts up from the southeast corner next to the road to the northwest by the lane at a mostly moderate incline until you hit the hillside which faces due east and rises from 1500 ft. where the house is to 1800 ft. at the top of the ridge. The village of Chelsea is only 4 ½ miles distant but 600 ft. downhill. When we sustain a severe thunderstorm, all the water quickly arrives in Chelsea leading to occasional flooding. Between the roadside strip and the hill is a five acre marsh created by centuries of outwash from the gingerbrook resulting in a thick over layer of peat on top of a clay hardpan. I have channeled the brook through the marsh one shovel wide until it goes underneath the southern fence, through a culvert under the road and out. The marsh still remains pretty marshy however, continuing to grow cattails, joe pye and boneset as the peat sucks up and holds onto various seepages off the hillside. The marsh is one of the aforementioned less-than-perfect aspects to the homestead. Agriculturally, that is. It's a habitat and that's good but perfectly, it would be the hayfield which we don't have.

Altogether, the homestead measures 50 acres in the shape of a trapezoid. The western line on top of the ridge is parallel to the eastern along the road. The southern is at right angles to those two and the northern follows the lane meandering northwest. Of that, 10 acres are farmed or lived on and 35 acres are forest. If we go back and look again at the requirements for a homestead and compare, this one scores pretty high. It opens to the south and the only frost pocket is the marsh which sits below our agricultural zone so no problem there. There is indeed a good stand of sugar maple comprising maybe 95% of the trees on the hill from which we have drawn countless gallons of syrup. There is spring water abundant above the house which gravitates to us. There is wood of many varieties available for construction projects and firewood. The soil type is pretty good. It qualifies as sandy loam, drains well and incorporates tons of organic material that we have added. There is not enough pasture land to keep as many animals as perhaps we would want and no hay land, but was that not a blessing in disguise? We will look into that question later. And 50 acres has turned out to be a good size for a homestead. It provides plenty but is small enough that I have trodden every square foot at some point and am on a first-name basis with most of our trees.

We arrived on the property in 1978. It was abandoned farmland. By that time it had been abandoned twice over. The original homesteaders had left evidence of their endeavors as two partially filled-in cellar holes, a house in the middle of the strip on our side of the road and a barn, opposite on the other side. The last inhabitants of those buildings departed after a terminating fire and the land began to revert to forest. By 1930, a neighboring farmer was roaming his cows through there as auxiliary pasture and by the middle 50's, he was gone and the land could abide by its own seasonal rhythms until we arrived.

This was a typical scenario for these marginal, hill country zones in Vermont. I am counting as I sit here and I come up with at least 6 cellar holes close by around the circumference of our property. All of them have crumbled in, have no evidence of any building material in them, and are growing trees out of their rubble. The properties around these cellar holes that would have been farms are now contiguous forest. There was a great disappearance out of this area just as there was throughout Vermont. There had also been a great influx of settlers once things opened up for the English colonials. Vermont has a history somewhat separate from the rest of New England. It was no-man's land between French Canada and English Massachusetts and Connecticut, and the Yorkers' New York and the Yankees' New Hampshire. It wasn't until after the peace treaty of 1763 ending the French and Indian Wars, more than 100 years after the settlement of the rest of New England, that English settlers began to pour into the area that became Vermont. It was like pulling the cork out of the bottle – Vermont became a state in 1791 when the population was 85,539 and by 1800, it had exploded to 154,465. In 1811, William Jarvis, who had been a diplomat in Spain, introduced the Merino sheep into the state at his farm along the Connecticut River, and by 1840, there were 1,681,000 sheep in Vermont. The state went from completely forested, except for some native corn fields east and west in the Champlain and Connecticut valleys, to denuded as settlers moved into any available land, cut the trees and jumped on the sheep bandwagon. But the Erie Canal was completed in 1825 and the railroads were headed west and by the time the civil war was done, the sheep bubble had burst in Vermont and everybody pulled out and headed west too. Those who remained were those who owned the bigger farms in the fertile valley bottoms and they switched from sheep to cows and Vermont was on its way to becoming known as a dairy state. The village of Chelsea today has a lot less going on than it did in 1824. Then it had two gristmills, five sawmills, two fulling mills, two clothier works, two carding machines, a small woolens factory, two trip hammer shops, two tanneries, three stores and a tavern. Today it has a court house, two gas stations, two stores and a breakfast and lunch eatery, and just about everybody commutes somewhere else to work.

By the time we showed up, our 50 acres had hardly any open land on it. After its presumed sheep time, it had been a side hill pasture for cows for a while and then left to its lonesome. The steep hill side had evidently been fenced off from the cows because it was wooded with 75 year old maple and ash but the rest was covered with what is known in the vernacular as "puckerbrush". Puckerbrush is young growth so dense you have to wade to get through it and in this case, it was comprised of maple, birch, ash, balsam fir, white pine and populus tremuloides – otherwise known as popple – all saplings 2"-3" thick and 20ft tall interspersed with old wild apple trees. Where the popple had got going sooner, and it is famous for taking over open land, it was 40ft tall and 8" in diameter. There was quite a lot of it tall and straight and it was going to turn out to be very useful to us. The northern boundary along the lane was lined with old maples, some of them having barbed wire cutting through them, and below them was a section so nutrient poor that nothing but lichens covered the soil. Here, a curiosity to be seen around 3 or 4 wild apple trees, tenacious survivors that they are, were perfectly defined circles just to their drip lines, of a dense growth of skinny maple saplings coming up through the apple branches and topping them by 5 or 10 feet. The lichen tundra offered no future to the maple seeds but the fallen apple mulch represented opportunity. I got to thinking that this little curiosity wouldn't be seen today because of the deer. Any fallen apples left on the ground today disappear rapidly. That leads you to the conclusion that the deer population had also plummeted as a result of the 'great denuding' and as the forest came back, so did the deer.

Another curiosity of the place which really caught my fancy was the discovery, while we were first walking the land, of a stoned-in spring down along the gingerbrook. It was intact, three feet deep with plenty of organic detritus on the bottom but the water was clear and cold. The really interesting thing about this spring was a wooden pipe plugged into the stone work draining the water down and out. It was 4" in diameter and just a short section remained, the rest having long ago rotted away. This spring is about 150 yards above that cellar hole by the road. Now we are talking serious history. Wooden pipe goes way back used by people either too poor to buy metal pipe or used before metal pipe was available. Making wooden pipe is a difficult and tedious process involving a long-handled auger. It was made in lengths of approximately four feet and the ends were maled and femaled in order to fit together snugly. It is hard to imagine somebody making 150 yards of it, so I suppose that they stopped somewhere convenient and filled buckets to carry to the house but there is no evidence either way. However there is evidence of another family along the way who wanted no part of trucking buckets of water and decided to modernize by putting in lead pipe. The lead pipe is visible inside the wooden and I know it went all the way down to the house because I came upon a section while digging a channel through the marsh for the brook. Before we set up our own water system, we used that same spring for drinking, washing and as a refrigerator. At that point it was I who was carrying buckets from that spring 150 years after them, feeling myself to be carrying an historical tradition and feeling myself to be plenty weary.

All right! Here we are with deed in hand; now what do we do? What's the plan? The entourage consists of four children, two mules, four goats, a bunch of chickens, ducks and turkeys; Buster, the out-of-Texas '54 Chevy; Two-Ton Tony a '52 Dodge; and a '64 Rambler station wagon. We have ourselves a challenge and the concise plan is: 1- build a house to live in and 2- clear land for grass and garden, and 3 – do it all ourselves and right away. Pretty straightforward plan you might say. Can't see a cloud in the sky; let's just do it. How did it go? The answer to this question is what this story is all about. Things will happen in this story as they do in every story – things that are surprising, things that are traumatic and things that are wonderful. There are many trails that wander off the main path that we might investigate and there are many characters that might make an appearance. The land itself is the main character and it made the first decisions easy. The SSW slope begged to have a house dug into it and exactly where was decided when I was pushing through the puckerbrush one day and just about bumped into the trunk of an enormous maple which I hadn't been able to see from any vantage point and 20ft further I bumped into another. Shade in the summer and sunlight after leaf fall on into the winter – the spot for the house should be right behind those two maples. The acreage in front of that sloped all the way down to the marsh following a contour from SE to SW and that looked right to terrace in our gardens. With those two main decisions made for us, we could proceed with the plan and all the others might fall in place or they might become a place in which to fall.

150 Year Old Maples in Front of House

BUSTER

Our story begins in Texas and we are going to begin it with Buster. Buster was and is a truck. But not just any old truck. A kind of special truck to which special things have happened. A Black Beauty kind of truck who has led a Black Beauty kind of life and has his own story that intersects with ours and carries us onward. The first time I saw Buster, he was sitting in the Austin city dump just on the outskirts of town beside one of those highways heading west. This was before the recycling era and everything just got dumped there and pushed into fetid, steaming piles. It was early summer, already topping 100°, and I was in Austin enrolled at the university taking advantage of the G.I. bill, having, thank God, recently split the U.S. army. It was 1972 and Buster was a 1954 Chevrolet pickup not even 20 years old yet but already a classic. He was bruised, beat-up and dented with a fading light green paint job but he had those curved rear cab windows and seemed to be dealing with his present circumstances with the quiet dignity of an old warrior. The present owner of the truck and curator of the dump, who also lived there with his fly-blown old crone of a wife in a dwelling that was indistinguishable from the general debris, put his finger in each bullet hole 1,2,3 and told me the history while intimating that he wasn't going to sell such a Gen-U-Wine truck to no Yankee. The man he would sell it to had to be the right man, not just any man (looking askance at me) and it would cost him considerable. The bullet holes were put in the driver's side by the game warden who had already warned that no-good-deer-jacking scofflaw Buster (for whom the truck was named) and when he caught him in the act one night and Buster paid him no heed and floored it, the warden shot three times (this being Texas). The last bullet hit him in the back, putting him out of the deer business and out of this story to be replaced by Buster the truck. Which truck still sports those holes and the chrome plated swiveling spot light which only deer-jackers and cops usually have. But I figured that just maybe the curator of the dump couldn't resist the lure of cash-on-the-barrelhead so when I presented him with a wad of twenties totaling $200, he grumbled the whole time how I didn't deserve that gen-u-wine truck, being the obvious godamn liberal Yankee that I was but he took the money and the day I went to pick up Buster was the day Jo arrived from Vermont with her two kids and a cat.

Buster with bullet holes and jacking light.

Jo probably didn't count on driving 2,000 miles to spend her first day in the city dump and maybe wondered what exactly she was in for but there I was with an old truck and a new family and we never looked back. I was as ignorant about family as I was about old trucks but Jo took care of the one and Buster looked after the other. I had never subscribed to that adolescent American passion for messing with automobiles so Buster just had to keep rolling on his own volition. I knew Buster had a mind of his own when, after driving an overnight flat dump tire to the local gas station every morning looking for air, one morning that tire was miraculously hard so we set out like children of Eden for the mountains of New Mexico. The brochure, mysteriously arrived in the mail box, promised us a free pass to heaven if we'd just come and visit to "7,000 ft. cool". So we headed west into the Texas panhandle in the middle of summer driving through the mirage shimmers until we realized Buster was blowing suicidal quantities of black oil onto the highway. We fixed him up good by filling him with a whole case of "motor honey"- the stuff that when you pop the top and hold it upside down, even at 95°, nothing comes out without being encouraged. That kept him humming sweetly to Ruidoso and we bawled up the mountainside to 7.000 ft. cool to collect our free pass when Buster stopped dead in his tracks halfway up. We left him beside the road for the night while we hitchhiked down to the motel which was apparently our gateway to the Promised Land. Buster you trickster, I said to him the next morning, stopping exactly halfway like that, as we freewheeled backward and I slammed the steering wheel over so we did a 180 and that Chevrolet bonnet bird was pointing downhill and feeling like Slim Pickens riding the bomb, we rocketed towards town hoping Buster had his brakes honed. I could hear him chortling as we homed in on the traffic light where the mountain road met the highway and, by the patron saint of General Motors, if that light didn't turn green and the traffic cleared out and we skidded around the corner, kept rolling to the motel, turned in and shivered to a halt right in front of number 8 where Jo and the baby said "Hi".

I could tell Buster was just sitting there grinning to himself like he had engineered he whole thing just for the sheer fun of it so we kept in mind that this truck was a cowboy trickster as we blew the cockroach out of the fuel line, headed home leaving paradise behind and began planning and preparing to Buster our way out of Texas on to the Green Mountain state.

The best reason for keeping old trucks if you're on the homestead is that you yourself can fix them Lift the hood and everything is right there staring you in the face just as plain as a new truck isn't. You can figure it out; you can buy new parts and you can fix the problem and be back on the road without severely depleting your bank account. Try to find one that doesn't have a computer in it. Buster didn't need a computer to tell him what to do but he needed some surgery to keep him from seizing up on the road north. I kept the shop manual open next to me on the ground and solicited advise and sealed him up and then built a tiny house on his back to accommodate ourselves, a baby, and two goats - all of whom we wanted to get to Vermont. The Buster-back-house I put together out of 2x4 and plywood discards from building sites and added two flat side windows out of a '56 station wagon such that the goats could watch the scenery and Americans speeding by on the highway would swerve and fishtail around us, pointing and gabbling. The key to the Buster-back accommodations were two large pieces of plywood hinged together which lay flat so we could sleep front to back, or raised and hooked to keep the goats segregated while Jo and baby could migrate back and forth singly or in tandem through the back window to the front seat. An inner-tube from a truck tire sliced on the bias served nicely to seal the passageway. The very idea of seatbelts never even crossed our minds. The goats were Tulip and kid, who we will talk about later, and they were our milk supply and our investment in animal husbandry. I don't think that they enjoyed the trip but they put up with it displaying the fatalism that their race has acquired from their many-thousand-year association with mankind.

Buster kept the trickster under his hat until we were cruising the highway through St. Louis hoping to air out the goats on the other side of the mighty Mississippi and he stopped dead where the interstate runs 40ft below the actual city streets. I scrambled up the berm to encounter two shirtless and grease covered Chicanos working on their truck and promised them nothing but wouldn't they help? It took them a half-hour to find the entrance ramp and get down there and they rolled up grinning and shouting I trade you trucks and I tell them just a little nudge and I'll pop it in first gear and they knock bumpers and soon we're ramming down the interstate at 40 mph and the boys are whooping and laughing and waving their hats out the window until finally Buster's had enough of fooling around and barges into life and we cross the bridge and set the compass northeast, where he'll have to trade his cowboy hat for a wool cap.

We put the chains on him and hit the snow roads that first winter after we had bought the land and traveled back and forth from our rental, cutting down trees to open things up for the house and transporting firewood back to the home stove. There is a four mile hill climbing out of Chelsea going east and we were Bustering one of those loads there in second gear on the way home when the deputy flipped on his spinning light, slammed his fire-engine-red wrecker around in a 180, boomed back up the hill all smoke and fire jabbing his index finger repeatedly to the side, pull over ye scum, and proceeded to cut us off and run old Buster into the ditch just in case he might pull a fast one on him. He took me to the jail and impounded Buster. The charge? Driving in Vermont with Texas license plates. I could tell Buster was remembering his old scofflaw days and loving every bit of it – the law chasing him again. Deputies especially can get over excited about things but we changed the plates and got back to work and work is what a pickup is all about. Buster was indispensable to the building projects – hauling, pulling and carrying. By this time, the house was off his back and I was cutting the tall, straight popple just around the house site to be used as rafters and joists and they were too much for the mules to pull so Buster yanked those sticks out of there one at a time bulling and jamming through stumps and over rocks until we had them all piled above ready to be skinned and rolled onto the frame. It was a hectic time for Buster transporting everything and everybody and even a kitchen sink so by the time we had put together the first building and winter was coming on fast, he was parked out of the way and due to his grumpiness in the spring, I couldn't raise a spark in him and unaccountably I left him to his dreams. The insidious conspiracy that is time somehow clamored our attention and years passed and Buster stayed right there and his tires began to submerge and the pucker brush grew up around him and slowly the green flash dissolved in the northeastern rain leaving him rusty – solitary, noble and rusty – he was abandoned. I had the same excuse everybody uses in these circumstances – I was just too busy to tend to him. Buildings to construct; corn, beans and squash to grow; babies to father – an endless list, but Buster was not without influence. It was that baby who had Bustered across the continent along with the goats, then coming into driving age and sensing the "cool" factor in tooling around school in that amazing truck, who was to rescue Buster from the clutches of Isaac Newton. Ben got together with Doctor Dan, the rig man, who could fix any rig, human or mechanical, wood, steel, or bone. They filled his cylinders with green snake oil and soon had the engine purring. They changed out the 3 speed transmission for a real one that had a granny gear. Then we scoured the rust and painted him green and he was back on the road. You might laugh at that granny gear but it was the best thing that ever happened to the old boy. The 3 speed was just fine for cruising the flatlands in Texas but having that low, low first gear transformed Buster into a Gen-You-Wine Green Mountain truck. You can crawl up and around these side hills, a load in the back, with the engine just about at idle speed. These days I wonder how I managed to do anything around the place without Buster. Always something to haul, relocate, carry and there he is ready, now with wooden bed and sideboards – somehow he has repositioned himself as king post of the homestead. The canny old cowboy had turned indispensable again. Wasn't a thing you could do but that you had to have Buster for it. The boys loved to joogle on down the dirt roads on some made-up mission, lording it over the pathetic excuses for trucks which cringed on by and just knowing the power of a genuine truck.

Now when Buster gets parked for the winter, not far from the spot where he'd almost disappeared into the pucker brush, and the snow builds up to the bullet holes, and the jacking light dangles at its own peculiar angle, and Buster dreams his slow moving dreams of steel, and he falls into a reverie of cockroaches and old Hereford bulls and wicked, wonderful thunder storms and wild northers come out of the panhandle and hot, buzzing star blasted nights and the light flashes on and there is a doe staring right at him, her big dark eyes with such long lashes, pools that lead him subterranean, her legs a-straddle, her ears cocked, so beautiful; he shivers with anticipation and waits to hear Buster's rifle.

Capers

There are many different breeds of goats in the world just as there are of all the domesticated animals. Some are kept for meat and are correspondingly shorter legged and stout. Others are milkers, and, like dairy cows, are finer boned, slimmer and longer legged. Some are cold country critters like French Alpines and exhibit the same characteristics as other cold-adapted animals – short ears and a thick coat. Others have come out of Africa and have the opposite traits – long ears and a sleek coat. One of these latter breeds is called Nubian. They were popular around Texas in the 70's and we picked up one whose name was Tulip. However, before Tulip, we had experienced the basic goat beginner's tragedy. We had just acquired two white goats only days before we went out on a visit leaving them tethered and coming back, we found them dead and eaten by dogs. The lesson was and is, never tie up a goat but if you must, then never to anything longer than two feet or they will invariably strangle themselves and, if you absolutely have to, always in a place secure from other trouble. Tulip's floppy ears extended to the tip of her nose but the ears of her newborn kids were an inch or so longer in proportion. Nubian kids are one of God's most beautiful creations. They have sparkle eyes, twinkle toes and almost from day one, that bounce around as if they came with springs in their feet. We kept them for a while in a cardboard box overnight in the kitchen of our rental in Austin and when we opened the back door in the morning, they would leap out, skid the corner, bound down the back steps, jump across the small stream and find their mother. One on each side, one to each teat, bump, bump, bump almost lifting her in the air before settling to suck their breakfast. I had grown up a suburban lad and consequently knew nothing about anything and Tulip was my first foray into animal husbandry. Jo had grown up on a dairy farm, but before the day when girls might be expected to participate so she was less clueless than I, but together we were innocent enough to do foolish things and get away without consequences. Before Jo arrived in Austin with her two children, I had discovered for rent an unusual place for a city property where the landlord had trucked in an entire house and plunked it down on some cinder blocks on a flattened space next to a brook/drainage ditch. It was within a couple of acres of wild Johnson grass dotted with Siberian elms and sycamores. In order to drive down in there, I had to beat out the cement curb with a sledge hammer. Heedless of any written or unwritten laws to do with wandering livestock, I let Tulip and kids roam as they would. Perhaps because God is kind to fools, we actually had no trouble with our neighbors and after that brief fenceless idyll in city limits Austin, we packed Tulip and one of her doe kids in Buster along with baby Ben and took those African goats to Vermont where the coming winter promised to provide some –30o nights.

Before finding the land with the Gingerbrook running through it, we rented a two story clapboarded farmhouse adjacent to a nice barn located right on the highway. Tulip was there with her two kids in the barn when we left one day on a mission. Returning home, while still in the driveway, we noticed the front door wide open. Oh, oh. The front door is wide open and when we left, it was closed. The first thing we noticed was that the rubber plant in the foyer had lost its leaves. Then we saw a trail of black pebbles leading right up the stairs. Tulip and kids were in our bedroom jumping and shitting on the double bed. What an outrage and you can be sure that we never told the landlord this story. O goat, trouble is thy middle name! Murphy's Law was written with goats in mind – if it's at all possible, they will do it. Another goat, unrelated to Tulip, I found one day in the upper pasture hanging upside down in an apple tree. She was hanging by a rear hoof, which had caught in a crotch. She had obviously been tempted by low hanging fruit and figured to climb right to it. The leg was broken and we had it splinted and plastered and she eventually recovered.

If you are looking for a milk goat, it is worthwhile to check the teats before bringing her home. It makes the chore of milking much more enjoyable if you can squeeze with your whole hand. Many goats have quite small teats and you can manage by using just thumb and forefinger and stripping out the milk but we were just lucky that Tulip was so endowed and not only did she raise her many kids, she also raised our kids with her milk. Goat's milk does not separate into skim and fat like cow's which is one reason for its health claims but making butter is not possible unless you invest in a separator. We so did at one point however I don't recommend it. Cleaning that separator each time is an extremely tedious chore and the resulting butter comes out pure white. If you seriously want your own butter, get a cow.

 Goats reproduce quickly. They become sexually mature at an unhealthily early age and have a gestation period of about three months. If you want to push them, they can produce two batches of kids in each summer season. Tulip once birthed a perhaps record-setting four kids at one time, so it didn't take long before we were dealing with a herd and a herd is what we wanted. We were looking to clear out the regrowth from the old pastures back to their original edges – either stone walls or obvious lines of large maples - and this was a job for goats. Goats are browsers. They will certainly eat grass but they prefer leaves, buds and bark. The pasture closest to the buildings, about 2 acres, was wall to wall with mostly maple saplings 2" to 3" in diameter and 20ft tall. I fenced off sections at a time with strands of electric, which mostly kept them in as long as there remained visible edibles, and cut down a swath every day for them to defoliate. Anything small enough they skinned and stripped on their own. All this while they provided us with milk products, fertilizing pellets everywhere and extra kids to sell. The saplings, along with some white birch and white pine that had come into the abandoned pasture, were then sliced into firewood when hefty enough and the rest went into brush piles. As the pucker brush came off and the sunlight hit the ground again, the grass began to come back along with broad-leafed weeds and wildflowers. In that field there were, and still are, several large maple trees. One of them blew over in a thunderstorm several years after the field had been goated. We had been hanging sap buckets on it and when I began cutting it up for firewood, I noticed that I had sliced right through some old tap holes mummified inside the trunk, so I sliced again close and came away with a 2" cross section of the tree trunk. Ordinarily a section of maple like this would check wide open within a few days of drying time, so hoping to hold it together, I slathered it with tung oil. That did work and that piece now hangs beautiful on our wall, but the reason for telling you this is because it offers a visual record of high tide and low in that field going back to the beginning of the twentieth century.

One inch thick maple round showing tap holes and scars

By following the tree rings, you see the tree starting out in the open in about 1910, booming right along until ca. 1965 when it really slows down until ca. 1980 when the rings expand dramatically until it came down ca. 1997. Now you could believe that was just a coincidence but by 1980 the goats had cleared out all the pucker brush, that big maple was freed of competition and could then use all the surrounding nutrient for itself.

History seen through growth rings: pt.A=1965. Pt.B=1980

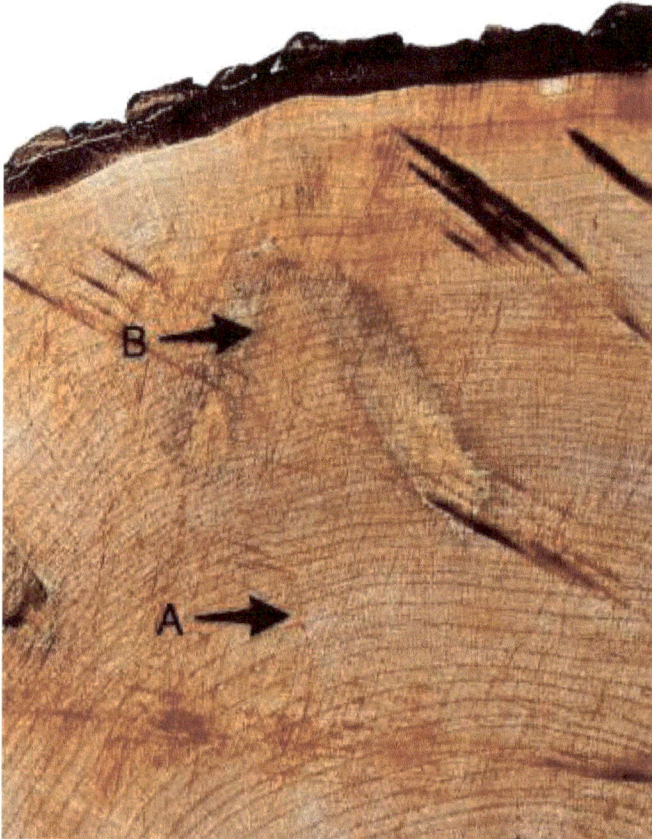

M & M

C.W. seemed like a sad case – a goofy boy seen walking around town in bare feet and hand-me-down clothes. A silly kid who would never amount to anything. Fifty years later and worth a million, he disappeared one day with his money and a younger woman, rumored to be gone to Florida. He left behind his wife, his son and his business – and what a business the silly kid had put together! He figured that people always had things they wanted to sell and there would always be someone else who wanted to buy. All you had to do was to get the two together and take your cut from the transaction. Even a small percentage on each sale multiplied over several decades ends up as serious money. By the time I first walked in on the scene, old C.W., his son and wife and their two sons were running a thriving auction empire. They had set-up an auction barn and yard right off the north-south highway in East Thetford, a small collection of buildings in the Connecticut River valley marking one side of a bridge crossing into New Hampshire. East Thetford is south of North Thetford, east of Thetford Center and down from Thetford Hill, which is actually the town center, attractive in the Vermont way with well-kept large white houses and arching maple trees. The town of Thetford abuts, to the south, the town of Norwich that has become over time a bedroom community for Hanover just across the river in New Hampshire. Being the home of Dartmouth – the college, the medical school and attached regional hospital – Hanover-Norwich radiates gentrification into the surrounding countryside. Doctors, professors and associated well-employed persons, have been buying into and moving into places like Thetford for many years, however, on auction day in East Thetford, you would never know it.

C.W. initially set up his auction business to deal in livestock. The Connecticut River valley through central Vermont and

New Hampshire was quality dairy country and C. W. grew up among farmers. He knew that they always needed to sell newborn bull calves or pick up a new heifer, or get rid of an old cow for some money while she was still on her feet. He provided the venue. Once a week, every Monday, in East Thetford it was auction day and the trucks rolled in bringing cows for sale. That's the way it started, but it soon took on a life and energy of its own. People began bringing in workhorses, then pigs, and goats and sheep and chickens and ducks and geese and guinea hens and pigeons and rabbits. And then, why not old tools? And syrup pans and worn out balers and hay rakes and your 15 year old Chevy because you needed some cash right away; and 5 dozen eggs and 3 crates of oranges you just brought back from Florida. You could bring just about anything semi-farm related to the auction on Monday and go home with some money in your pocket. And there would be canny old C.W. sitting up on the dais chortling and yelping out the numbers and exhorting the money and promising this is a good one boys; what'll ya give for her? It became an irresistible show every Monday and people poured into E. Thetford from the surrounding hills on both sides of the river. Instead of the usual occasional vehicle humming through E. Thetford on Rte. 5, on auction day, there would conglomerate a welter of old pickups, cattle trucks, salt-eaten derelict sedans and horse trailers. Not just the big dairy farmers from the valley, and certainly not the literati magnetized to Hanover, but the salt of the earth came – small farmers and homesteaders and trailer trash came – people who had two beefers, or a pony or three goats or a flock of laying hens all came. Professional buyers and dealers who knew how to buy low and sell high were there. The meat men buying for the slaughter houses were there. Toadies and flunkies and hangers-on, some armed with wooden canes to beat the cows into their pens, were there. Latter day peasants with hands like rawhide, weather ravaged faces, and clothes to match, were there. Such a fermenting brew of humanity to astound and amaze. Never had I seen a flux of faces and bodies like this outside the frames of Jan Bruegal's world. Also was there an occasional lipsticked and rouged woman wearing high leather boots and high hair, perhaps like the one I imagined running C.W. off to Florida.

I watched one Monday as such a female tantalized and beguiled poor Freddie Miller into what, I learned later, was his shame and disgrace. Freddie was a very little man in his fifties, maybe sixty, at the time. He had a strange, misshapen face and a high thin voice and had lived alone all his life. Somewhat of a gnome he was and if you thought about it, you could imagine that he never once had a woman. Easy prey for the lady with the high-heeled boots. And what prey he was! Because the thing about Freddie Miller was that he was rich. He had put together and maintained one of the most extraordinary general stores in the country. It rambled over and under, back and forth and up and down through a big, old building in the tiny burg of E. Topsham and if Freddie didn't have that item, you didn't need it. Every little thing jumbled head to toe from tire chains for a 1939 Reo Power Wagon to a wheel of aged cheddar or a CO_2 fire extinguisher. Freddie had it all and he was canny as a fox. He was notorious for always coming out ahead on his deals. So, after many years of this, Freddie was sitting on quite a fat wad and ripe for the plucking. It was a slow motion train wreck – everybody could see it coming except Freddie. That perfume, that lipstick, and that smile just for him. He married her and on their wedding night, the locals put on a shivaree beneath their window hooting and hollering and banging pots and pans, so Freddie threw them down a shower of cash and she locked him out of their nuptial chamber and was gone by morning soon to be followed by her pot of gold. .

I had started going to the auction, easing Buster in with herd, not just for the anthropology of it all, but to learn what was to learn about local ways and local economies. After a bit of watching and listening, I began to participate somewhat. I bought and sold a few goats. I brought home a mated pair of geese and we hatched some goslings. We bought a spate of ducks to harvest some duck eggs. Small stuff, but I came to be somewhat of a regular there. Then one day a young woman led two ponies into the auction ring. She was crying because she loved these ponies, which she said, were actually mules, and didn't want to let them go, but because of X, Y, and Z. she had to. Their names were Mickey and Maud. They were matched in size and color – dun or light brown with a black stripe down the back. A matched pair of mules! Holy Shit! And she's crying about letting them go! I bid. I bought them for $200. They were twelve hands big – that is 48" high at the shoulder – and had ears about 9" tall that were full of fuzz. Mickey was three years old and Maud was five at the time. The year was 1978. As I write this, we are at 2013 and Maud just recently lay down in the pasture and died. 40 is a ripe old age for an equine. She would have been a centenarian in human years. Mickey met a different fate, but we will get to that later.

At that time, I knew nothing about working with mules, or horses for that matter. I just knew that mules and homesteads just naturally go together. 40 acres and a mule? We had 50 acres and two mules. Whoo-eee! Where to start; was the first question? Well, as the auction moved on with its own momentum, an old boy approached me saying he had a set of harnesses that would fit them little mules. That was the first step but I was so ignorant, I had to study photos of draft teams at work in order to figure how to arrange those harnesses and hitch them up. I wasn't a complete greenhorn with equines. I had ridden cow ponies for a couple of months on a ranch in Brazil. It was owned by the famous King Ranch and they were running imported Texas quarter horses trained so well that all you had to do was point them at the cow in question and hang on. Most of the time you drowsed through the day waiting for some cow to come in heat which you would then cut out of the herd and drive to the inseminator. There was no bull. All the

30

cows were artificially inseminated. They had been hybridized by the King Ranch, were called Santa Gertrudis and were built more like pigs than cows. Nothing but steaks on those critters. They were stocky, fat and brown but, in with them, were kept two Brahmas. Like reincarnations of Ganesh, they were gods suffering life among the riff-raff. Tall and white with hump and horn pointing skyward, they kept themselves apart with dignity and grace and when the vaqueros whistled a certain cadence, they would walk to the open gate and through to the new pasture and all their flock would follow them out. The vaquero's job was to open and close the gate. The cowboys amused themselves by sprinting and then reining their mounts back onto their rumps to see who could leave the longest skid mark. Otherwise, they smoked and drank yerba matte. They hung their matte gourds with silver straws from thongs around their necks and would stop by the corn cribs on the way out early in the morning to put some husk in pocket for rolling cigarettes with tobacco pared off a hard, black, almighty hunk they stored in a leather pouch

Howsoever it went, pretending to be a cow puncher in Brazil wasn't going to qualify as basic training for farming with mules: so gee, haw, whoa and back; who was going to train who, was the question. Maud was handsome, willing and well-proportioned in the mulish way. Mules don't muscle up like horses and have thinner legs, smaller hooves and skinny necks but are very strong in a mysterious way. Mickey, on the other hand, in the words of a friend was "narrow chested, ewe-necked, cow hocked and lazy". She did have a pretty face though and was to prove tough and resilient in her own way. They were both she mules. You can't really call them female because mules are, in a way, sexless. You breed a male donkey (a jack) to a mare and you get a mule. If it happens in reverse, you get a hinny - an animal that, for whatever reason, everyone feels is useless. You can also get a boy mule out of the mix but he is sterile as is the girl. She mules are preferable. They are not as recalcitrant, they are steadier, and they are more willing. But Jack mules are often employed anyway. As an example, there was the big red mule called "El Macho". He teamed with a friend of mine who was in the Peace Corps in Panama. El Macho was beautiful and had a fine temperament and willingly carried my friend up and down the mountain to the Guaymi Indian village where he lived up close to the Costa Rican border. To walk up that mountainside was like climbing a stairway to heaven but going through hell to get there. The trail was a series of muddy pools like mini terraces that had been created by legions of mules and horses plunging one hoof after another up the climb. So the feeling you got riding that Macho and having him carry your baggage too, put you in a closer relationship to God.

If all you want to do with your team is skid logs, you only need a set of harnesses that are good enough not to separate under the immense stress put upon them; padded collars the right size; 4 heel chains about 2 feet long which connect the tugs to the whiffle trees (AKA whipple trees or three piece evener); and a medium duty chain about 10 ft long to come off the center of the evener and hook to the log. The whiffle trees can be made out of lengths of hardwood 2X4s and put together with pieces of steel strapping and specialized hooks. These I was able to figure and duplicate by studying the contents of a big box of busted and rusted and torn and worn pieces of work horse equipment given to me by Eubert, a 90 year old neighbor who had never thrown away anything in his entire life. His last horse had died 10 years prior and the only time he had ever owned a motor car was in the 1920's and he disliked it and never used another. Eubert lived about 5 or 6 miles up out of Chelsea village and he was the last person by many years to drive a horse and wagon to town to pick up supplies. One day he parked beside the hardware and feed store which backed right up against the stream running through the village, and while he was inside, the horse spooked and dragged the wagon down the steep bank into the streambed and proceeded to gallop downstream trying his damnedest to get away from that wagon racketing to pieces behind him, bouncing over cobbles and smashing into boulders. That was far in the past when Eubert invited me into his ancient barn one time to inspect his horse drawn equipment and just at the door, I was banged in the face by one of those big white-faced hornets. Eubert was standing right next to me and said, "Now I don't know why he went and did that. They never bother me at all." Eubert sold me his manure spreader. He asked me what I'd give him for it: I said. How about $25 and he said: That seems fair. He also sold me a one-horse mowing machine and a one-horse disk harrow – that is, they were just right for two little mules.

I was raised to be a fair and liberal minded boy – to treat all people with respect and all animals with kindness. However I had never actually lived with animals-not even a dog or cat- so my notions were based on what I had read in many a childhood book; stories such as The Black Stallion, Old Yeller and The Jungle Books. So, I figured that Mickey, Maud and Bob would have no trouble getting along as long as I talked nice to them, treated them well and explained patiently the nature of the job before us. O.K. guys, let's do it, shall we? Surprisingly, that sort of worked for the first few days until we graduated to a moderately heavy log that had to be pulled across a very innocuous brook in order to get home with it. They stopped there and decided they didn't want to pull that log through that brook. We prefer not to, they said. I attempted to persuade them using logic and rational explanations. They responded by looking around at me and shrugging their shoulders. That's when it hit me – the first of many real-life lessons the homesteading life was to offer – that these mules knew me for a wishy-washy liberal, a no-account easily disregarded – and I realized that I had better damn sure get them going right then and there or go back to reading children's books. So I barked and growled and told them that this was no longer a team of equals; that I was the boss and they were going to damn well do what I told them! They blasted through that brook and we never looked back.

When you are working with a team, whether skidding logs or mowing hay or pulling a sled, you almost always want them to move at a walk. Things just tend to happen that can destroy you, them or the equipment, and the faster you're moving, the less chance you have of avoiding these things and the worse the destruction tends to be. The second feature of a good team is that when you tell them to whoa, they stop; and they stand there unmoving until otherwise directed. This is a prime safety factor. The third feature is that they backup; and back up strong if you need it. Mickey and Maud didn't oblige me with any of these critical traits. They didn't want to walk anywhere – they preferred to gallop. Hitch them to a log and they were off! And I was off! – running through the puckerbrush holding on to the reins , trying to get them to slow down, getting whipped in the face by saplings springing up in their wake and jumping back and forth over the log to avoid getting crushed as we cornered around stumps and trunks. They stopped all right when you wanted but you could never count on them standing. They were impatient. They wanted to be off again. However, contemplate for a moment all the undesirable side effects of a sudden surge forward while you are back there hitching up a chain or unclogging the cutter bar or re-calibrating the heel chains on the evener. My solution was to always hold the reins with one hand while attempting the task with the other – not a recipe for easy living. Since we were always skidding in the direction of home, another strategy that often worked was to park them facing away from the head of the log while I hooked on the chain, then wheel them around, hitch and go. A most powerful motivation for them was the lure of the barn.

A team that backs nicely is a real pleasure – M&M of course did not back at all. On one occasion, coming down out of the woods with a sled full of firewood, we managed to straddle a smallish tree and run the head of the pole right into it. There was no going forward and if they would just push it back just a wee bit, we could pull the pole to the side and slide on past that tree. I ended up telling them to close their eyes and steel their nerves, and then fired up the chainsaw right under their noses, pulled the tree out of the way and off we went again down the hill, over the bridge, across the field and up to the woodshed.

Homestead Solutions

These 'solutions' which are to be found scattered throughout the book are things which you might be tempted to buy outright or to hire done but which, in the homestead spirit, you may make or do for yourself.

Solution #1

Nothing could be finer than coming down off the hill through the snow hauling a sled-load of cut firewood with your horse or your team. You like it; your mules like it; your horse likes it; it's the sled that takes a beating. It has to be built rugged. We have shattered several variations before making the model illustrated here which has survived already I have lost track of how many years. The runners receive the bulk of the action so to make the strongest runner possible, search out a hardwood limb like the one pictured which has grown into a severe bend but which has enough width to be sliced into two identical runners. A natural curve is very strong and will never break. The runners pictured here are 8ft long and 4" wide. The limb has to be thick enough to give you two identical runners when slabbed and then sliced down the middle. The floor is made of 2" planks lag-bolted into the runners. The draw bar is a 3" steel pipe with three holes drilled into it to accommodate the pole and the angle iron braces. (It is always a good idea to have an old bed frame or two stashed in case you need a piece of angle iron.) The two outside holes could be used to bolt on shafts if you've switched to a single horse. The superstructure depends on six hardwood poles set into one inch holes in the runners. Containing the load are boards screwed to the poles. This seems to be somewhat ticky-tacky but it works; it's rugged enough to contain close to ½ cord and is simple to replace every couple of years. Something else that needs to be replaced occasionally but which is critical to the long life of the runner is a wooden shoe. This is affixed to the bottom of the runner with ¾" trunnels made of the same wood as the shoe (maple in this case) so that it all wears at the same rate.   The shoes can be cut from a maple trunk 4" in diameter sliced in half lengthwise, then pegged to the runners and bent around the curve with the help of a series of shallow cuts on the underside at the sharpest point. These shoes abrade to nothing after a while but you just put on another pair.

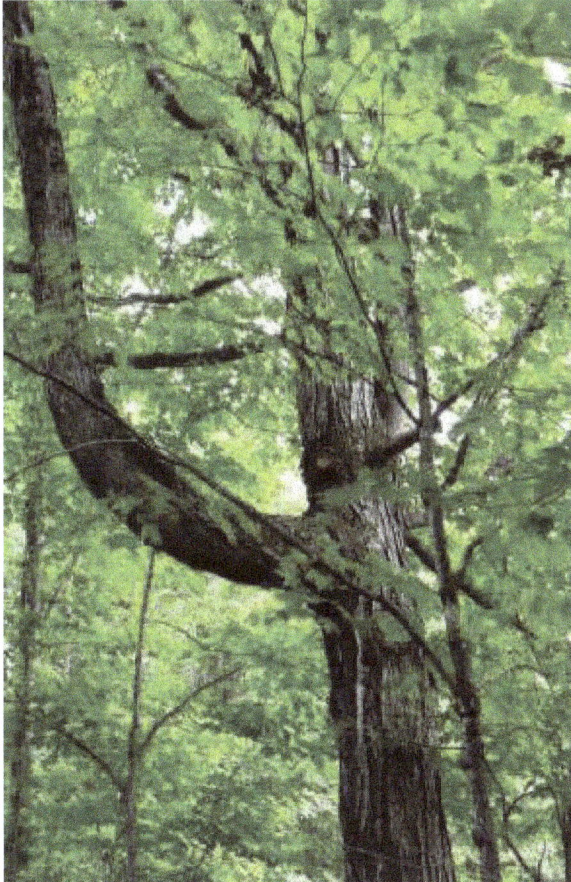

The right maple branch to cut into sled runners

Don't get the wrong idea about Mickey and Maud. They weren't ornery, nor stubborn, nor faint hearted. They busted their little fannies doing what had to be done. If they had bad habits that made things dangerous at times, the blame was not theirs but mine. I think a rule of thumb around equines is this: if something goes awry or even if something godawful happens, it is your fault, not theirs. You weren't careful enough; you didn't anticipate; you didn't check and recheck harness and equipment; you were daydreaming; and especially you failed to keep in mind that what you've got here are free spirited animals who don't necessarily share your perceptions and whose first and overwhelming reaction to anything untoward is to bolt. Somebody other than me – that is, somebody who already knew how to train and work horses, or somebody of a different character who might study up before plunging in, might well have ironed their quirks soon enough.

However as time moved on, they did get ironed some and I got ironed plenty. They rode, drove and skidded. They did everything. They did it at full speed and they did it for fifteen years. They rode the kids all over the place. Riding Maud while she trotted was like riding a train. Her legs moved rhythmically like pistons and her back stayed level and flat so you felt like you were running atop the rails. They skidded the new homestead open for houses and barns, pastures and gardens. The second growth forest, once felled, needed to be translocated to its ultimate destination as sugar wood, stove wood, saw logs or construction poles. They did it. They pulled whatever conveyance good, bad, or crazy I thought to put behind them. They pulled a wagon homemade out of 60's Saab rear axles; they pulled a mowing machine; they pulled a sled for maple sap and a sled for fire wood; they pulled a disc harrow, a spike tooth harrow and a flexible tine harrow; they even pulled a snow roller. The snow roller was one of my most brilliant creations. It was made from a junked galvanized tank 10ft long and 3ft in diameter. I fabricated a framework around the tank out of hardwood poles and bolted an old spring metal seat to the back and the mule pole to the front and thought that it looked mighty fine.

The most likely question to pop up here is: Why would anyone even consider doing such a thing? Of course, there is plenty of historical precedent in New England for rolling the roads with horses so I felt I had tradition on my side. There was also some method in my madness. We had no way to plow our driveway and no money to pay someone to do it and, at the time, we owned no four wheel drive vehicle, so . . .the idea was to park down at the road and walk up the rolled-smooth way pulling kids, groceries and sundries behind us in plastic sleds. Which we proceeded to do. The drive was quite steep so the roller was always parked at the top facing downhill, waiting for the next snowstorm. M&M would roll it easily down to the road but could never hope to get it up through unrolled snow. To add more weight to the rig, I got the two boys to ride along on the framework. Ben, on one side, was maybe 8 and Will on the other would have been 5. So . . . one morning, post snowstorm, we barreled down the drive and just as we approached the bottom, several good old boys from the Washington "snow raiders" or "freeze fighters" or whatever they called themselves, howled on by doing about 50 mph on their snow machines. M&M freaked and hit the road galloping.

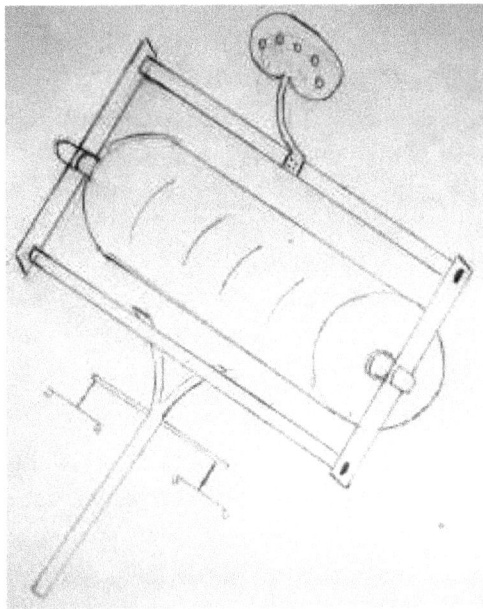

The roller pounded the ditch at the bottom of the drive with such an impact that the bolts holding the seat pulled out of the frame and I landed on my back in the snow. I was up running to see the whole caboodle under a vast roostertail of snow disappearing down the road at top M&M speed. Ben had the 8 year old presence of mind to leap off into the snowbank while I was running and screaming at Will to JUMP; imagining in microseconds all the worst possible and gruesome outcomes. He contemplated the beauty of the individual flake adrift in the vast universe of snow for a while, then jumped and came up laughing. And the Washington "snow tigers" (sic) enjoyed themselves no end by herding the mules finally to a halt far down the road. It made their day. Any time after, when I would run into one of them, all he'd want to talk about was racing them crazy mules down the road.

But, you ask, why did the seat fall off the snow roller? Wasn't it a result of incompetence and stupidity? During those years, I was afflicted plenty by both of those qualities but, in this case, the answer is no. It was a result of ignorance. Ignorance meaning not knowing as opposed to stupidity meaning never knowing. Ignorance can, in theory be overcome but stupidity is yours forever. In this case, my ignorance was of the rot-resistant qualities of different woods. I had chosen to build the roller out of poles from what I knew to be the strongest, heaviest hardwood in the local forest. The tree is officially named hop hornbeam because its seed clusters resemble hop flowers, but it is also called leverwood or ironwood. It is found sporadically scattered throughout our woods never growing very thick or tall and seems to die out under the canopy of sugar maple and white ash. Being so dense, it makes splendid firewood and it grows into a natural straight pole. However, as I discovered at the demise of the mighty snow roller, it rots very quickly once cut and exposed to the weather. After just a couple of years, those heavy bolts ripped right through the ironwood. Given the selection of hardwoods in our bit of forest, the right choice would have been white ash. Our woods are dominated by sugar maple: perhaps 80% of the hardwoods are maple. Maple is, needless to say, a splendid tree, beautiful and useful in many ways, but not in construction exposed to the elements. White ash is also a very handsome tree, growing tall and straight trunked and even tops out the maples on our hillside. It is the wood of baseball bats. It is lighter than maple or hop hornbeam but has considerable flexible strength. It too will rot when left outside but I think that an ash frame would have supported that seat until the time came when we picked up a nasty monster of a 4 wheeled Jeep and proceeded to rage and roar and bully our way through the snow to the house, relegating the roller tank to the metal recycler.

Mickey and Maud were capable of extraordinary feats of power and endurance when presented with the opportunity. One sap season we combined all our sap buckets with those of a friend and strung them along both sides of the maple-lined lane that works its way up and beyond the hill behind the homestead. There were perhaps 900 buckets that extended for about a mile and M&M were hauling the sap in a 120 gallon tank aboard their sled. The sap season that year started with very little snow on the ground and the lane soon turned to mud. Those mules humped that sled back and forth countless times through the mud, Maud with her legs going like pistons, Mickey valiantly keeping pace, along the flat, down the steep hill where the ledge protrudes in ridges through the eroded dirt, then catty corner through the farm, down to the lowest point where the syrup pans were set up waiting. They seemed to love it. In the heat of a long haul, their ears would be pointed dead center and forward. The mules' ears spoke their language. You knew what was going on in their heads by watching their ears. They could rotate them in a vertical plane almost 180o from front to back. If you were on their case and they were listening, both ears would be facing back toward you. If only one ear was swiveled at you, they weren't taking you too seriously. One ear might be at 90o and the other straight forward – they were checking out something to that side. Ears flat back on their neck - look out, they are angry, or perhaps chasing a coyote out of their pasture. Ears relaxed or drooping a bit – they are tuned out or dreaming; but when they suddenly perk and rotate together – something is happening over there, or if you're in the woods loading up, they have heard someone coming and that someone wouldn't appear for a full five minutes – their hearing was that acute. However, when their ears were pointed full forward, say at 20o past vertical, everything about them was focused on the road ahead and going right at it.

Due to a perpetually drippy winter nose, I acquired the habit of carrying a red bandana handkerchief in my right rear pocket. This practice often carried into the following summer and as I browsed the pasture with M&M, Mickey would wander over to have her ears scratched and Maud would sneak up behind, yank out the bright red handkerchief and canter off triumphantly. It was her favorite game. I would run after her yelling and cursing. Give me back that goldanged handkerchief you miserable piece of gristle; and she would run circles around me with her nose high and her neck arched first to one side and then to the other, proud as her majesty's hunter. Sometimes I'd get the handkerchief back and sometimes she ate it. Perhaps it was not altogether a game. She could have been motivated by that delicious crusted-on salty snot.

They were playful in other ways. After a couple of years, when there was the definition of a pasture fenced with no grass yet but piles of brush and downed trees scattered about, M&M would start a romping session at the top corner by snorting loudly, stamping and then rocketing off diagonally downhill to the lower corner where they would skid to a stop, point their noses in the air, snort, snort and snort, wheel about and race top speed back to the start They would do this sometimes for fifteen minutes. It was usually in the evening, getting quite dark, fireflies out, and they hurdled and careened over and around all the brush, logs, and stumps. You couldn't help but laugh and rejoice at their crazy vitality. Sometimes for fun I'd say to the kids, "Lets fire 'em up!" and get the mules snorting and running by whooping and running around the pasture ourselves. We did this once but left the gate open and were left wondering who was crazier as they bolted through at full gallop out on to the road and away on a lark. It took us hours to track them down and bring them home. They were always lured by the song of the open road. They would jump over or see a weak spot in the fence, or in the days before any fence, when they would be tied around in neighboring openings to various little hawthorns to graze whatever they could, they would pull the rope and be off The neighbors didn't seem to mind. Even later, when Mickey was gone, and Maud was retired and a little stiff and hard of hearing, she would be pastured with one of our draft horses who were so terrified of the electric fence that they wouldn't cross the invisible line even if the wire had been carried away by a cross country moose; and she would spot the opening and wander out to stand dreaming in the middle of the road oblivious to any truck crawling up behind her and tantalize the horse to where he would dare to leap the non –existent wire to join her and off they would go; Maud at a stiff little trot. Big draft horses are so heavy and have such large hooves that they connect so to the ground that a spark will fairly leap off the fence at them. They intensely dislike even the possibility of this so that you can shut off the charger for the rest of the season, or for some horses, for the rest of their careers.

Maud may have been sterile, but she surprised us once by displaying maternal feelings. She adopted a newborn calf. She had been pastured with some cows and when one of them dropped a calf onto the grass, Maud came over to investigate, chased the cow away and proceeded to act as if the calf were her baby. Equines feel themselves to be superior to cows – they always boss them around and chase them away. Maud began to

43

make funny little noises and then straddled the calf with her back legs apart so the he could get to her non-existent udder. We watched him nuzzle for a while and then relocated Maud so milk could flow and life could grow.

After about 15 years into it, we dug a deep hole near the house and buried Mickey there. We were coming down the hill in the snow with a heavy load of firewood in the sled and she slipped and the momentum of the sled pushed her down and her right front leg snapped. I cut her out of the harness and she actually walked on three legs back to the barn. The vet came, proclaimed it hopeless and put her down. If you recall what I said earlier, you know who was at fault. Of course, it was Mickey who went down, not Maud, but anyway the thing happened as a result of my decision as to time and place.

Maud went on to be teamed with several good, bad, and ugly replacements before being retired in favor of heavy horses. One was a loaner donkey named Houriet (Hooree) who was so wily he could pretend he was killing himself while actually Maud was doing all the work. Another was a beautiful, tall mule named Millie. (Almost all she-mules are named with an M – in fact they are often referred to as Molly mules.) She was so much bigger that I had to offset the evener giving her 1/3 of the length and Maud 2/3. Just after her arrival, I managed to get her and them stuck in an absurd no-exit situation and she decided then and there that I was a damn fool and she was not going to work for me. And she didn't. She refused to do anything more and I sold her so she could start anew. I had run smack into the stubborn mule of myth and legend. I have thought about this since and have come to believe that to explain that behavior, you need to know that mules are more sensitive than horses. You can terrorize a horse into working for you but you can't a mule. If you beat a mule or resort to screaming at her, she won't forgive you, won't forget and will get "stubborn" on you. Horses, of course, are not insensitive. They are extremely perceptive. However, their way is that of a child, whereas a mule is sensitive like an adult – they bear grudges.

Maud's last teammate was a black pony named Billy. He matched her in size and was a working fool. To show me how he pulled, the man who had him for sale hitched Billy to a stationary tractor and asked him to get up. He just about turned himself inside-out trying to pull that tractor. He was feisty in a way ponies can be and horses aren't. He was a gelding but that didn't stop him from trying to hump any mare that came into range. They might be twice his size and would kick the bejesus out of him, but he'd keep on coming back for more. Billy and Maud worked out well for a few years. He might have been feisty, but he didn't have Maud's true grit. He just gave up on one occasion when they were hauling sap after a March storm that left snow up to their bellies. He wouldn't help out Maud until I offered him a drink out of a full sap bucket. He slugged down a gallon and a half, thought about the finer things in life and decided he would rather leave this situation behind and get himself back to the barn.

We traded Billy for a big, elderly white mare who did the same work alone that M&M had done together – except in slow motion. Maud retired to a new career as weed eater and companion equine. That must have happened in the late 90's so you see she was able to browse away quite a few years. She was a companion to draft horses but needed not their companionship. Occasionally I would hear the horse in the far pasture running and whinnying so I knew something unusual was happening and would go to investigate. The problem was that he or she had lost track of Maud. She was snoozing in the shade while the horse followed its nose munch by crunch oblivious until suddenly realizing he hadn't seen Maud for at least ten minutes! Where was she? Time to gallop around screaming for her, Maud not even bothering to open an eyelid. On another occasion, we headed into the woods to bring in a hefty ash log that I had cut from a tree which had blown over in a hurricane. This log had rolled downhill into a pretty good hollow which, coincidentally, had been created by the infamous hurricane of '38 whose trademark is the "hump and hollow" topography left on many a Vermont hillside by the uprooting of so many trees. We let Maud trail along to keep 'Pudgie' happy and then tied her off to the side. Pudgie, a very large and immensely strong Belgian, moaned and complained that he couldn't pull this log out of that hole and gave a few desultory fake attempts at trying so I left him there hooked to the log and walked Maud down the trail a few hundred feet towards home. I went back to Pudgie and he yanked that log out of there in a microsecond and headed to catch up with Maud.

Maud was always able to grow a quite amazing winter coat – so thick and fuzzy that snow would rest on her back and never melt. She never got cold and was so positive about it that the coat wouldn't come off until July. As she aged and her backbone started to show and her locomotive began to look more like a caboose, especially in the spring when that fuzz and fur was half shed in raggedy patches, I would look at her and think, "By God, she's a train wreck and can't last much longer"; but she always shined up and spirited up by mid-summer until one year, she didn't.

Maud and Pudgie, 2008

Those Human Beings, Part 1

The world is full of individual humans, any one of whom could fill a biography but some just strike your fancy and this series placed here and there throughout the book presents a sample of characters we have encountered along the way.

It is possible to come in off the lane above the house to the northwest and follow a drivable path downhill around the house, through the orchard, past the cider mill and out southeast onto the town road. It's a diagonal through the heart of things that would cut off the square corner where the lane meets the road. At any time we might go in or out in either direction but we were extremely surprised one fine summer day while we were at work on the new house, to see a little old man on a little-old bicycle come in at the top and coast blithely and serenely, as if he were cruising through Central Park, down, around and out the bottom.

We looked at each other quizzically. Did you see what I saw? Was that a vision? Might that have been an elf or some likewise otherworldly being? Where was he even coming from? How did he get here? The lane is all steep and corroding ledge coming out of square miles of no-man's land. We were in due time to uncover the answers to these questions but only after encountering the same little old man pedaling the shoulders of the state highways sometimes many miles from home. His bicycle was a throwback to another era. No gears, no derailleur, small wheels and handlebars that instead of laying out horizontally, pointed straight up like the horns of some toro bravo to be seen in the arenas of Spain. This arrangement allowed him to sit up, back perfectly straight and pedal along at a constant leisurely pace. We came to know him somewhat. His name was Theo and a child of God he was at this stage of his life just sailing along. His skin had taken on that translucent quality seen in the faces of painted Renaissance angels and his affect was gentle and quiet but always with a hidden twinkle as if he wasn't unaware of life's subterranean pathways.

He loved those bonny summer days when the siren song of the road beckoned and he would get family or friend to transport him and his bike to some predetermined location usually at the height of land somewhere so that he might wend his own way back. He was in his eighties then and would be out for most of the day but nobody worried about him. He paid his way home by searching out cans and bottles discarded along the roadsides. He had installed a flat basket over the front wheel and the five cent bottle deposit law had been an incentive and a great boon to his cycling life. He cleaned up the highways and byways, filled his basket with bottles and cans and paid his mileage as it were. He often carried with him an umbrella which he would unfurl to hold aloft and catch the prevailing winds.

We talked to him about our own byway wanderings searching for cider apples and he said: "Did you see those oak trees up on Sky Acres"? No, we replied but we found them the next time we went back, a clump of red oaks each 15" in diameter where typically oaks are not part of the natural forest. "When I was a boy waiting for my parents to finish visiting in Sharon down along the White River, I dawdled out in the street. It was in the autumn and I filled my pockets with acorns and when we got to home, I pushed then into the ground at the corner of our property by the road up on Sky Acres." Theo was an old man whose passion was riding that bicycle through his beloved countryside and now and then they would ferry him to Sky Acres so he could coast down the steep hill and peddle on home along the blacktop and he would stop at the oaks and daydream about being a little boy picking up acorns in the fall.

Bovinity

We had been living with goats for what seemed like an eternity when we responded to a piece in the paper about a woman who kept Scotch Highland cattle. "I've seen pictures of them. They are pretty cute. Let's go check them out." We had no plans or expectations that day but we came home with two bovines. After talking with us, the lady made us an offer we couldn't refuse. "If you would like that brown and white cow there, bred to our Highland bull and about ready to drop, you can have her in exchange for keeping our future herd sire bull until we need him back." She couldn't keep using the same bull for very long because he would end up breeding his own daughters, so she was always planning the next sire in advance. The boy that came home with us had a long fancy Scottish name in the registry but was called just Fuzzy, and the cow's name was Bossy. Bossy is such a common name for cows not because of their temperament but because it is generic: the Latin word for cow is "bos".

I was certainly intimidated to begin with. I knew nothing of bovine psychology and from a goat keeper's perspective, these animals loomed very large. And a bull! El toro bravo! All those familiar stories of bulls chasing and maiming people and even killing unlucky farmers. And this Fuzzy came equipped with those massive horns that Scotch Highlanders are known for. However, he turned out to be more of a Ferdinand type bull and by putting grain on the ground in front of him, I could approach behind his horns and get a rope around his neck to control him. Bovines, more than any other domestic animal, will do just about anything for a bucket of sweet feed. It works to coerce them with that bucket as a reward. Fuzzy stayed with us for two years before she wanted him back but besides escaping the fence and savaging a couple of fruit and nut treelings with his horns, he caused us no trauma. I watched him once seriously challenge a large brush pile to a showdown. It was a piece of work building that brush pile out in the pasture, but he looked at it cockeyed one day and decided it needed to be taught a lesson. He ravaged that pile with such gusto, snorting it and thrashing it with those long horns, backing up and charging, windmilling his way into it, that all was strewn far and wide. One guy's work is another guy's amusement.

The coming of the cows coincided with the coming of the grass, and the goats did that for us. By the time they had stripped away all the pucker brush, they had deposited a dung pellet on every square inch of the pasture space and the grass came on of its own accord, fertilized and without any direct seeding. However one of the best things about introducing cows to the homestead was getting rid of the goats. Those damn goats were good for us in many ways but I didn't realize until I began snuggling up to Bossy, that I just wasn't a goatie kind of guy. Those wily, cunning brigands were always conniving their next scheme. You are never far away from trouble with goats unless you have the wherewithal to do everything about them the right way: which I didn't. A real goat fence was beyond our means so I cobbled up three strands of electric wire with an old timey battery-powered charger but this only contained them when it suited their mood. Otherwise, they were in the garden or snacking on apple buds. Cows, on the other hand, will stay in a field behind only one strand of electric wire placed at waist height. You can also tether cows in unfenceable places and if they get into trouble, they will lie down and wait for you to come. If you tether a goat, it will likely strangle itself, and if you tether a horse, all hell can break loose once it winds the rope around its legs.

Keeping a milk cow on a homestead yields multiplying benefits – benefits that you might not think of to begin with. Once Bossy dropped her half-Highland heifer calf, and we started milking and things settled into a routine, she spent her nights in the pasture with the calf and her days tethered away from the calf. This accomplished two things – first, she created and then maintained our "lawn", and second, that's how we shared her milk with the calf. We put a halter on her, used a twenty foot rope and a pointed steel bar driven into the ground and rotated her clockwise around the home buildings all summer. The feed selection started out sparse but she mowed on and left her patties behind, and after a couple of seasons, the "lawn" turned downright luxurious sprouting various kinds of grasses, clovers, weeds and wildflowers. Daisies, black-eyed susans, queen anne's lace, red and yellow hawkweed, yarrow, wild strawberry, bladder Campion, elecampane and of course, and best of all, dandelion. How mysterious it seemed that all these flowers and grasses somehow appeared from nowhere. How did all those seeds get there? Well, dandelion presents no mystery and most of the others, I suppose, arrived in the hay we were importing. We know that some seeds can rest dormant in the soil for many years waiting for favorable conditions to sprout. Many are transported and defecated by birds. Witness the immediate and incredible barrage of blackberries and raspberries that happens after a clear-cut in the forest. Be that as it may, Bossy was our lawnmower – maybe "greens keeper" would be the better term. She ate her way around and around, avoiding a few of those ill-tasting wildings, but lassoing the rest with that great tongue first sweeping to the right, then to the left, eating, shitting and magically transforming greens into milk. She especially loved dandelion as do all cows. Such a maligned, persecuted, poisoned and hated plant that continues to come in triumphant. It is beautiful, vibrant and healthful and, if it is loved by cows, that is proof enough of its nutritional power. Dandelions won't grow in poor soil. They are indicators of fertility and I rejoice to see that glowing yellow carpet in the spring. Dandelion greens in the pot; dandelion wine in the bottle; dandelion milk in the frig; and honey bees delirious covered with orange pollen bringing it home to feed the explosion of new growth in the hives.

Bossy was half Guernsey and half Hereford. That made her brown and white and heftier than pure-bred milk cows. It was a good mix for a homestead cow. First, She didn't want to produce so much milk that you needed to feed her a lot of grain just to keep her weight up or so much that you felt you couldn't keep up with it in the kitchen. Second, she would throw a beefier calf more appropriate for a future meat animal. Cows would prefer to give their milk to their calves rather than you. For that reason, commercial dairies take the calves away from their mothers right off and never let them suck. If you leave the calf with the cow and want milk for yourself, you have to do two things. One: separate the calf for a period of time, as we did during the day, and two: when starting to milk her, bring the calf to her and let it nuzzle, then tie it off to the side and proceed to take the quantity you want. We used about a gallon a day and Bossy would not only hold back her milk flow for her calf but also stop the flow at about the gallon level every time as she became accustomed to the routine. You wouldn't think a cow could do that but I'm your witness.

Only a gallon a day – it seemed like a deluge. Milk, cream, butter, yogurt, yogurt cheese and cottage cheese; and there was always more so we started selling yogurt in quart canning jars. Somebody began calling it Jogurt. Yogurt cheese is something like cream cheese – you put the yogurt in a cheese cloth, hang it up until it drips dry and there you have it. However, taking only a gallon for yourself still leaves a lot of milk for the calf. On four gallons a day, those calves grew fat and fast so I thought about giving her a second calf. Bull calves are an unwanted byproduct of dairy farming so they can be had for cheap. However, Bossy didn't really like the idea. She would kick and butt the little fellow, so I had to help until he very quickly would get his sea legs and figure out how to get his share. He (that is: they, because we did this many times) would wait until her own calf started always on a front teat, then he would dart in from behind where she couldn't see him and nurse the back teats.

Most of these calves became meat. They were born in the spring and slaughtered late in the fall after a summer of milk and some grass so they would be categorized somewhere between veal and baby beef. We would sell one of these and that would pay our hay bill for the year. Our household meat would come from an animal held over for a winter when, still being quite small, it would not consume a whole lot of hay, pastured the next summer and slaughtered the following fall. No grain involved and extraordinary how economical it was and how much family food was provided by an animal only a year and a half old. That bull calf not yet two is not old enough to start acting "bullish": he still feels himself to be a calf and is tractable but the real bonus is that he is old enough to inseminate the cow. Thus the animal you are raising for meat also acts as your breeding bull in the fall before he is slaughtered. He has had a summer of milk, a winter of some hay, and a summer of grass, and he will give you a couple of hundred lbs. of meat. Of course, you don't need to keep a bull given the availability of artificial insemination but this system gives you a win-win. But you could call the man, tell him which breed (out of dozens of choices) you prefer and he'll come when she is in heat. With just one cow in the field, it can be a little difficult to detect, but with two or more, when one jumps on another, that one is in heat.

Getting from a slaughtered animal to T-bone steaks on the plate posed another whole set of challenges. Our homestead philosophy wanted us to do everything ourselves when at all possible, so it wasn't pretty but we did it. Start with a meat saw and a bunch of sharp knives. Once the skin is off, saw him in half along the backbone. Put a length of rope through the back leg above the tendon, carry the halves to the shop and hang them from a beam for a week or so (cold weather). Carry the half into the house, put it on the kitchen table, get out Joy of

Cooking which has a diagram of all the cuts and see if you can duplicate-which you can't- and you don't, but you cut him into all sorts of pieces anyway with a goodly amount going into hamburger, then you wrap it all in freezer paper, label and send him to the deep freeze. In those days, the Country Store in Chelsea maintained an entire freezer room, in which were dozens of individual lockers that were rented out to the locals. This was a legacy from way back when it was unheard of to have a freezer in your house and it hung on in Chelsea until well into the 90's when it had become an untended mess, and a new owner mercifully eliminated it.

The production of meat and the resultant slaughtering of animals was my least favorite aspect of our homestead life. We also slaughtered many a chicken, some turkeys and an occasional pig. My distaste for the whole thing finally led me to stop killing any animals and eating mostly vegetarian, but given the exigencies of children's protein requirements and the unbeatable economic advantages, it was what we did at the time. However, if you are going to eat meat, you can't do better than raise it yourself. And you certainly can do worse – a lot worse. Any commercial meat that is a product of industrial agriculture or isn't organic is something you should never feed to your children or eat yourself. This is especially true for veal, beef, pork, chicken or turkey. Most of these poor animals often never see the light of day, are kept in filthy and overcrowded conditions and are overfed with questionable stuff that is laced with antibiotics to keep them alive under such conditions. Of course, you don't have to do the butchering or slaughtering yourself. You can hire a professional to come and slaughter and then take the sides to a butcher to have them hung and cut up. In the case of fowl, we used to have a man come, who had converted a trailer into a mobile butchery. He was accompanied by his daughter who helped kill, pluck and gut, and his wife who had had a stroke and wanted to come along for the ride and the entertainment. He had rigged up a special lift to get her in and out of the truck. On the side of the trailer he had painted "We Kill, You Chill".

Bossy contributed to our well-being in still other ways. A friend once said to me half joking that is was worth keeping cows just for the manure. When they are not spreading it themselves during green grass season, and they are inside for the winter, you can put together a truly powerful pile of fertility. When you start spreading that pile round, the plant world really perks up. If you make a pile out of just horse or mule shit, it will ferment and heat up all by itself, melt the snow off and steam away all winter. But if you do the same with cow shit it will just freeze solid unless you judiciously mix in enough bedding material such as hay, straw or shavings. The difference is the moisture content but you can get that cow pile to heat up too so that it is ripe and ready in the spring. There is a covenant between plants and animals that goes something like this: we feed you and you feed us. It works across the board but the plant world secretly favors bovinity. There is some mysterious biochemical miracle at work in their labyrinthine digest that produces the most favored plant food.

The bossy barn, as it came to be called, was situated in the lower level of our first building (AKA the shop) where she had to come in through a people door, step over a sill and jump up onto a wooden platform which had been originally built to keep baby Will up and out of trouble and then modified for Bossy with a gutter and a manure window. It was snug in there and a friendly place to milk but there was no water so we developed the daily routine of going to the Gingerbrook for water. On her own, she would go out that door into the woodshed, out another door to the outside and walk 200 yards through the snow to the brook, drink her fill then turn around and run back to get her ration of sweet feed. That was all regular routine until one winter a white gander of ours, who was spending the winters out and around in the snow, began to feel that Bossy was an unwanted intrusion into his winter domain. Ganders are worse than either roosters or tom turkeys when they turn screwballed. They lower their necks, spread their wings and come forward hissing and will use the leading edge of a wing to beat their victim. The blow from that wing can result in serious damage. So this gander developed a grudge against Bossy and began to waylay her as she exited the outer door. The gander would fly into her face and beat her about the neck with his wings. Sometimes he would land on her back aflapping so that as I watched them careen away, they looked like a flying cow. Bossy naturally grew to fear and resent this persecution. She would pause at the outer door, then plunge and hit the snow at a gallop, udder all a wobble, trying to outrun the ghastly ghost. The gander would then sometimes latch onto the hairy end of her tail as it waved past and then they presented what seemed a wild goose chase. It all came to a dramatic ending one morning when the gander seriously miscalculated and got in front of her as she made the plunge. She rumbled on, over and through him such that he never recovered. Bossy preferred sedate to hassle and harry but it took her a couple of weeks to really believe the ghost was gone and she could revert to her leisurely jaunt to the brook.

Another testament to the miraculous nature of cow shit was (and is) its ability to bring back old apple trees from the brink of extinction. Wild trees that had seeded and sprouted on the land when it was open pasture and then had gradually been smothered by woody regrowth during the 30 or 40 years of abandonment, were just hanging on in the shade of the competition when we arrived. Once I had cleared around them and trimmed off all the dead and dying branches. I hit upon the idea of tying Bossy to each one in turn. In the spring and fall when there wasn't any grass and before and after the snow, I would tether her to one of these wild apple trees and leave her there for a week or so and bring hay and water to her so that urine, shit and hay all were mushed into a circle around the tree. I continue to do this today with other cows and these erstwhile stunted wild apples are now looming high and mighty and put out regular harvests of cider apples.

Homestead Solutions #2

A Hemlock Hedge

The lane that runs up the hill on the north side of the property is only a couple of hundred feet from the house and although it discourages the average traveler, it does see a certain amount of four wheel and motocross traffic. The steep sections have eroded down to successive waves of ledge and the flat sections often sprout huge mud holes. Both of these situations seem to attract certain loud sorts of characters which prompted me to want a hedge between us and the lane. There was and is a line of old maples there with miscellaneous saplings and brush growing in and around them but I wanted a solid, tight hedge as both a sight and sound barrier. Hemlock is a deep woods climax forest tree which lives for hundreds of years and grows to immense size but I had heard that it could be kept pruned and shaven into a hedge. I thought that I could transplant young plants while they were still dormant in the spring so I headed out with a shovel to a nearby back road where I had noticed a bunch of little hemlock. I didn't plan this but the timing was such that it was the worst of mud time when the ground has just thawed and lost all integrity so that it seems more like jelly than soil. After trying to shovel out the first one in these conditions, I thought, what the hell, and tried to pull it out with a hand around the trunk. It slid out of the melt with all the roots intact, even down to the fine feeder roots. Leaving the shovel behind, I walked along popping the little hemlocks out of the ground until I had 40 of them which I right away, before they had a chance to realize their new situation, plugged back into the earth every five feet for two hundred along the lane. Merely levering the soil open with the shovel enough to slide the roots in and then stepping them was how they were put in. This seemed to me to be a miracle at the time that all these baby hemlocks survived and have grown into a hedge now 10ft high and 6ft wide. Every spring the new growth gets sheared and shaped and the many hemlocks appear to have fused into one long organism.

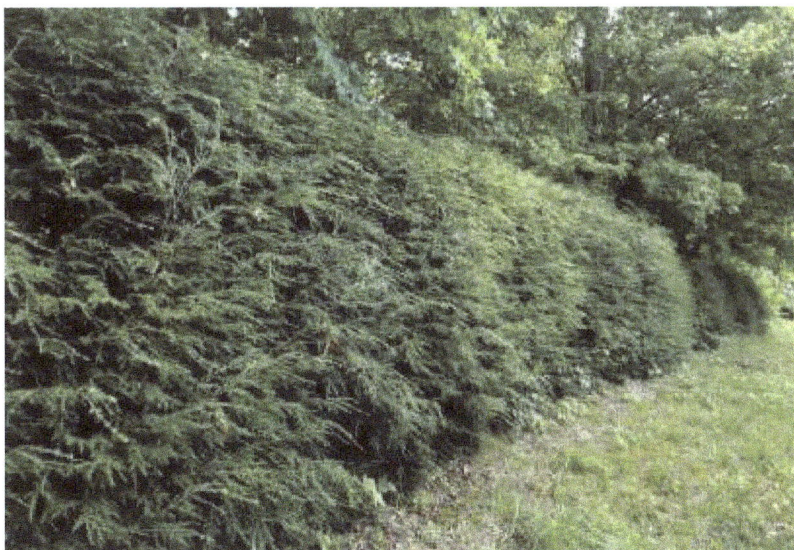

The Cow who Mooed Once

Once upon a time there lived a cow with us who had shaggy auburn hair hanging over her eyes and horns that were longer than any other cow east of the Mississippi. I measured them from time to time and even as this cow got to be quite old, her horns continued to grow. When she was 15, her horns measured 61" wide from one tip across her head to the other. She would use these horns to expertly scratch an itch anywhere on her back or sides. She would also waggle them at somebody, a stranger to her, who approached her without getting properly introduced. However she knew exactly to where these horn tips extended and never in the years I spent close to her did she touch me with one. I would lean my chest against her forehead to scratch her in that special place just behind the horns in the center of her head and she would be still and waggle not. I could extend my arms in that position and barely hold both horn tips.

We practiced ESP together. She was very receptive. She was often in a pasture with a draft horse and sometimes I wanted her in the barn but not him. If he saw me or heard the barn door clattering open, he would come charging over ever hopeful for a treat. But if I didn't want to deal with him just then, I would walk quietly to the edge and beam in the direction of the shaggy cow. She would look up, stare at me, get the message and head slowly to the barn without attracting the attention of the horse. The other thing very special about this cow was that she never mooed. Most cows at some point during their day, will stand around and bawl either for specific reasons or just for the sheer joy of sounding off, but not Vicki – she never mooed. She had a calf once and after the calf was gone to someone else's farm, Vicki gave her milk to us and to facilitate, she would stand quiet anywhere in the pasture not tied up while I squirted a pail-full.

There are two pastures on the homestead, an upper and a lower, both enclosed by one strand of wire that could be electrified but isn't. I would put Vicki in one but if for some reason it didn't feel right, she would leave. At first I thought she was running away, but when I searched for her, I always found her in the other pasture. It was not as if there were open gates in either. She would leave one pasture and go into the other without somehow leaving tell-tale signs like broken wire or knocked-over fence posts. She did this mysteriously several times. She wasn't trying to run away or escape – she just decided to change her scene without waiting for me to do it. One very hot summer day, I searched for her and finally found her in the lower pasture standing right in the Gingerbrook where it runs into shade beneath a covey of balsam fir. She was panting and sweating in the heat and had gone to the coolest spot on the homestead to pass the day. Vicki did leave one day however and a neighbor called to say that she was munching on their lawn. I took the low road to retrieve her, didn't find her and started back up the high road through the woods. I noticed signs of her but didn't actually see her until I made it back all the way to the house where she was lolling about right in front acting like she had been there all day. She was magical and mysterious and I think that time she was actually playing with me and leading me on.

When I tied her to apple trees during the fall and spring before and after the snow, she would wait for me to come with hay, grain and water and never would she moo. I would leave her at one apple tree for a few days and move her to the next until all the trees had been slathered with cowshit and the grass or snow was coming and the circuit was finished for the season. This one time however, I thought Vicki has been at this tree for a while now; I should move her. Then another day passed and I thought – I really should move her. But I was too busy or lazy and yet another day went by. The next morning when I appeared hauling a bale of hay toward her, Vicki looked right at me and let out with an enormous, anguished MOOO. Holy Cow! She about frightened me out of my boots. She was seriously complaining about my treatment of her. She was the cow who mooed only once.

Growing Your Own

If homesteading is about anything, it's about growing your own. It's about doing your own and making your own but above all, it's about providing yourselves with quality food. When first coming onto this piece of land, we were confronted with too many decisions, some to be made immediately, followed by others cascading off the originals. The first decision of where to put the house was nicely made for us by the location of the two old maples, and once we could envision the house tucked into the SSW facing hillside, we could see the gardens being down in front running like terraces along the contours of the slope. All was such a mass of second growth you could hardly walk through it. There were some openings within the trees however and before we did anything else, we transported some rhubarb and asparagus root and stuck them in as soon as we could dig in the spring. That was the beginning and 35 years later, they are still our first fresh eats of the season. My plan for transforming the young forest into garden involved Mickey and Maud. As yet, there was no barn so they had to stay out all winter. I figured I could create garden and at the same time give them some shelter by fencing them into the trees. We fenced a plot approximately 30ft by 75ft right in and around the trees and kept the mules there all through snow time. Freeze or thaw, blizzard or sunshine, they stayed out unfazed through it all. By the following spring, there had accumulated a serious covering of muleshit and hay mixed in with the fallen leaves and detritus of the forest floor. Then I chainsawed down every living stick in the plot, making sure to cut flush to the ground (a good way to eat through a saw chain quickly). This regrowth, I calculated, was in the 40 year old range but only the popples and balsam poplar had busted out from the adolescent scrum to gain some height and girth. Many were 12" to 15" thick and these I laid end to end to define the bottom of the terrace and the rest went into the construction or sugar wood pile... After that, we hooked up to the disc harrow and ran back and forth over top of the stumps trying semi-successfully to mix the manure into the earth. Then, we poked holes in it and put in some seeds, starts and seed potatoes and wondered what would happen. The corn came up dark purple instead of green but forged on and once its roots reached down past the manure layer into the earth, it gradually gained its righteous green and went on to give us a good crop. The tomatoes and potatoes however, grew to prodigious leafy heights and produced hardly anything edible. The squash and pumpkins went bonkers threatening to overwhelm all like kudzu but again yielding limited fruit, all symptoms of excess nitrogen as a result of the vast quantity of manure and urine to hit the forest floor. But that was just the beginning, and as the plot leached, mellowed and incorporated, we had a base of fertility that just wouldn't quit. We continued with that same winter animal paddock technique until we had fashioned two full terraces along the contour S to SW. These terraces are about 300ft long and 30ft wide and the length of them all got the same treatment. Over time, other equines were added to the mix, along with young Highland bulls and heifers. No one seemed to mind wintering in the snow and it would be years before there would be shelter built for everybody.

If you absolutely clear cut a section of woodland, even small diameter second growth, it is extraordinary how much wood comes off. We were able to fuel the sap fire for a bunch of years with the firewood harvested from this clearing operation. There were balsam fir, popple, white birch, balm of gilead and some skinny maple and ash just coming on. The smaller stumps, cut at ground level, disappeared fairly quickly after being split by the disc harrow and rotting or chopped out by a mattock furrowing a seed row. The largest stumps maybe lasted for 10 years as we disked over and planted around them, before disintegrating and disappearing completely. The terraces became permanized and impervious to wash out by the vigorous growth of grass next to the log rails. The repeated action of disking sends the soil slowly gravitating downhill. Whatever rocks that appear get thrown against the logs and the witch grass knits everything together, so even after the logs are long rotted and gone, the terrace remains well defined. The grass swath receives all sorts of goodies from garden soil on the slopes above and is so luscious that I scythe it every season and use it as the green basis for the compost pile. Another plant that thrives in that zone is comfrey which also contributes its nitrogenous leaves to the compost. Even some wild apples have sprouted there and I have thought to leave them, graft onto them and prune them so that they grow out along the line of the terrace.

Another often mentioned strategy for converting virgin territory into garden soil that actually does work is the use of pigs. Again, here is an animal that provides both meat and manure, and at the same time, excavates your garden for you. We only ever kept one pig at a time and to accommodate them, I put together a movable pen 6ft square with a base made from saddle notched logs and a superstructure of four poles and hog wire. I could push or pull this rig from one spot to the next. A piglet would stay in place for days whereas three months later, he would tear up fresh ground in a matter of hours. Soon a hog could graduate to moving the pen along by himself by snouting underneath one of the bottom logs and lifting and shoving forward six inches. A pig is quite a savvy critter. He learns and responds and relates. It wouldn't be long then before he would be lifting the whole thing far enough to rummage right out and commence to run around chortling and whistling. However, a bucket of grain in hand would bring him trotting along behind and back in the pen. But I knew the game was up once they had figured in their wily little piggy brains that this was the way to get extra treats during the day and it was time to think about slaughtering

To get a pig to do something for you, the best way is to make friends with him so that he will follow you anywhere, and the best way to do that is not necessarily to scratch him behind the ears but to bring him special treats. You can't tie a rope that will stay anywhere on a pig's body except around an ankle and you can't push or pull a pig any distance whatsoever; he just won't go. You can get him to move short distances – but only backwards – by putting a bucket over his head. He will vigorously try to back out of it, and if you're good at the game, you can maneuver him this way and that to where you want him. But you can see that you would much rather have him trotting along behind you. I learned from a farmer in Ecuador that it is possible to stake out a pig by tying to a back ankle. That is the only place on their bodies where there is enough angularity to keep a rope from slipping off. This farmer however didn't use rope but rather a rubber strip cut out of an inner tube 2" wide and 20ft long. He didn't knot it either. He cut a slit close to the end long enough to push the strip back through thereby forming a loop which was then pulled tight and left on the leg the whole time so that the pigs trailed these behind moving from place to place.

I learned this but didn't practice it when I should have once bringing a pig home from the auction in the back of 2-Ton Tony. She was supposedly tied to the headboard of the old Dodge but as we chugged up the last hill before our driveway, she sailed out over the 3ft high tailgate and disappeared into the woods. That is when she became the famous and fabulous jumping black pig of South Washington. Tony's bed was 3 1/2ft off the ground; add to that the 3ft of the tailgate and the declining slope away from the back of the truck and you have an approximate 7ft drop. When we finally caught up with her after a week of feral wanderings and excited neighbors, she looked as if she might as well have sprouted wings. Totally black she was except for the twinkle in her little piggy eye and when we boarded her into a pen to keep her close, she jumped out over the top. I kept adding another board and she kept jumping over (or was she flying?) until she eventually gained the status of myth and legend in the family. I took that pig for a ride one day and haven't heard the end of it since. I had heard of someone in the environs who kept a boy pig for breeding – a boar – and that gave rise like a bubble in the bathtub to the "why not?" idea of grounding our flying pig with a collection of piglets. A litter of piglets offers a riotous, rollicking presence to your homestead. They are a careening bunch of little destroyers enjoyable enough until they quickly grow past their charming phase.

I threw the jumping pig into the back of our old Jeep and set out for the boar. The Jeep was of that variety which had two seats up front and a small carryall section behind, with a tailgate and floppy plastic windows. No sooner were we on the high road than she decided that the back was not suitable to fully enjoy a ride in the country so she squeezed between the seats and set up like co-pilot next to me. She hung her head out of the window like any dog might and enjoyed herself mightily – queen of the road! Things progressed just fine and we got to the boar all right but, navigating as a team, we lost our way en-route. We turned into a farm to ask directions and as we approached, I noticed a man standing in the driveway acting strangely. He was pointing and gesticulating, jumping up and down and laughing his fool head off. What was the matter with this guy, I wondered, until I realized that the butt of his joke was us. Man and pig out for a little jaunt in their automobile. Ever after, when I would run into that man, he couldn't help but say to me something like, "Hey, it's the guy whose pig takes him for a ride in their Jeep". However, to get back to the topic of pigs in general, I feel that they are not actually a good fit as a homestead food source. They will eat grass somewhat and especially clover but basically they eat what you eat, only a little less fussy, and are correspondingly expensive to raise. The exception would be if you could find an alternate, free-for-the-taking food source like one neighbor who collects all the out-of-date dairy products from a local company. He runs the cartons and plastic containers through the rollers of his hay conditioner to squeeze out all the milk, yogurt, butter, cottage cheese, cream etc. into a vat and uses that to raise a bunch of pigs every year. One other negative about pigs is that they are well-nigh impossible to slaughter by yourselves on the homestead. We had to hire someone who came with a crane to lift the pig off the ground; a large tank capable of holding 100 gallons of water; a propane flame thrower to heat that water; a bench to operate on; and the specialized tools used to scrape down the skin. As opposed to other large animals that are skinned when slaughtered, pigs are left in their skin, only scraped clean of scruff and bristle. That's how you get your cracklings. Ourselves, we didn't actually keep that many pigs and soon stopped with them. To this day, I refuse to eat pig meat. I feel that there is a little known being locked inside that porky body which unfortunately the whole world looks at and sees only meat. The pigs are trapped inside their own delicious meat and are trapped by their own voracious greed.

Fertility is the end-all and be-all of growing your own. Fertility in the vegetable garden, in the fields, in the berry patches, and in the orchards. How you get there has been pretty well documented. It is compost and manure; manure and compost, and all the organic material you can import and parcel out either as mulch or just as stuff to throw around. The bible on this subject (I should say; one of the bibles) is the famous "Farmers of Forty Centuries". The question there to be answered is: How did people in China, Korea and Japan farm the same land for 4000 years and provide for themselves year in and year out while Europeans who arrived in America left behind played out soil after sometimes a single generation? The answer of course turns out to be the truism – feed your soil and it will feed you. In those places, absolutely nothing organic was wasted and everything went back into the soil. Farmers would build outhouses along the highways next to their fields inviting travelers to please stop and deposit their contributions. They dug out the muck from the bottom of irrigation canals and drainage ditches to throw back onto the fields. They pollarded trees for the leaves and twigs to tramp into the rice paddies. They even pulverized the carbonized mud bricks of their old stoves and put that into the gardens.

We personally have yet to smash up any bricks but we have taken the basic lesson to heart. All the organic material that is either produced on the homestead or imported in the shape of hay, straw, food or fiber stays on the homestead and nothing leaves that isn't sold as a finished product. For instance, we have managed to keep a raspberry patch flourishing since first setting it out soon after our arrival by mulching. Every fall we rake and dump quantities of maple leaves in there but furthermore, we relegate all our discarded fabric and clothing to the raspberry patch. No synthetics allowed. All cotton, wool and leather go in and disappear. Holey socks, used up leather gloves, old sweaters and bags of sheared wool all go in. Sheared fleece takes quite a while to disintegrate but supplies plenty of nitrogen in the process and makes a terrific smothering mulch if you want to use it in other places. I have used it around young apple trees and it is generally free for the asking. Another advertisement for the power of organic material to bring about change is seen in the area around the cider mill. We built the cider mill up against a steep bank in a cut-out next to the road. That set-up allows you to come in at the top and go out at the bottom. The cut-out was created years before as a result of the town road crew excavating for gravel and fill. The area was basically an old gravel pit with not a blade of grass to be seen. It is now bright green with plenty of clover and several fast growing apple trees. This transformation was accomplished through no fault of my own. I did nothing except throw apple pomace around and sluice the mill floor with water which runs out the door onto the (now) greensward. Quite a tonnage of pomace has come out of that cider mill over the years both from our own apples and the squeezings of many others. Pomace was thought by the ignorant to sour your soil and not be useful as fertilizer but that is clearly not the case as is shown by all the clover growing also in the field below the mill where I fork it about every cider time.

There is much to say on the topic of what to do with one's own "humanure". It was well done, the coinage of this new term for an old problem. Without being actually euphemistic, "humanure" has a nicer ring to it than say, the down and dirty people shit or the silly deep doodoo. But shit it is and it is what ties us unquestionably to the animal world. The difference between us and the gods is that the gods don't have to shit. Gods live purely on ambrosia, which I translate to mean 'pure energy'. Living on pure energy would allow you think, act or change yourself to a swan or a bull to your heart's content without concerning yourself with any waste product. But alas! Back here on earth, people have to come up with different ways of dealing with their #2. When the world was young and sparsely populated, people just shit (or is it shat) anywhere, presumably at a distance from their dwellings. A lot of people around the planet are still doing just that. When I was in highland Peru and I would ask where should I do my business, even in a good sized town, they would direct me "over there". 'Over there' turned out to be a barren, stony and often cactusy area not far off where everybody shat (or is it shitted?). This sounds worse than it is because the altiplano of Peru is very dry and quite cold and the feces quickly dries, turns to powder and blows away. That sounds better than it actually was as I found myself compulsively singing, "The answer my friend is blowing in the wind" while squatting among the dried-up turds. A more terrifying humanure disposal system that I experienced was in the little village called Tasbapaunie located on the Caribbean coast of Nicaragua. There were built outhouses on stilts that extended out into the sea such that wave and tidal action would carry the shit away. The village was comprised of a string of houses built on the strand not far from the shore interconnected by a grassy common that was maintained like a putting green. However, it was not maintained by the people but rather by an assemblage of roaming animals. There were horses, dogs, chickens and pigs wandering around like equal citizens and by some miraculous ecological balancing act, there was no shit of any of the animals in evidence anywhere. They all had to scrounge for a living. As far as I could tell, none of them was fed purposely as we might a pet or a farm animal, so it was a free-for-all for anything they could get, including each other's shit. The pigs played a major role in this play as I came to find out the first time I used the outhouse on stilts and was startled by a loud snortling and looked down between my legs to see a large pig standing in the wash looking up apparently waiting for his breakfast. Somewhat discomfiting it was at first but I got used to it and acquired a new perspective on the old saw – "one man's trash is another's treasure". The same sort of thing would happen while walking the high trails in the Andes where each lonely homestead would feature at least one vicious, skinny cur of a dog who would miraculously show up as you squatted among the rocks to eat your leftovers.

At this point, I could start to rave about flush toilets, either qualifying the system as the quintessence of civilization or else the sum of all our stupidities. I will do neither as the subject has been well exhausted all over the map. I will just say that the flush system does a miraculous job for cities but that it makes no sense to force installation of septic systems in the country. To think about the potential fertility lost every day to the flush toilet is a mind blower. If a city system could be figured that would separate the humanure flush from the general sewer pipage, the manure part could be reclaimed without the toxic chemicals and the heavy metals. That would render the city flush somewhat reasonable but I see no reason why people living isolated in the country shouldn't have composting toilets. Even such an enlightened state as Vermont mandates a septic system with each new housing construction. They are expensive to start and trouble later on. So when we started, we couldn't handle the expense and didn't want to flush anyhow. Instead we planned to have an "inhouse". It began life as an outhouse and then became an inhouse as the construction surrounded it.

We had been reading a book devoted to the construction and design of Japanese houses. In this book, the author maintained that the situation of the typical Western bathroom was barbaric and uncivilized. The idea of bathing and shitting in the same room made no sense to the Japanese at all. They of course are quite particular about bathing so the excretion function was always placed at the other end of the house from the bathing function. It might be that Westerners are less fussy or the explanation for the modern bathroom may have to do with plumbers and the advent of the flush toilet. Plumbers would insist that it made more than sense to concentrate your pipage in one place instead of stringing water lines all over the house. However that went, we agreed with the Japanese concept and when the house was built, it not only incorporated a separate 'bath' room but also a 'shower' room both upstairs with their own sinks to accommodate different people doing different things at the same time while the inhouse resided down and out a side door.

The construction of the house entailed slicing into the hillside and pushing the excavate to the fore to create a level building space. This created a bank at the front into which I cut a notch with pick and shovel 6ft long, 3ft wide and 4ft deep. I concreted this into a tight box with a door in the front and a hole in the top. A piece of luck appeared in the town dump as a perfect little throw-away outhouse with roof and seat intact. We set this over the hole until it became the star performer in a celebratory bonfire inaugurating the inhouse. The inhouse features a built-in exhaust pipe with a fan. There is no odor in the room unless there is a power outage, which has happened but now we have it covered with little solar panel. There occurs a curious phenomenon when it's 20° below and the wind is blowing. The fan begins to vibrate and howl in a husky voice, giving rise to the inhouse myth of the "Doo-Doo Munster". We keep the pile covered with sawdust or shavings and clean it out once a year. I wheelbarrow it to a different location each time, usually near an apple tree, and leave it to transform in two years to dark, sweet compost that you may crumble between your fingers. Our humanure adds its small contribution to the fertility of the farm. Even though I feel that it would be safe to use anywhere, I follow the conventional wisdom and don't put it on any vegetable that may be eaten raw. I often put it on the dry bean patch before planting or around any fruit plantation. It is not necessary to build an entire inhouse to accommodate your own humanure. Some friends of ours set up a system with a home-made wooden throne which takes a five gallon bucket under it. They keep it supplied with sawdust and compost it outside. Even just collecting your urine in a jar would make some little contribution. Ladies I'm sure that you can figure the logistics of that one.

Our main-stream compost basically comes out of the chicken coop. We usually keep about 20 hens and one rooster. The coop has a dirt floor which we cover with shavings. Everything that comes out of the kitchen year round goes right into the coop. Instead of sending kitchen scraps to an outside bin where coons, skunks and various rodents might rummage, we give it all to the chickens. Edible or not, it all disappears. Banana skins, citrus rinds, cabbage stems, egg shells, meat and bones, snap-trapped mice – everything goes and is either eaten or scratched into the litter. I wait to dig out the coop until the comfrey flowers. Comfrey is the prime green ingredient in the compost pile. It is highly nitrogenous and is easily propagated and increased by slicing the thick root into pieces and planting in rich locations. We started a row next to the south wall of the horse barn where the roots could feed underneath the stalls. The growth there is explosive and it all goes into the compost along with cut grass and nettle. Nettle is another powerful plant worth establishing just for compost production even though it is also highly nutritious eating. Cut the comfrey, grass and nettle, dig out the coop, mix in last year's corn cobs and dry bean stalks, add lime, wood ash, phosphate, green sand and azomite and then stand back and let it ferment. That will feed the root crops, the salad bowl and the greens, whereas the manure pile accumulated out of the horse barn is used to fertilize the corn, squash, tomatoes and cabbage.

You can see that chickens play a key role in our fertility cycle. However they do consume a whole lot of grain – in our case, organic corn and barley. If you are familiar with "Diet for a Small Planet", you might question the advisability of "misusing" perfectly good grain feeding animals instead of eating it directly yourselves. It is a question and a conundrum. However, life without a constant supply of fresh eggs and with a never ending breakfast of cornmeal mush would become a less joyful affair. I think the question is more applicable to ruminants than to animals that will not thrive or can't survive on just grass. You could free-range your chickens and that would help to lower you grain consumption somewhat. I decided against that option after chasing wildly after a hen-toting fox cursing and yowling and attempting to outrun old Reynard himself. I failed to impress him (or her) with my empty threats and she even came back for more. Instead I throw into the coop handfuls of clover, dandelions or violet leaves. Violet leaves are very high in Vitamin C and once established, will compete easily in your lawn or pasture. That doesn't substitute for free-ranging but it does lead to a dark orange egg yolk. A fresh farm egg is a far different item from a supermarket egg. It is characterized by its color (not pale yellow); by its compactness (the white nestles close around the yolk); and by looking sunny side high (the yolk perches right on top). We manage to keep the flock going in perpetuity by hatching our own. We no longer eat any and I don't cull so they just cluck on into old age until one night they fall off the perch and I bury them in the manure pile in the morning. Inside a coop where all the hens lay their eggs on top of each other, it's impossible for a hen to set and hatch a clutch. I have come up with a system to allow this to happen. Once a hen has become 'broody' – a condition somewhat like catatonia that is easy to recognize – I transfer her to a separate box caged in away from the others. This can only be done in the dark and the new box is also kept dark for 24 hours because she is attached to the place where she started brooding and will abandon the new box with its eggs – feeling them not to be her own. When she awakens to the new dawn a full day later, the eggs under her will have become familiar enough that she settles to them and broods for 21 days to hatch usually between 8 and 10 chicks.

Besides providing raw material for compost, chickens have contributed to homestead fertility in another way. If you raise a certain number of chickens for meat, you can keep what you need for your own, sell the rest and pay off the cost of the grain. It is a big up-front investment in feed but you end up with chicken meat for no cost and more importantly for this discussion, vast swaths of chicken shit slathered across selected areas. Certain parts of the homestead on the high end of the terrain were so leached out with soil so poor that only lichens and moss could survive there. This was where we fenced in the meat birds to begin with. We would order in 50 chicks of those all-white 'monster' birds that, if you feed them commercial mash, will often grow so fast that their legs won't support their bodies and they end their days sitting next to the trough.

We fed them whole grain organic corn, soy and barley and as they grew, we expanded their enclosure and moved the fence along. They did well under those conditions and the lichens did not. The grass came on like gangbusters and those areas are now part of our orchard, growing apples, plums and a booming butternut tree. Those chickens, after being butchered by 'We Kill, You Chill', leave behind one last addition to farm fertility – a large pile of white feathers.

Homestead Solution #3

When you build your barn or buy your barn and you really should have water available right there, you may go out and buy what is known as a frost-free hydrant. Or you could make one yourself at a fraction of the price. The basic idea of the thing is to provide out-door water through the winter without resorting to extreme measures involving heat tape or useless insulation. This works by burying the susceptible parts below the frost line and allowing the water to drain out of any exposed part. Let's just say that you are starting with ¾" plastic pipe which you have laid in a trench at whatever depth you deem necessary (mine is only at two feet and doesn't freeze). As per the accompanying diagram, you go from there to a ¾ shut-off with a built-in drainage nipple. Before you put it in, you take off the handle and weld or braze a ¼ rod onto the stock long enough to end up above ground and then braze the handle back on. The rest of the plumbing gets the water up and into your buckets or trough. The key to this system is the drainage nipple. It has a cap with a rubber gasket to keep it from leaking. However, in this case, you want it to leak so unscrew the cap a few turns making sure that it will stay put but allow the water from all the above ground plumbing to drain   To prevent the water from pooling beneath the drain cap, dig a deep hole to begin with a fill it with gravel

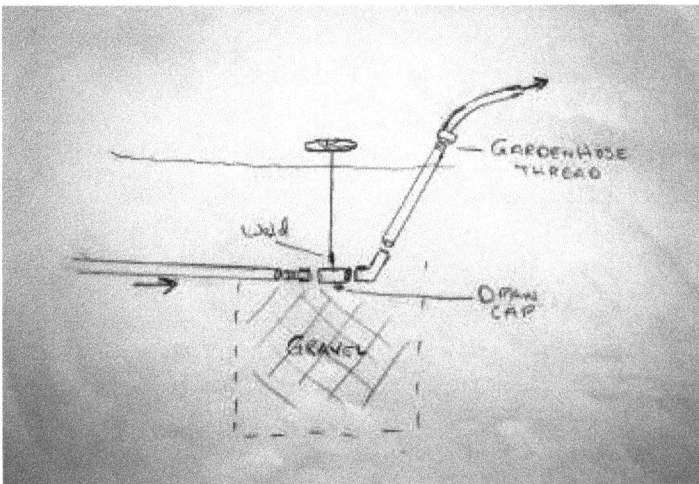

Feed Thyself

I suppose the hanging question in regards to 'growing your own' is: can you really feed yourselves from a few acres of farmstead in central Vermont? Well, yes: if you are willing to subsist on beans and potatoes. And realistically, no: but you can come pretty close, so let's discuss how. Let's start with the food that you really can provide for yourselves – those crops that you may harvest, process, store and eat without extraordinary effort. The indigenous American staples are the most conducive to homestead labor. They can be planted, tended and harvested entirely by hand. Potatoes, corn, beans and squash: none of these need any tool other than a hoe to deal with from seed through harvest. I think that this is one of the reasons that the Industrial Revolution came first to Europe and not the Americas. The staples in Europe, discounting turnips, mangels and such, were the small grains: oats, rye, wheat and barley. What a lot of work to deal with them! What motivation to come up with a contraption to do it for us. First reapers, then binders, then combines and the machine age was off and rolling.

Potatoes came out of the Andes after the Spanish invasion in the 16th century and have become a worldwide crop producing more tonnage than any other. Believe it or not, the country that produces the most potatoes is China. Potatoes create more food per allotted space than any other crop, unless for some reason, you have a love affair with mangels. Our first summer at Gingerbrook, before there was any garden space, we harvested a potato crop by placing some sprouted spuds on top of the sod in an open spot and covering them with hay. We store our harvest in wooden boxes in the root cellar and eat them until May when they start sprouting in the dark. If you plant a row of earlies in April, you can start eating them again in July. Potatoes are by no means fool proof. You have to deal with the Colorado potato beetle and occasionally the dreaded late blight comes floating in on the wind and the entire crop can be destroyed. That's what happened to the Irish in the 1840's when the lucky ones emigrated to the U.S. and the unlucky starved. In highland Peru, where the natives still subsist on potatoes, they make it through the dry times waiting for the next harvest by freeze drying some of the previous. They spread them out on the stony ground, stomp on them to express some of the moisture and let the high altitude sun and the cold, dry nights dehydrate the potatoes. The end product is called chunu. It makes the most god-awful boiled dinner you have ever tasted but it's better than starving. When they are eating fresh potatoes, the Quechua always boil them with the skins on. It turns out that potatoes offer a store of vitamin C but its concentrated around the skin so if you peel them after boiling, the vitamin C will have migrated into the center and become available. They are protected from scurvy and the lowly spud also yields a surprising amount of protein – it is a sustaining food. I have been with people in small highland villages where potatoes are the only thing they will have for a meal. They would sit around a terra cotta pot boiled over a llama dung fire (there are no trees for firewood) and reach in with their fingers, slide off the skins and drop them on the hard earth floor to feed the guinea pigs. The Peruvian Quechua grow dozens of varieties of potatoes. They come in all shapes, sizes and colors and each has its own name. Most of the world grows its potatoes clonally and the Quechua do too, but they have the opportunity to continually produce new varieties through cross-pollinated seeds. I brought home 10 varieties of potatoes from Peru in 1977, each one widely different from any other. I planted them all and some did better than others but they all disappeared in the fire of 1985. Or so I thought until two years later when I noticed some potato plants growing beyond the fringe of the garden. They turned out to be one of the Peruvians – an oblong purple called 'papa runa' (potato man). It had held its own on its own through a couple of winters and saved itself for us and we are still growing it today.

The other three American crops, the famous three sisters, corn, beans and squash, play equally big roles in feeding us. Corn (known as maize everywhere else), we use in three different forms – sweet, pop and flint. One other type of maize is called flour corn. It differs from flint in that it is soft with a white, starchy center. Flour corn is favored by tortilla makers because it can be ground by hand. Flint corn is hard and shiny, has higher protein and in general is more northerly. The last type of maize is dent corn. That is the corn grown around the world in uncountable acreage for animal feed. These five types of corn have been man-made and manipulated for so long that there are now countless variations of size, color, shape and flavor. We chose one of each of the three and saved the seeds year after year from the best ears so that now the plants are completely at home here. These are 'open-pollinated' varieties: you can't save the seeds of hybrids and have them come true. We used to count the growing season as 90 days (it now seems to be at 110-115) so that the corn had no time to dawdle and it didn't help to protest occasional chilly nights. The flint corn is an 8 row long, slim ear that is yellow but throws in a percentage of shiny, dark red ears. This flint corn supplies us with our corn meal. We pick it by hand and then disk over the stalks. It needs to be hung up under cover in order to dry sufficiently for storage. Along about late winter, we shell the ears and put the corn in large canning jars for keeping. Shelling a tight ear like this flint is no easy task and we were lucky to get a corn sheller rescued from an old barn. It is a cast iron, hand crank relic of the days when they were serious about making tools to last. It has 1909 stamped on it and it spits out the cobs from one end as fast as you put them in the other.

Sweet corn ain't what it used to be. Due to genetic manipulations, you can get yourself seed that will give sugary enhanced, supersweet or even 'synergistic' sweet corn. If you really go off the deep end, you can even grow corn that will kill any worm that tries to bore into it without any help from you.

These varieties are crisper, stay tender longer after picking and how sweet they are! Needless to say, you can't save those seeds and anyhow we are happy with our "old fashioned" corn, have always been and don't intend to grow anything else. Our sweet corn is a white variety which we acquired through the Seed Savers Exchange maybe 20 years ago. It was a quick grower when it came and by selecting seeds over time, it has become more so. Plant it the end of May and eat it at the beginning of August. Summer without sweet corn wouldn't resonate. It would be like winter without snow and you sadly sequester your toboggans. In order to save your corn seed, you have to be somewhat careful. If you are growing two types or three, as we sometimes do when we plant popcorn, they will cross-pollinate and your flint corn will go sweet or your pop, flinty. It helps that they tassel at different times so that there aren't competing armies of pollen in the air. Other help comes from double rows of mammoth sunflowers planted along the edges where their hairy leaves catch the flotilla, and from locating the blocks at a distance from each other. We try to eat fresh as much of the sweet corn as we can as a rite of summer. But the daily more-than-you-can-eat gets cut off and put into the freezer to be pulled out for winter meals.

Popcorn is a wonderful thing. There is a wonderful set of words in Latin America for popcorn – "palomitas de maiz" – little doves of corn. It has an air of mystery about it. There's some magic involved in those transforming explosions. It seems straightforward when you buy that packet at the store. You dump them into the pan, apply heat and voila, they pop. However, if you grow your own, maybe they pop and maybe they don't. It turns out that the kernels will only pop if they are carrying the right amount of moisture. What's the right amount? If they're too green, they won't pop, and if they're too dry, they won't. A climate controlled curing room would do it but that's an unlikely addition to your homestead, so our solution is to hang it in the house to dry, keep running test batches until they pop and then shell and seal them in canning jars. There are not as many pop varieties as there are of the other corn types. Most of them are short season but not as short as the type we settled on – Tom Thumb. It's a tiny plant that puts out a 4" ear that is finished and drying on the stalk long before anything else.

Saving your own seeds is of course possible for every vegetable but hardly feasible on the homestead. For many vegetables, it's tricky or troublesome for various reasons. For some, you have to worry about cross pollination from similar species which then renders the seed untrue to type, and for others that flower and seed their second year, you have to bring through the winter to replant and even then, you might have to isolate them to keep them pure. Squash would be an example of the former, and carrots of the latter. Squash seeds seem like good candidates for saving. They are large, easily extracted and dried for keeping. However, first of all, hybrid seeds in general don't come true and are not worth saving. Secondly, from among your open pollinated types you must isolate the members of the three different squash and pumpkin families away from each other to prevent cross pollination leading to unexpected seed variations. In the case of carrots, you must select a good one from the root cellar in early May, plant it and soon it will send up a flower stalk which then proceeds to mature seeds. The trouble here is that the world outside is full of wild carrots – family members, some of whom are poisonous, who are sending their pollen aloft perhaps to find its way to your sweet, little domestic carrot.

Saving seeds yields a lot of advantages. You are independent of the seed companies; you are not likely to run afoul of any genetic tomfoolery; and you can raise plants that become increasingly adapted to their actual microclimate and fertility situation. It is also possible to overcome the problems mentioned above – after all, the seed people do it all the time. However, the advantages have to be balanced against the hassle factor. With everything else you might have to do, do you have the inclination, patience and attention to detail necessary to pull it off? Some things are better left to the professionals and we decided to limit our seed saving to the easier crops – corn, beans, peas, tomatoes, peppers and occasionally, a special type of turnip.

This brings us to the third of our native American crops and the one to which we devote more space than any other. It is also the one which is the workhorse of homestead nutrition – dry beans. Green beans go into the freezer, canning jars or dilly jars for year-round eating but they are merely salad to the dry beans' meat. There are hundreds of varieties of beans. We have even contributed a couple of our own to the worldwide total. Beans usually self-pollinate and come true but we've had new variations pop up on occasion and have even saved one for years because our son liked the look of it and we call it 'Ben's bean'. I was once swapping stories with a California farmer who said that at harvest time, he just mowed down the rows of beans and left them right there to dry before threshing. I thought this to be highly improbable until I realized that it never rains there – day after day of hot, dry weather. That is surely not the case in Vermont. If you tried that method, you would end up with a mess of mildewed or rotten beans. By the time the beans are ready in late August or early September, the nights are cool or even frosty and the morning dew is heavy and not likely to dry out before midday. The situation is not conducive to drying the pods so you have to get the plants out of the field. I clip them off at the base so as to leave the roots in the soil, then bundle them with twine and hang them beneath the metal roof of the cider mill. It warms nicely there beneath the September sun letting the mature pods crisp up and the still-green pods ripen further and dry. I don't thrash those beans until sometime in Jan or Feb so that they hang through sub-zero temperatures. I feel that this helps considerably in limiting seed borne diseases. In midwinter, I stuff those bundles into grain bags, bring them into the house and jump up and down on them to break up the pods and liberate the beans. Reggae seems to provide a coincidental rhythm for stomping bean bags. We have an ancient wooden machine called a 'fanning mill' that I use to winnow. That's very handy but you can do the same by dumping from one bucket to another in the wind. The dried, powdered leaves and stems and stalks all go into next season's compost.

In reasonable fertile soil, beans will thrive without any extra manure. They actually enhance fertility by fixing nitrogen which you would aid by leaving the roots in the ground. The system of planting in long, narrow plots makes it easy to move from year to year so that you can rotate in such a way so that the same crop isn't replanted in the same spot for at least four years. Corn is planted after beans and is heavily manured. Potatoes are planted after corn and not fertilized at all. Squash is planted after a root crop and also manured off of last winter's pile. Roots are alternated with leaves and take compost dug in deep. Tomatoes and coles each take a dollop of horse and cow in the bottom of their planting holes. But beans specifically have been moved around to all sections over the years so that the nitrogen-fixing bacteria are present everywhere and there is no longer need to inoculate.

Less we forget, the topic in question is feeding yourself. So far we have meandered through potatoes, squash, corn and beans. Potatoes, you can eat your own reasonably for nine months of the year from a relatively small plot. Beans, you can have all year round depending on your tolerance and how much planting space you wish to devote and it's surprising how little space yields how much bean. Corn, we don't consider a staple (except for popcorn!), so we limit the plantations to 30ft of terrace. We love our cornbread and our polenta but we eat it only occasionally and the same for sweet corn, which doesn't necessarily come out of the freezer every day. The people who traditionally do use corn as a diet staple (that would have been everybody from Texas to Panama) have learned that you can't eat it every day and not go red-necked unless you treat it in a special way. That is because corn meal consumed regularly tends to bind up a vitamin B, which leaves the back of your neck flushed. That plus light skin and hot sun will turn you into a redneck. The traditional eaters of tortillas and tamales treat their cornmeal with a wood ash slurry or lye to make masa harina or hominy and this solves the problem. You can also leave your cornmeal mash to sit overnight to ferment with a culture like yogurt and that will also take care of it. As for squash and pumpkins, you certainly can drown in their abundance, and if you consider both summer and winter varieties, they will feed you for perhaps 8 months of the year. The first zucchini, if you start her inside and put her out pushing your lucky frost date, you could eat on July 1. And your last winter squash, maybe a big hubbard, might make it to April. But meanwhile, if you grow the whole variety of winter squash, you will have to seriously devote yourself to consuming the lesser keepers before they start to rot on you. However, every night when you kneel at your bedside in your pajamas and send your thoughts into the unanswering ether, don't forget to sing praises to the mighty zucchini. How generous and loyal it is! I haven't patience for those who cast aspersions upon its jolly green giants. If a few happen to grow right by you, then chop them up and feed them to the chickens – they love it – or throw them into the blender and use the result to replace the milk or yogurt in your pancake recipe, but complain not about too much being a bad thing. While diddling around in the garden the other day, I found myself singing or murmuring as it were, a little zucchini hymn so as not to be selfish about it, I thought to share it with you. It is sung, more or less, to the tune of that world famous ditty "Beans, beans the musical fruit ...".

'Zucchini, zucchini that bountiful gourd. The more you grow, the more you hoard. The more you hoard, the better you feel. So let's have zucchini for every meal!"

Two other indigenous Americans that aren't really staples but are nice to have are tomatoes and peppers. It is hard to imagine life without tomatoes but I don't put peppers in the same category. We've always grown enough cayenne and jalapeno to generate some local heat and to make a few rounds of salsa, and we put some green peppers in the freezer but it only amounts to 'icing on the cake'. As for tomatoes, it's not difficult to fall in over your head and grow too many of too many exotic varieties. We try to limit to 50 plants, which we give plenty of space and do not stake or cage. We grow a selection of 'heirloom' tomatoes and save our seeds, trying new ones occasionally thus participating in mankind's perpetual search for the most flavorful tomato ever. So far the vote tends to favor one called 'Cherokee'. The fruit that is not eaten fresh is juiced and canned as sauce that might also later be reduced to paste in the winter when the cookstove is going.

So far we have been eating pretty well except for April, May and June and the next candidates won't help us much in those months either. These are the Eurasian imports – the roots and the coles. These are strictly perishable root cellar items and once you start moving through April, they know, even though it's dark in there and still cool, that it is time to set the stage for the next generation. Carrots, beets, onions, garlic, cabbages, daikon, leeks, turnips and rutabagas, they all begin to turn flaccid, soggy or moldy and to send out shoots or leaves of various descriptions. Except for garlic which is harvested earlier in the summer and hung up to cure and dry, the others all go into the root cellar in October –November depending on how soon the real cold comes in. Along with apples, carrots are the unquestioned aristocracy of the root cellar. You can successfully grow and store plenty of carrots, as is the case with the rest of the root cellar denizens. But carrots get special treatment. The onions and garlic get hung up on twine and the others get put in wooden boxes and stacked; however, carrots get layered within boxes of maple leaves so they are not touching and then stacked. The boxes come down one at a time as the carrots are used and the maple leaves get thrown into the chicken coop along with carrot nuggets too small to bother with. The temperature in the root cellar gets down into the 30s by mid-December and hovers close to freezing the rest of the winter before climbing again in March. Some years we have eaten carrots in the first week of June. The humble cabbage deserves an extra word here. I continue to find it extraordinary how well and how long they keep through the winter. We put two to a box so that they are not jostling and even in the spring when you peer into a cabbage box and see two balls of black and gray mush, if you keep peeling, you will eventually arrive at a pearly white center that is still sweet and edible. Not raw however. Jo slices and dices it and cooks it in a frying pan with vinegar and oil equal parts. Those would be the last cabbages left and you have to admire and praise their little hearts.

The root cellar is a walk-in built into the earth at the back of the house. It has two pipes to the outside – one cold-in and one warm-out. The inlet has a fan to better take advantage of those November nights that drop below freezing. Along with the vegetables, boxes of apples are also kept in there. They are boxed and stacked by variety – the shortest keepers disappear by December and the longest we don't start eating until February. Some are still there in June but they go to the chickens. We have read about apples and ethylene gas affecting your other vegetables in the same room but we have not bothered about it and don't really notice any problem. The room is bracketed by shelves, where all the canned goods are kept along with vinegar and oil and a miscellany of edibles and drinkables that might be transferred to the refrigerator in the summer when the temperature inside rises to 65o.

We are still in the process of answering the question 'can you feed yourself?' and I fear the end is not yet in sight. The individual vegetables so far mentioned or discussed are those that I feel are possible to do on a small scale by hand or horse and come out with enough for a family for a good part of the year. A serious root cellar, I hope has become obvious, is a necessity. The lean times in the spring can extend in proportion to how deeply invested you are to canning and/or freezing. These are the times when you are likely to pay more attention to your neighborhood co-op. One more character from the above line up that we can't let go by without discussing further is everybody's favorite hot breather – garlic. It's so hot but it likes it so cool – cool and moist, and nothing fazes it except hot and dry. Plant it late in the fall before the first snow and miraculously it is the first green shoot of the spring. Those spring freezes, sometimes all the way into June, don't bother the garlic at all and it's ready to harvest by mid-summer. Once dried and cured, it will stay good into the following spring. We have patches of garlic that have gone feral which can be harvested early somewhat like scallions. These ferals are slowly expanding and are so tenacious that they are out-competing the grass. They have grown into early spring swaths of green that are five feet in diameter. Everything about garlic is easy and once you get going with the variety you like you don't have to buy in any more seed. The only drawback is in its seed to fruit ratio. One kernel of corn yields 100. One bean yields 60. One tomato seed yields many fruits and uncountable new seeds. One garlic clove might only give you back four more. It just means that a larger percentage of your harvest needs to be saved for next season but garlic grows close together so you can pack a lot of crop in a limited space.

O.K. I imagine by now you are saying to yourself: But surely the entire chore of staving off starvation can't be given only to vegetables. What about other good stuff that we like to eat? Well, how about fruit? Fruit. Contemplate the word.

Contemplate the visions bubbling up in your mind. Contemplate how the canny plant world has seduced the animal world with fruit into serving its needs. Contemplate the irrepressible joy that arises when you think about fruit. You don't wonder that herds of monkeys will traverse miles of jungle canopy to get to a massive fig that is ripening its fruit that day. Or that bananas and citrus get shipped around the world from the tropics. Or that a flock of waxwings will arrive at your blueberries and strip them clean before you have a chance to harvest any. I digress, but the point is – don't resist your impulses: plant fruit when and wherever you can. Don't do what I did, telling myself that I was too busy with more important stuff to fool around filling up empty spaces with fruit trees. That is what I do today and have been doing for a while but I skipped the first ten years by not going for a full orchard to begin with. The usual limiting factors were in play - time and money - but the some that were planted and made it through childhood and adolescence are now full-fledged beauties. They have been followed by a mismatched flotilla of variously aged others with the youngest being pencil thin grafted saplings. With the number of apple seeds scattered around the place by way of the cider mill and all the resident apple trees, seedlings are always springing into view through the grass and if I find one in a good spot, I will graft to it my favorite variety of the moment. I get a little thrill when I see a new one show itself but more sooner than later, available spaces will get too tight to squeeze into.

Here is a list of fruit that we have grown and eaten here and expect to continue to do so: Apples, pears, plums, blueberries, raspberries, blackberries, elderberries, currants, grapes, apricots and peaches. All these are completely cold-hardy except the blackberries which occasionally lose their top few buds in a particular winter and the peaches which are a recent gift of the warmer climate. We put in a Reliance peach 25 years ago and it promptly winter killed, but we thought to try again recently and have been rewarded with our own succulent peaches. There is hardly anything better than a ripe peach right off the tree. The berries we expect a crop from every year but the larger fruit can easily skip a season from time to time but it's very unusual to have no apples whatsoever.

Every fruit that you plant is not going to make it. Everything happens to fruit trees. Borers chew into them and riddle the trunk. Meadow mice and voles strip the bark and eat the roots. Deer rub the velvet off their antlers against the trunk and eat the dormant buds. Fungal and bacterial cankers eat into the limbs; bulls escape from the pasture and shred a young tree with their horns; the electric company comes to make a repair and flattens one with their truck; a rogue mowing machine shreds one to pieces. You mourn the loss of each one – they are your babies – you've invested yourself in them all but you learn from each loss and you plant more and increase the protection level. Encase them in plastic grow-tubes to start. When they emerge from the top of the tube, take it off and circle it with a stout fence. In the winter, wrap a guard around the base of the trunk. Don't remove the fence until they are large enough and tall enough to withstand the assaults of bull, deer and machine. Don't grow dwarf versions of anything so that they really will grow up tall and stout. Unless you are planning an eventual pick-your-own operation, you will want the first branches to come out at five feet above the ground. You will eventually be thankful for this when you can mow under the tree without getting on your hands and knees and you see the deer balancing on their hind legs trying to reach something edible. Believe me, you won't mind picking your own from a ladder. These grow tubes are a relatively new thing which I think are terrific. If you are starting with small grafted saplings or even unbranched, bare rooted trees, the tube protects them from many destroyers. Borers, rodents, deer and machines are kept away while a warm, moist microclimate inside fosters faster growth. However, it seems that there must be a downside to every new miracle fix and in this case, it might come if you experience extended periods of hot, rainy weather inducing a fungal riot inside the tube. I also lost a promising young apple tree once by leaving the tube in place under the first branches. Carpenter ants set up shop inside and excavated the trunk to create a metropolis that suited their megalomaniacal ant dreams but killed the tree.

Plums are a homestead wunderkind because they are so vigorous and require no tending or pruning. If you start by buying one, you can soon turn that into an entire plum village for no additional expense. Buy a Japanese-American youngster and set-in next to it a wild American for pollination and then wait for root sprouts to emerge. Wild Americans are easy to find and transplant – they live roadside just about everywhere and can be located by their white flowers first thing in the spring. Plums like to live in thickets and so go about creating them by sending up shoots as their roots extend. Amazingly they may reach 20ft from the parent trunk. These sprouts are all clones of the root stock so if left to mature, they will not produce edible fruit but they offer themselves perfect for grafting. Duplicate the original if you love it or beg, steal or barter scions from other types and before you know it, you're plum crazy!

You could also go homestead crazy with another easy-to-propagate fruit – grapes. Our first grape came from a piece of root which we chopped off an incredible wilding that screeched us to a halt along a back road because it featured a trunk the size of your forearm and reached all the way to the top of a 80ft maple. I thought to train it along some left-behind telephone cable but it expressed its disapproval by never yielding a single grape while secretly planning a bust-out. It worked its way along the ground toward the nearest tree and then launched itself skyward. By the time I noticed, it was well on its way so I shrugged and thought, "O.K. do it your own way". Feeling liberated, by the next growing season it had reached the top of the 20ft black walnut and in its exuberance, broke down some branches and loaded the tree with grapes. There were so many that I ran them through the cider mill, squeezed out their juice and fermented out a batch of wine. Sour grapes make sour wine; we are still drinking it but it's hardly a candidate for Vintage Vendors so we've started other sweeter types.

The Grape that would not be denied.

You can multiply grapes to your heart's content by either transplanting pieces of root or taking cuttings in the early spring and sticking them in the ground with some rooting compound. Yet another ideal homestead fruit that will expand itself infinitely if allowed is the blackberry. Start with just a few plants or roots, put them in a place with plenty of grow room so you won't resent their incursions in the future and they will multiply and spread into a thorny paradise. There are many variations on the blackberry theme but look to find one that grows straight and tall (8ft) and yields fruit the size of your thumb. If you are lucky, you could find one such in your home area and transplant. If not, one called the Himalayan blackberry fits the bill. Most varieties featured in the catalogues will not make it in this cold zone but if you live farther south you might even be able to go thornless. Blackberries really respond to plenty of nitrogen and a slick way to feed them is to summer your laying hens in the patch every once in a while.

The berries are the quintessential homestead food and on top of the list are blueberries. Blueberries are what permaculture is all about. Plant them, get the soil right, keep the fertility level up, mulch them heavy, and then, with maybe an occasional pruning cut, nothing else except picking berries for the rest of your days. Well, maybe you'll have to deal with the birds to see who gets to the berries first. We have found that hanging those owl-eyed balloons with flash tape seems to work. 10 to 15 plants, after they gain their maturity, will keep you rolling in blueberries. Blueberries are long-lived and sturdy but it takes them a while to grow up. You can really speed up the process by giving them plenty of nitrogen in the beginning. Even resorting to ammonium sulfate could be worth it before then settling back into compost and acidic mulch when the plants are sized up. Blueberries are neat, clean, live forever, and stay where you put them. Elderberries are rampant, rambunctious, brittle, shaggy with dead branches, and wonderful. They thrive in moist locations in rich, humusy soil and will feed the birds and honeybees as well as you. The tiny berries are tedious to pick and occasionally I'll lose control and stuff an entire spray into my mouth and using my teeth as rakers, pull the stem through leaving a mouthful of berries and tiny stemlets. Currants, black, red and white, like blueberries and elderberries, don't require much attention once they are established. Raspberries and blackberries however are somewhat more demanding of your time. They both put fruit on canes the second year. That leaves a forest of dead canes from the year before. You can either try to ignore those to your peril or cut them out every spring. The raspberries also need to be top pruned in the fall otherwise the snows will flatten them. The tall, thick canes of the blackberries usually manage to stand up through the snow but there is often a mess in the patch to be cleaned up in the spring. 100ft of raspberry in rows 10ft apart will keep you well supplied, but with blackberries, you will get to decide with your scythe what size limit to impose on the patch. I don't try to tame blackberries into rows. I started a few transplants in an open area and then just let them ramble until that season when I thought – 'that's probably enough' and now I just keep it mowed around the periphery. Both these berry patches are permanent fixtures however – they have maintained for many seasons with copious mulchings on the rasp and plenty of nitrogen on the black.

There is one more fruit that you might not consider but which maintains itself, and even slowly spreads when completely left alone, and delivers a vitamin C punch – rose hips. Our hedge of Rosa rugusa comes from seeds which we transported from plants growing alongside the beaches on the coast of Maine. I should say – our 1 1/2 year old daughter transported them – in her diapers. Rosa rugosa, sometimes known as 'beach plums', grows rampant in the sand on the Maine coast and Maya, attracted by the bright red fruit, plucked and swallowed her way along the beach. Rugosa hips are plump and full of seeds and when the dirty diaper pail got home, it was obvious we had a load of future roses all fertilized and ready to go. I skinned out a strip with a mattock and Jo laid out the diaper contents all along it. As I write this, Maya is approaching 30 and the roses are rampant and loaded with ripe hips. They look like they will go on forever and not only do you get the rose hips, you also get the roses. A few of the bushes also feature white flowers. The typical to-do with rose hips is dry and store them to make tea during the winter but I also like to grab one as I walk by and scrape off the thin outer skin with my teeth. They make quite a seed packet and you have to work at it so as not to swallow any seeds.

I'm a proponent of pigging-out on fruit in season. It just feels right and healthful and part of the party that is summertime – and the plants take great pleasure in your crunchings and slurpings and comings back for more. They want you to want their offerings. Their mission in life is fulfilled by your yearnings. However, even if you gorge right off the bush, that will still leave plenty for putting by before they ripen right past you. Can, dry, freeze, jam, ferment or juice – each fruit poses you a choice. Peaches, pears and plums sure are fine coming out of a jar with a light syrup. Blueberries dry like raisins but we like to put a bushel into the freezer to whip up frozen into smoothies throughout the year. Raspberry and blackberry jam can't be beat but jam is 50% sugar, which we don't like to buy so we limit the quantities. Rhubarb really likes being canned. Elderberries, like blueberries, are a nutritional bonanza so we prefer to freeze them so as not to subject them to heat. Apples offer their own cornucopia of possibilities. Early ripening apples ready in late summer or early fall are usually pretty tart, go by fast and are good candidates for sauce. Later varieties ripen according to their own schedule so you can use them out of the root cellar in succession from October until May (although very few apple varieties will last that long in unrefrigerated storage). Some people choose to keep their apples in the form of cider. They will bring 50 milk jugs to the cider mill, then fill an entire freezer with them and bring out one a week for an entire year. Others will do the same except they will put the 50 gallons in a barrel, let it ferment and enjoy theirs hard. We keep our cider in the form of juice by pasteurizing and preserving it in canning jars. This apple juice can also be used as the base liquid for other fruit juices. Take any of the berries and put one cup in the bottom of a half-gallon jar, add honey or syrup to your liking, and fill the jar with 180o apple juice. Let it sit for a couple of weeks until the berry has infused into the juice, then pour, strain and drink a raspberry, elderberry, blackberry, blueberry, grape, or currant, apple nectar. This technique will also work using just boiling water instead of juice. The best drink of all in this category can be made with chokecherries – you've got to try it to believe it! This is contagious. Once you get started, you may fill all the shelves in your cellar/pantry before you catch yourself. A variation on this theme is called 'shrub' – or was called shrub and therefore probably still is. This involves using cider vinegar instead of juice or water. This time fill the jar half way with the selected fruit and top off with vinegar. Let the vinegar infuse with fruit, then strain and mix one-to-one with honey. Now you have a thick, syrupy and sour concentrate of fruit which you mix with water, hot, cold or fizzy according to your taste and you'll never buy another sodey pop for the rest of your days.

Cane sugar is an item that is hard to do without. There are times when it only will fit the bill. But you've got to buy it in from the tropics and you may cut down on its use by substituting your own maple or honey. Maple syrup is strictly a north country affair which takes a bit of organizing to produce and I'll talk more about that elsewhere but honey bees will thrive just about anywhere. Well, perhaps not anywhere. They have recently taken some hits from unexplained sources, maybe pesticide related, but if you live out of agribusiness territory, you can still have reasonable luck with them. We usually have just one hive and sometimes two if I capture a swarm. A colony doesn't usually maintain for longer than three winters but meanwhile they have paid for themselves and you start with a new one. Dealing with bees seems like a daunting proposition and I remember feeling intimidated at the beginning. Intimidated and scared. The single best remedy for those feelings is to suit yourself so that you now feel invulnerable. I once picked up a box full of bees and comb that I has set aside and I lifted it upside down and the whole show crashed out onto the ground Pure and sudden terror! A swirl of extremely angry bees hit me in a cloud and I ran as if the very furies themselves were unleashed to persecute me to the ends of the earth and the end of time for such stupidity. Honeybees have a memory and they bear grudges. They didn't forgive me for a long time and anybody else walking by that hive would be stung without question. To repair the damage and get that hive back together, I needed to discard my blasé attitude and clothing and suit up so that no bee could get into me. And I have done that ever since. That allows you to calm down, work slowly and smoothly, and concentrate on your actions rather than worry about getting stung. With one reference book and a few simple operations every year, you can expect to harvest some honey. In this locale, we will get from 30 to 75lbs from a hive depending on the season. This is without really knowing what I'm doing and basically leaving the bees alone. It is helpful to find a two-frame honey extractor to have on hand for the job. When they are friendly, and most hives are, honeybees are wonderful company about the homestead. They are often on flowers next to you in the garden and you can get just an eyeball away to watch them stuffing pollen into their leg pouches. Your relationship to flowers changes with honeybees as your guides. You see some cells in the comb packed with bright purple pollen and you recognize it coming from the outrageous purple anthers of the marshmallow flowers. You end up bringing in plants like the globe thistle when you see those ping-pong flowers each with four or five bees on it. And at fruit flower time, or when the Basswood in front of the house is in bloom, and the whole world is abuzz, you feel quite thankful that you can share your space with honeybees.

Are we still hungry? What else can we grow for ourselves? How about nuts? If we eliminate hazel nuts, which we have never tried to grow, this category presents an extreme case of delayed gratification. If you start today by planting a butternut or a black walnut, you might have to wait 25 years or more for your first nut. Hickories take even longer to mature. Persian or English walnuts are not cold-hardy in this climate so they're off the list. However we have waited and we are now rewarded by prodigious quantities of nuts – occasionally.

There's no predicting the next nut year – perhaps every three or four years the squirrels will start to collect and squabble and begin snipping off green nuts before they are ripe cascading them off of Buster's hood. It is not necessary to pay the nurseries for either of these trees. Find a local tree, collect fresh nuts (some people will be happy to have you clean up their lawn), submerge them in nursery bed, cover with hardware cloth to thwart the rodents and transplant when they come up. These seedlings will end up the same size as your boughten treeling ten years later   Nut trees have that mighty packet of energy to call upon so they leap into being to start but then they might cause some worry by seeming to stop growing for a year or two. They have utilized the nut packet and now they are putting everything they can metabolize into pushing a taproot far underground. Especially if you have a pocket of soil that will accommodate that root as far as it wants to go, then your black walnut will commence to add on 18" a year to its branchings. After 30 years, your walnut might be 35 to 40ft high. Butternuts are a questionable investment at this time. They used to grow prolific around Vermont and other cold-climate locations but have now been added to the list of trees in trouble. A contagious canker is decimating them, however we have found that you might keep them healthy by maintaining maximum fertility in a wide circle around them – compost, rock phosphate, lime and mineral supplements.

Black Walnuts and butternuts are both a devil to crack. If it weren't for the fact that they contain so much energy, it would seem that you expend more cracking and extracting than you get eating them. It is fun to do with kids – you crack and they extract – but you can tell that this is not going to be a serious addition to your home-grown diet. So let's move on to something that really could be. This is the topic of meat. I have saved this till last because it may be the most important portion of your diet or it may be the least. I have already mentioned that we have virtually stopped eating meat but that we raised our own plenty for quite a few years. We stopped because I despaired of killing animals but that is only my own conundrum and doesn't diminish the fact that growing your own meat is the easiest, most economical and most proteinacious food that your homestead could provide. "Easy" is perhaps a word that hardly applies to anything you might attempt on the homestead and now that I've written it and am sitting here thinking about it, it would seem that what it took to arrive that plate of mashed potatoes on your dinner table was a whole lot 'easier' than that beef burger. However I think that there is some sense to my madness and it has to do with quality and quantity all wrapped up in one big convenient package. A bull calf slaughtered in the late fall of its second year will yield you hundreds of pounds of meat. All at once, that's a serious addition to your lunch possibilities. If the infrastructure were already in place, the grass, the fence and the barn, and the man came to slaughter, and you sent the carcass to the butcher to be cut and wrapped, it would seem like an enormous windfall that came quite "easily". This is, of course, beef that we are talking about now. Beef, or sheep or goat, is grass concentrated in a form that you can eat and grass is the base upon which the homestead sits. Grass (we would define that as just about anything green that might grow in your orchard, pasture or hayfield) not only grows your animals and miraclizes your milk, but continually cuts to make your compost, and mulch and feed your fruit trees. The economics of raising meat this way is unbeatable. You have to provide hay for the cow that winter but after the calf is born in the spring, they are out on the grass. The calf drinks milk until he is weaned when they go inside for the next winter and meanwhile you are also getting your share of that milk. If you buy in another bull calf to join in on the grass/milk bonanza, that one can be sold as veal, which will pay for last winter's hay. Meanwhile, your meat animal, still a calf, will only consume a few bales of hay the next winter and will go on to bulk up on grass the entire summer following. That meat has cost you almost nothing and the bull calf never became old enough to get "bullish" on you. We didn't want to pay anybody to slaughter and butcher but also in the spirit of doing it all yourself, we convinced ourselves that we really knew what we were doing. All you need are something with which to hoist him off the ground, a couple of very sharp skinning knives and a meat saw – and perhaps some prior knowledge obtained either through books or by watching a professional.

Raising fowl for meat can be another profitable homestead enterprise. Chickens, turkeys, ducks, geese or guineas – some are more attractive propositions than others. Ducks, geese and guineas all can forage most of their own living given the right circumstances. However ducks really need a living pond to make a go of it and guineas are entertaining but so close to the wild that you would need a rifle to harvest them. They are indigenous African birds at home on the open savannas; they like to fly and don't like being cooped. They will wander widely, roost in the trees and lay 20 eggs on top of each other in a communal nest. They raise an unholy ruckus from time to time and either you will find that entertaining or perhaps downright irritating. Geese are a good fit for the homestead because they will grow solely on greens. They don't need water other than to drink, and they will mow a pasture down smooth and leave behind a layer of fertilizing slime. They have the added attraction of propagating themselves without any attention from you. A matched pair might raise 6 to 10 goslings every year. Geese are long-lived and cold-hardy, and they are feisty as I've described elsewhere and will do things like attacking passing cars trying to bite the tires if they get themselves into the road. A goose is a big bird and it's a piece of work to pluck and clean one. The feathers are strongly attached and don't want to come out but at least a goose is nowhere near as heavy as a turkey. If you keep feeding him, a tom turkey can weigh up to 50 pounds. That one wouldn't fit into anybody's oven so perhaps at some point you just stop feeding him. All that weight is just grain in another form. Turkeys and chickens, even if they free range, will eat volumes of grain to get to slaughter weight. The economics of raising them for your own food will work to your advantage however, if you raise extra birds for sale. Figure out how many extra you need to sell to pay for all the grain you have used, and if you've grown them plump and clean and organic, you will have no trouble finding customers. They will also pay for a professional like "We kill, You chill" to come and process the whole bunch for you. We would do up occasional birds for ourselves as we needed but faced with the prospect of slaughtering 50 birds, it would be a case when the Misery Factor came into play.

The Misery Factor comes into play to define your bottom line. At what point might you just say no? To arrive at your decision to go or no go on any proposition that might need your input, you could weigh a whole series of factors including time, money, degree of difficulty, available help, weather, tools needed or urgency, but after cogitating the whole list, you sometimes give precedence to the Misery Factor in the end. The thought of killing, plucking, gutting and cleaning 50 fat chickens would send me into a spiral of funk that drops me into the lap of the Misery Factor. The MF often has to do with the weather. You might just say no or you might postpone. An eager-beaver friend asks you hike a local mountain with him and it's a hot summer day – the Factor says no. It's turned 20 below and you had planned to cut and haul firewood today – the Factor says wait for a warmer day. Occasionally the Misery Factor might coincide with the 'Monkey's Raincoat'. The Monkey's Raincoat comes from a Basho that goes something like this:

The first rain of winter

Does anyone have a coat for this monkey?

It's that day in October that skips you into November and into hypothermia when the temperature drops into the low forties and the rain drizzles all day and you were planning to pick up apples for a big squeeze the next day. It's the MF and you retreat until tomorrow and fire up the cook stove. Or perhaps a mason friend proposes doing a chimney job together but it looks ugly and so after consulting and mulling, the Misery Factor wins out and we happily say no. Of course, one man's misery is another man's walk in the park and your own misery threshold can waver and mutate according to that day's body chemistry but you wouldn't be homesteading to begin with if your MF level charts out high on the scale – you would be in an office thinking about the next coffee break.

At one point, we kept rabbits for meat. Rabbits, of course, breed just like – rabbits. You might start with just one pair and before long you could populate a village. The local feed store will sell you commercially designed rabbit pellets which will grow them quite fast, however the homestead advantage here is that rabbits will do just fine eating grass, legumes and other leafy greens. Cut-and-come-again plants like clover, alfalfa, comfrey, violets and dandelions will keep them happy in the summer and high quality second-cut hay will do throughout the winter. Rabbits are traditionally kept in cages off the ground with mesh bottoms to allow the turds to fall through. You can build your own and we did that for a while, but in the spirit of free play, we wondered if we couldn't liberate them somehow. Trying to keep them in a pasture is pretty much out of the question – even if they didn't tunnel their way out, the hawks would gradually pick them off. So at one rental property, they free-ranged an open barn floor alongside goats and chickens and at another, they lived in a dirt-floored cellar. They frolicked and procreated happily in these settings, however as an efficient, agricultural, meat-producing system, it wasn't one for the record books. Rabbits are vigorous burrowers and in these cases, they tunneled right under the foundations of the buildings to create underground nurseries and entire villages even sometimes leading to escape hatches to the outside world. This also puts you in a "how do I catch these critters" situation whenever you would like to harvest one or two. It'll turn you into a trapper and a hunter. We brought one young rabbit into the house as a pet. It had a beautiful soft sorrel coat and we let it roam about the house at will along with the cat. The kids liked playing with it and it was housebroken to the extent that it left its fewmets in approximately the same place on a newspaper we set in a corner. Everything was hunky-dory until the rabbit grew up and he turned out to be a male. Our cat at the time was a female, not that it would necessarily have made any difference because the biological pressure to procreate on a young buck rabbit is obviously intense. He followed the cat around relentlessly trying to mount her until she got fed-up with him and started hissing, spitting and slashing. A few days later, we woke in the middle of the night to a thumping and crashing coming from the kitchen. The rabbit was spinning in circles, bouncing off one cabinet door to the next, out of control. He died soon after and when talking to a vet, we learned that there is an element in cat's saliva that is neurologically pathological to rabbits.

To top off your home-grown meal, you would probably like something to drink. Fruit juice is one thing and alcohol is another. Wine, beer or cider? Buying any of these can put quite a crimp in your budget, but how about making them? Cider, or 'cidre' if you want to go French, just about makes itself once you have done the work to press the sweet cider. Wine is trickier but possible from any of the fruits. We have made wine out of many, ranging from peapods (not recommended) to chokecherries (highly recommended). Beer, on the other hand, is a challenge and takes some real doing. I consider beer to be a health beverage. It is barley tea with an infusion of hops. The sugar in the malted barley is fermented into alcohol but since you are making your own, you can regulate the level to arrive at a nutritious, thirst-quenching beverage. Or, you can knock you own socks off if that is your ilk. Hops will grow rampant soon after you start them and they harvest and dry during the late summer. You can grow your own barley or you can buy 50 lbs. of seed barley, malt it, roast it and brew 25 gallons of beer for a cost of somewhere between 1 and 2 dollars a gallon   If you want to grow your own, I recommend planting it in rows so you can weed and harvest with ease. From every 100ft of barley row, you could expect to reap more or less 10 lbs of grain. Needless to say, bottles for all these beverages are free for the scavenging from any recycling place.

O.K. We have meandered our way growing and raising all these food possibilities to this point where we have to decide whether we have enough. How big is your family? How much meat do you want to eat? Where do you lie on the Misery Factor scale?   And where's the bread?   The bread. If you've noticed the absence from our crop list of wheat, oats, rye, spelt and rice, that is where we parted ways in trying absolutely to grow our own. We have successfully grown these grains (except for rice) and harvested them with a scythe and threshed them with a plastic whiffle ball bat and we continue to do things like growing oats for the straw to make infusions, however when confronted with a 50lb bag of perhaps the finest organic wheat in the world trucked in from the west for sale at a ridiculously low price, we became very happy to buy our small grains. It was no contest. If you buy your grain in bulk and you have a flour mill and you like to make your own bread and pancakes and desserts then it becomes very economical to eat the highest quality grain. Whole grain flour does not keep well and will start to go rancid after a period but the grain itself, if kept in a cool, dry place, will stay good practically forever. So, fear not to purchase 50lb bags and then grind the flour just as you need it. The same tactic works for other products we would not or could not grow for ourselves. Buy in bulk! Rice comes in 25lb bags. Long grain, short grain, basmati or even 'forbidden' black – beautiful stuff and if you store it in canning jars, it will stay perfect for as long as it takes you to eat it. We have bought olive oil in 5 gallon containers; citrus by the case; salt in 25lb bags; and organic sugar from Paraguay in 10 kilo sacks. Add to these the list of other boughten necessities such as spices, tea, chocolate, bananas, coffee, and various and sundries to keep us fed up during the lean time of spring and early summer, and you have the answer to my question at the beginning of this lengthy discussion – No, you can't really feed yourselves to the full extent you might hope but you can travel a long way down that road and enjoy the pickings as you go.

Those Human Beings, Part 2

Ennis

We had first noticed him running the roads. Driving the dirt roads on a mission between here and there, we would pass him and wave having no idea who he was. We were newly arrived in the territory and knew not a soul but this man we would see running sometimes miles from the spot where we had last seen him. We wondered about him and made up stories with the children imposing all sorts of fairy tale characteristics on him. Perhaps some wicked witch was compelling him to run out his days. Maybe he was fleeing the constant pursuit of a band of furies. Perhaps, like Charlie on the MTA, he was fated to run and run and never get off the track. When he showed up at the homestead one day as part of a surprise group to help hammer siding on the shop building, one of the kids asked why he was always running. He replied – because I love to run – an answer that deflated many a wild conspiracy theory manufactured for our own amusement.

Though not a fairy tale creature, Ennis was to prove a most unusual character. No college for him, he enlisted in the army after high school and was sent along with the 82nd Airborne to the Dominican Republic in 1965. His brother went all the way through the educational establishment to become a District Attorney in New York City but Ennis was the wild card in the family. He never did appreciate being forced to sit a desk in a classroom for hours at a time. Growing up in New Jersey, he liked wandering the Pine Barrens away from the houses. He liked running. He liked being in the Dominican Republic. He didn't feel himself to be an occupying army. He got on with the campesinos there. He admired their toughness and their humor. He watched how they lived, farmed, built their houses and got by handily on what they could extract from the land. He carried these people with him as he went from the army to working the British oil rigs in the North Sea. This was dangerous work in extreme conditions which attracted men from many backgrounds and paid very high wages. With this money he bought 100 acres of inaccessible forest in Vermont. Keeping in mind the campesinos in the DR, he built his homestead with an axe. He built a log house and a log barn by squaring the timbers with a broad axe and cutting the notches with a felling axe. The buildings are precise and tight. His land is very remote bordered by a disintegrating road that is hardly more than a trail and he lived alone always claiming that the only thing worse than being single is being married. His water supply was provided by a ½" black plastic pipe lying on top of the ground that ran continuously from a spring in the forest into a deep sink in the house without benefit of any shut-off valve. Running hot water he considered to be an unnecessary luxury. Any hot water used was heated in a blackened pot in his self-constructed fire place. He heated the small house with this fire place and cooked by tossing a can of beans into the fire declaring it ready when the can bowed top and bottom. He would brag that it took a master chef to cook this way without exploding the can in your face.

He had no steady employment and scraped by taking on jobs here and there and would scrimp on things or just do without. One day we came upon him beside the road dowsing into his truck's gas tank with a long thin sapling. It was on a very cold Thanksgiving Day and we were headed to dinner at a friend's bringing an already cooked and still warm 25pounder with us. As I rolled down the window to verify his gasoline problem and he leaned in close to talk, I could feel the warm, ripe turkey air flow up and out and smite Ennis deep in his olfactories. There he was on Thanksgiving Day stranded out of gas beside the road perhaps contemplating his next fire-heated can of beans when we smote him with the warm exhalation of turkey and stuffing. What was to be done but squeeze him in the back seat between the kids, put the roasting pan on his lap and take him with us.

He would often stop by just to talk and have a Jo meal on the side. He had a powerful need to talk. While living alone, he would gradually fill up with words like a balloon inflating until the pressure reached a critical level and he would show up looking to blow. He was intelligent and surprisingly well informed. Often we might pass his truck parked by the store in the village and see him inside with the daily newspaper perched on the steering wheel. He had entertaining mannerisms while talking. If he were making a certain point when one would normally use an index finger for emphasis, Ennis would point with a middle finger. Often he would use two middle fingers held out at the same time like a sheriff having drawn both six shooters. One particular evening after dinner he was telling stories as it began to get late and past the children's bedtime. At that stage in the construction of the first octagon house, there were not as yet any bedrooms so we all slept on the floor in sleeping bags arrayed around the barrel stove. As Ennis carried on talking, one child after another slid into their sleeping bags and snoozed off. Increasing hints like elaborate yawnings and unfurling pajamas had no affect and Ennis kept on talking. Jo appeared in her night gown and crawled into her bag and although Ennis had actually inched closed to the front door, he kept on talking. After still more time, he didn't appear to be slowing down so I slowly disrobed, keeping up my side of the conversation by occasionally muttering – "You don't say" and Ennis kept on talking. Finally I had loaded the stove for the night and settled into my own sleeping bag while Ennis, now standing by the door, hadn't stopped yet. I said to him before drifting away: "Don't rush Ennis but if you do leave, please turn off the light."

One morning at the crack of dawn, Ennis appeared looking mighty wan and bedraggled wondering what was for breakfast.

He had been here the previous night helping to diminish the contents of a keg that we had provided in celebration of finishing (enough to move in) the house. It turned out that after leaving and planning to walk the four miles home, he had only managed the 100 yards to the lower pasture where he had sat down for a 'rest' and only just woken up. He had passed the night on the grass with, as the poem goes, only the stars for a cover.

After Maya was born, Ennis took a shine to her and used to bring special gifts for her like 'The Little House on the Prairie' books. He considered himself to be an expert horseman and figured that every girl should have her own riding horse as a rite of passage. He was a man of many opinions and would insist on educating us about horses saying things like 'horses never lie down' or the best way to break a green horse was to ride him into three feet of snow in which he would soon tire and stop bucking. Be that as it may, he had been using an old-fashioned type Morgan mare as a skid pony and decided that she was the horse for Maya. The mare was a beauty. She was so dark that she appeared black. She was only 13 ½ hands but well-muscled and so willing that she would break her heart trying to pull whatever you might hook her to. One day in the early fall after the remnants of a hurricane had blasted by, Maya rode the mare up the lane and came back excited saying that without even being asked, the mare had jumped the numerous downed trees and branches blown across the road. That mare had chutzpah. There was no task she wouldn't attempt and no barrier she wouldn't jump. After cobbling up a few gates in the pasture to see if she were for real, we took her to the 'Tunbridge World's Fair' and enrolled in the kid's jumping competition. It was just one month after the hurricaned trees that they both came home with blue ribbons.

Ennis was as proud as if they were both his babies. Which was saying something because there were no babies in his life and certainly no women, until of course there were. All the faux-misogynistic rantings and the boastings of the contented and hassle-free life of the bachelor disappeared into a shower, hot water, a flush toilet, a gas stove and the other necessities that a marriage demanded. It didn't last too long but a baby girl came out of it and for Ennis who 'weren't no spring chicken', it was a wondrous miracle and the highpoint of his life and he has been the best daddy any girl could ever have.

The Things Bob Carried – With Apologies to Tim O'Brian

Occasionally when meeting someone for the first time and they will ask me what I do, if I'm feeling contrary, I will reply, only semi-facetiously, "I carry heavy objects for Jo." It's been a lifetime of carrying heavy objects. So I think to myself: What heavy objects have you really carried, Bob?

Bob carried buckets. He carried five gallon buckets. He carried four gallon buckets. He carried plastic buckets. He carried metal buckets. He carried buckets of water, buckets of sap, buckets of milk, buckets of cider, buckets of syrup, buckets of vinegar, buckets of honey, buckets of cement, buckets of sand, buckets of rocks, buckets of compost, buckets of manure and buckets of gravel. Bob carried boxes. He carried wooden boxes. He carried cardboard boxes. He carried boxes of apples, boxes of carrots, boxes of cabbages, boxes of beets and rutabagas, boxes of potatoes, boxes of canning jars, boxes of syrup jugs, boxes of pints, quarts, half gallons, gallons, boxes of books, boxes of used clothes, boxes of junk. Bob carried bags. He carried 100lb bags. He carried 50 lb bags. He carried 25 lb bags. He carried grocery bags. He carried bags of scratch, bags of sweet feed, bags of horse oats, bags of rolled oats, bags of wheat, bags of spelt, bags of rye, bags of buckwheat, bags of barley, bags of lime, bags of phosphate, bags of blood meal, bags of greensand, bags of cement, bags of sand, bags of plaster, bags of apples, bags of apples and bags of apples. Bob carried bales. He carried bales of hay. He carried bales of straw. Bob carried cases. He carried cases of empty jars. He carried cases of full jars. He carried cases of pints, cases of quarts, cases of half gallons, cases of apple juice, cases of vinegar, cases of maple syrup, cases of medium amber, cases of dark, and cases of grade B. Bob carried milk crates. He carried milk crates of canning jars, milk crates of empties, milk crates full, milk crates of milk, of cider, of water. He carried wooden pallets. He carried wooden cider racks loaded with pomace. Bob carried car parts. He carried tires. He carried batteries. He carried transmissions. He carried generators, alternators, carburetors, fuel pumps and back seats. Bob carried armloads. He carried armloads of kindling, armloads of stove wood, armloads of sugar wood, armloads of brush, armloads of stone, armloads of brick, armloads of rhubarb, armloads of sweet corn, armloads of veggies, armloads of chickens, armloads of goaties, armloads of calves, armloads of lamb, armloads of pig, armloads of babies, and armloads of children. Bob carried shoulderloads. He carried shoulderloads of 2x4's, 6's, 8's, 10's & 12's, shoulderloads of poles, poles for rafters, poles for posts, poles for beams, poles for horse equipment, poles for fence posts and poles for trellises. He carried shoulderloads of ladders, shoulderloads of rolled wire fencing, shoulderloads of rolled plastic pipe and shoulderloads of sap line. Bob carried tools. He carried axes and splitting mauls and sledge hammers and scythes and chain saws and wedges and wrenches and oxy-acetylene tanks and jacks and shovels and iron bars and rakes and hoes and ad infinitum those heavy objects travel from here to there.

You, Your Horse and Your Chain Saw – Building a Homestead.

The Homesteaders Bible (which only exists in my head) clearly states that you try to do things only with what you have at hand. You look at what you've got, plan accordingly and go from there. Only when you can't figure any other way, do you go out and buy whatever. So, with this philosophy in mind, we set out to construct our Gingerbrook buildings. It is no great revelation to think that you can frame your structures out of whole trees – peeled poles. This has been done and still is done all over the world but when you set out to build real houses this way – not just sheds – today in America, it feels as if you are doing something perhaps difficult. What did I know? I was a novice with no real carpentry experience so I could wade naively into whatever project and feel quite jaunty about it. We bought the land in the early winter and wanted to have a building ready to move into before the next winter. So I thought – let's build it out of the trees that are growing right here. Surely it can be done – cut them down and put them back up vertical, horizontal and diagonal so they looked just like a real building. That was the plan and the idea was to build a livable house without spending any money directly on the building materials. Possible? We will see.

The larger plan was to build a small building first and live in that one while working on the main house, then use the first one for a shop or storage space afterwards. Meanwhile I had to figure what to do with the animals. Mickey and Maud could just stay outside through any kind of weather all year round but neither goats or chickens would appreciate getting snow bound. However they wouldn't show up until the fall when we would move everything at once from the rental so I had time to peck away at that one. The location of this first building was dictated by the topography of the land and by the predetermined location of the main house. We wanted it close enough so that the two buildings could be connected at some point but we also wanted it right on a steep bank that rises as you get closer to the northern boundary – the lane. We wanted it on the bank so that you could walk onto the living floor right off the top of the bank but 30ft out, that floor would then be 10ft off the ground. We weren't going to do any earth moving in this case – the idea was to use the natural contour of the land. It was to be a saltbox with the long sweep of the roof facing north so we could utilize the whole length of those tall, straight popples that were standing right there in front of us. We planned it to be 30ft long and 15ft wide with a dirt floor underneath, a plank living floor and with enough space under the peak for a sleeping loft for the children. All the rafters and joists were popple logs and the posts were white pine. Those two trees were the fastest growing of all the second growth in that old pasture and were therefore the trees selected for the job. The building sits on concrete pads poured in hand dug holes. Somebody said you have to tie it down or else a hurricane will blow it away, so I put metal straps in the concrete and bolted them to the posts. I since have built a few similar buildings without tie-downs and they haven't blown away yet. All the trees were cut and hauled up above the building site either by Buster or M&M depending on their size and then skinned with draw knives. There is a beautiful tool called a spud expressly for this job but I didn't have one.

I figured it like this: Build one rectangular frame and put a floor on it to come in at ground level at the front; then build another on top of that one; then put up a ridge pole at the 20ft mark and attach the rafters to it. That's what we did and we joked that if it lasts 20 years, it will be a miracle but it is still there and not looking too bad. The popple joists were put on the long way and the thin ends hung out over the void by sometimes 10ft so we shaped them to a V, boarded them and called it a prow and made it a balcony which years later fell off in one mighty crash, the popple notorious for rotting in the weather. It was a beautiful sight that frame, the freshly peeled poles gleaming in the sun but if we are not going to freeze to death this winter, we had best cover it up. That was done with second hand boards that I had been accumulating from tear-down houses and barns. The planks for the floor came out of abandoned buildings at the copper mines in Strafford, Vt. These mines had been the center for copper ore production in the entire country at one point in the middle of the 19th century and besides the abandoned buildings, they had left several football fields worth of a surreal red desert of tailings which is now a 'superfund' site. There was enough used lumber to cover the whole building with 'clap boards' which I assume were just the thing before 'claberds' became all the rage. I took the chain saw then to the walls to cut out windows and doors.

Shop door made with slabs.

The doors I made, and the windows were some automotive glass out of fifties vehicles and some framed mullioned glass taken out of old houses and sheds. The fifties featured cars with side and back windows that were straight and flat, and in the late seventies, there were still plenty in the junk yards but they have since been devoured by the crushers. All the cutting was done with chain saws which is fine for logs but aggravating when you're slicing up hundreds of boards, however relief did arrive later when electricity came in from the pole that was on the property by the road. The ceiling/roof was nailed to the rafters with the last of those old boards and here is where the first direct expense intrudes – we put on roll-roofing to top it off. We lived in that house for three years before the main house was available and I'll tell you more about our life style there later on, but the point here is that the building was possible the way I had envisioned it for very little direct expense. There were other expenditures of course but we took to frequenting auctions and coming back with things like a double kitchen sink enclosed in its own ugly metal cabinet with built in shelves for $5: or a box of used copper sweat fittings for 50 cents with which I coppered the water from the spring line to the sink: or a derelict oil drum stove which provided the cast iron pieces to put together a heater with another 55 gallon drum. I 'weatherized' the house by stapling flattened cardboard boxes to the clap boards. I italicize the word because we were always quite aware of the weather outside our walls – the older kids slept in sleeping bags upstairs and would report that on a snow blowing night, they could feel the snow dust settling as if scattered by fairies on their faces.

That method of whole-tree construction - framing buildings with poles and then boarding it in – I used on all the other structures that were to come on the homestead. I considered it to be a success with that first building (which I will from here on call the 'shop') and we had the trees unlimited and we had the mules to skid them out and we had the chainsaw to carpenter them to size. We built a goat shed, a chicken shack, a hay barn, a cider mill, a sugar house, a horse barn, a healing cottage and an octagon house and we used variations of the method on all of them. The goat and chicken housing I threw together in desperation and managed to get them through the first couple of years before I could do something more permanent but the others could be worth spending some time discussing They didn't happen all at once – the horse barn had to wait 15 years to finally be built. Mickey and Maud, when they finally got some winter shelter were in a lean-to addition to the shop under where the prow had crashed and it wasn't until they were replaced with work horses that the barn had to happen. The octagon house will require its own chapter but let's combine all the other buildings into one showcase structure for the purpose of discussion.

They are all gable-end buildings; they are all framed with whole trees; they are all carpentered with a chain saw, a framing hammer, a maul and nine inch spikes, a chalk line, and a level. They all subscribed to the dictates of the Homesteaders Bible which says "Thou shall not spend the money which thou hast not or even the money which thou hast".

Let's take a brief detour first to visit the hay barn which bares my homesteader's soul. I love this structure for its utter simplicity. I needed some place right now to store the winter's hay so I threw together an A-frame and covered it with used metal roofing right to the ground. It contains four sets of rafters 25ft long and six feet apart connected by old boards two feet apart from bottom to top and kept from keeling over by nailing on long diagonals on the underside. It is situated on top of a knoll where the rain would drain away on all sides and before the metal went on, I lifted each leg just enough to slip a flat rock underneath so as to potentially keep them from rotting in contact with the earth. It is open on both ends and holds about 500 bales now but is infinitely expandable if needed by adding another set of rafters to either end. The first few years' worth of bales sat off the ground on a grid of slim poles one foot apart but over time, loose hay and chaff have covered and infiltrated to form a high and dry floor. You would think that the hurricane would not hesitate to blow that one away but it hasn't moved yet. Started as a temporary expedient, it has become a permanent haybarn.

Now let's get back to our showcase structure. This is where the balsam fir comes into its own The popples tall and straight had all gone into the shop or into lumber to be used later or into the ground as backstops defining the garden terraces, and the remaining random pasture pines had also gone to the sawmill and been stickered for the future. The balsam fir grows plentiful around the Gingerbrook. It grows straight with a new whirl of branches to mark each growing season and the great advantage it has over spruce for this job, is that it peels easily – especially in the spring, the bark will come off in long sappy strips It grows slowly and consequently there are many to be found in the 6" to 8" range. That is a good size for posts, sills, plates and collar ties. These buildings are all in the range of 30ft long so two 15 footers will get you there top and bottom. They are also about 15ft wide, give or take a few feet, so your collar ties and gable end plates can be the same length. That calculates to 14 poles 8" to 6"fat and 15 ft long for each building. The spot where the sugar house now sits nestled up against the brook just by the bridge, was a paradise of balsams. I cut every last one, peeled them and resurrected them into an entire building. It was a piece of work that didn't require the services of M&M and I chalked it into the column of minor miracles. After you've got your long pieces together, then you can collect the posts. Say they are 7ft long and you need four for the corners; two under the lap joints and two more on each side for good measure – that's ten posts altogether which don't need to be all that hefty because this roof will not be very heavy. If the rafters are two feet apart, that makes 30 of them and if the building is 17 ft wide like the horse barn to accommodate three 10'x 10' stalls and a 7ft wide pass through, they would be about 12ft long, but they can also do fine at only 4" thick so you can slice a lot of them off the ends of trees that you have already cut. The diagonal braces which you need to keep the building from see-sawing to the ground, can also be cut from the left-over tops. That would be two for every post, about four feet long and spiked in. O. K. Now you've got the entire skeleton of the building lying on the ground. It was a lot of work figuring, cutting and skinning but all it cost you so far was sweat, some equine energy and chain saw gasoline. No lumber yards; no trucking; no electricity and you're ready to put it together.

You could use 30 footers for the plates and sills but they would be too big on one end, too skinny at the other and altogether too ornery to manipulate on your own. So there is one slight how-to problem which I have watched people struggle with and that is how to line up the half-lap cuts on both ends of the pole. If you are dealing with a 6X6 for example, the cutting of a half-lap is easily figured and done but on a round log, it gets tricky. Set the pole on a couple of saw horses and dog it so that it won't roll on you and then measure half way down on one end, attach a chalk line there and run it to the half way point on the other end, and snap. This ensures that your two ends will be on the same plane. Then draw a line with your level across the cut face from the chalk mark and do the same at the other end. Now keep the chain saw on both of those lines until you've cut back as far as you think the lap should go – six inches should work – and the two ends are now conforming in line and level. This way you can connect all the way around making two rectangles 15' x 30' (our make-believe building) between which you sandwich the 7' posts and on top of which you now put the rafters. Each lap joint takes a post underneath to support it and the whole thing is spiked together down into the posts. And now set the whole thing on the largest, flattest stones you can find and maneuver into place. The sill may not be quite level – not to worry – there is plenty of flex in this structure. In fact, these buildings will move up and down irregularly as the ground freezes and thaws underneath those stones.

Sugar house in summer

Or if you are going two stories like both the shop and cider mill which come off of steep banks, the first frame is planked over and another identical is put on top. The collar ties go on to keep it from spreading and now a ridge board can go up supported by short (depending on your desire for pitch) posts sitting on the middle of the ties. You could in theory nail the rafters together and tip them up in pairs but a ridge board is the way to go, especially if you are working alone. There is hardly any pole that is perfectly straight but there is almost always one aspect of it that shows pretty close to straight so every pole that you end up using in one of these constructions has to be eyeballed first and then placed flat side up. This is especially true for rafters since you want the roof to run in a straight plane all the way across – or close enough. Looking at your rafters, you also have to decide on an average width to shoot for at the plate. Some will measure 4 ½" and a few will measure 3" so let's make the rafters sit 3 ½" above the plate. So its shim and trim to get them all even and you could make a template for the angle cut at the ridge.

The key ingredient most important to putting up all these buildings for next to no money is finding used metal roofing. People are always replacing their metal roofs because they have become rusty or there is some insidious leak that no-one can find so if you can cozy up to some roofers, they will give you the stuff to take home. The corrugated sheets that go on vertically will work but much better is old standing seam. On this, you pound the seams flat and lay them overlapping horizontally like clapboards. This requires a nailing board every two feet across the rafters. Although; don't nail this roofing, screw it on with grommeted hex head screws. There will be old nail holes here and there in the metal but it doesn't seem to matter – if it does, prowl across the roof with a silicon gun.

Most sugar houses in this area are made to be weather tight. The philosophy is that fresh air moving across the sap pans will cool down and slow down the boil. When you open the door and walk in, you can't see anyone for the cloud of steam. If you get down on your hands and knees, you can then get an open view of the sugarmaker's boots. I decided that I'd rather have fresh air and burn a bit more wood so that building has no walls other than the stacks of sugar wood that close in on two sides. But let's look at the walls on the other out-buildings. Unless you have garnered an endless supply of tear-down boards, this is the point at which you need to start hauling logs to the sawmill or better yet, bringing the sawmill to your logs. The siding on these buildings involves a lot of rough-cut 1" boards. They all go on vertically, nailed to the sill log and nailed to the plate, and then nailed from plate to rafters on the gable ends. For the horse barn, that is sufficient. For a building that you want tighter, a second layer of board gets nailed on the inside of the first covering the gaps. This could be called 'reverse board and batten'. The cider mill is done that way except that the outside layer is done with slabs. Slabs are usually free for the asking at saw mills and even though they come in all kinds of convolutions, they can be straightened well enough with your chain saw. The ones that are cut off of bull pines and are 16" wide and 4" thick you might as well slice up and use for sugar wood but with good luck, a goodly portion of the slabs will be 8" wide and perfectly straight sided. Either way, the inside boards will cover the irregularities of the slabs and those slabs cost you nothing. Your own sawn boards will cost you the sawyer's fee but that would be a small fraction of the lumber yard price. Sawing your own lumber also allows you to use just about any tree species. Much of the inside layer in the cider mill is sawn from balm of gilead which I was clearing out anyway but which nobody considers is useful for anything except its 'balm'.

Cider Mill with slab siding and recycled windows

Windows are a friendly addition to a building and they too can be added easily and cheaply. Start with a framed window that you salvaged or that you picked up at a garage sale and put it up against the inside wall at the spot you would like and pencil around it. Then nail four boards to the penciled lines and take your chain saw a cut out the opening one inch in from the boards. With the addition of a couple of swivel holdfasts, the window will now sit in that frame. To prevent water from running down the glass into the wall, make another cut angled down and out along the bottom deep enough to accommodate a skinny window sill. If you can garner a small supply of old clapboards, these work nicely for that job. I have mentioned elsewhere that I took a chain saw to the face cutting out one of these window openings. That is the dreaded 'kickback' and if you are preoccupied and not paying attention, it could happen to you too. But it is a straightforward procedure – when you plunge the blade into the wall (or anything for that matter), make contact first with the bottom of the tip, not the top. Doors for these out buildings could be banged together fast using boards vertical with a couple of nailers across the back but my favorite door is in the cider mill and that was just sawed right out of the reverse batten wall. I used the same routine as with the windows, then put on two horizontal straps and cut it out fixing hinges to the straps. From the outside it looks like part of the slab wall. If you are lucky, you may scrounge some big, old barn-door hinges in order to hold up a heavy door like that. Now, a final note about these buildings – their value according to the tax man is zero. Contemplate that one for a moment!

Who needs a Hero?

Every story needs a hero. The hero might be the one who rides in at the last minute with guns blazing to save whatever it was in that story that needed saving. Or the hero might be some inscrutable wizard pulling strings out of sight, or a small child who sees a way out that no one else can see. Or even a bare-chested thumper who dies courageously sacrificing himself for the greater good. Heroes appear to come in all sizes and shapes and often are not celebrated as such – or are 'unsung'. But let's do some singing here. The story told here, more or less following the building from scratch of the Gingerbrook homestead, has had a lot to say about the place and its animals, its plants, its trees and the ways and means of survival, but not much about its people and their home economics. The hero of this tale is of course Jo without whose magic and mighty labors it is hard to imagine any of it coming to pass.

The weather had warmed, the summer was coming on fast and although the building that was to become the shop – the building that we were to live in while we constructed our house – was nowhere near finished, we decided to move in. The roof wasn't on yet so we stretched a sheet of plastic over the planked floor and set up housekeeping underneath. There were four children, the youngest still in diapers and the others being four, seven and eleven. There was no running water, no stove, no dining room table, no beds, no washing machine and everybody had to be fed, washed, provided with clean clothes and monitored. The entire area was a construction zone. While the shop was being finished, the concrete walls of the octagon were being formed and poured. It made for a chaotic paradise for little kids and a dangerous one. The children needed to be watched continuously and booboos tended to continuously. Jo did it all. She cooked on a wood-fired hibachi and heated water there also: water that had to be hauled up from the ancient stoned-in spring down by the gingerbrook. She materialized meals for all of us plus whatever hungry male friends who arrived to help. She always had snacks available for the kids. She washed babies in a plastic five gallon bucket and diapers in a pot. She washed clothes in a galvanized tub. She breast-fed a one year old. She programmed activities for the kids. She read stories to them in the middle of the day. She kept track of their myriad playthings. Bob meanwhile was carrying heavy objects. Carrying heavy objects for Jo or playing with Lincoln Logs or chasing goats back into their electrified square of puckerbrush or moving Mickey and Maud to their next stake-out. That was the easy stuff and he took it all for granted as it was happening, but in retrospect, it seems an inconceivable output of energy and intelligence for Jo to have carried us all through that period.

Ben, Will, and Jo scrub time

And that was just the beginning. Things lightened somewhat after we moved from underneath and outside onto a floor and inside following the covering of a roof and some siding at least to waist height so no kids would fall off the edge. This allowed Jo to make the great leap forward of heating water on the cookstove and oh joy, to tap into running water once the pipe was laid in from the spring, and to wash clothes in an old wringer we found somewhere. The wringer-washer was parked out on the prow where it could slosh to its heart's content and drain out over the edge but that was strictly a summer time affair which still left Jo washing clothes by hand during the winters. Washing and wringing on the prow was not an unenjoyable affair however. The prow jutted ten feet off the ground into the trees and a clothes line running 50ft to a white birch allowed a T-shirt to come out of the slosh, squeeze through the wringer and reel right out onto the clothes line. During a sunny summer day, you could be doing something far worse.

We inhabited that building for three years before moving in to the octagon. Jo made sure that everybody stayed well fed, clean and educated. Day after day she produced nutritious and delicious meals. We grew organic what we could to start with and she bought organic. She bought 25lb and 50lb bags of oats and raisins and made granola. She bought 50lb sacks of whole wheat flour, rye flour and spelt and baked bread. There was always fresh bread for sandwiches and toast. She got organic peanut butter by the 12 jar case and began making jams and jellies first from wild fruit and later from home-grown. She bulk ordered 25lb bags of black beans and bags of rice. These bulk purchases represented an original outlay of cash but in the long run yielded a very low per-meal cost. She had a pot of soup simmering on the stove-top all the time. She would butcher our own chicken and throw in the pot any available vegetable and wild green. She would feed us dandelion and nettle greens. She would pick the flowers with the children and make dandy beer or wine. She gave us oat straw infusion to drink. She made yogurt from the goat's milk by putting jars in the cooling oven to incubate overnight. Once we exchanged the goats for a cow, she skimmed the cream and made butter and then made cottage cheese from the skim. She would make cheese with that yogurt by hanging it in a bag to drain. She cultivated culinary and medicinal herbs and harvested wild roots and flowers to make tinctures and essences. She gave these away to everybody and anybody who might need some help. She consulted over medical or health issues in person or over the phone. When we first hooked up to the telephone, we were joined on a party line but the other party soon begged for their own private line because people were forever calling to talk to Jo. Some insisted on giving her money for her time and knowledge and herbs but she never charged. You would think that she ought to have in order to contribute to our home economy but the rewards came in subtle ways. She generated enormous good will and as a result, things sometimes just appeared or happened for us. Occasionally she would look up and see Bob go by carrying a load of heavy objects.

Jo attended home and hospital births for women who wanted her close by. She stayed by death beds for the same reason. She birthed one more baby of her own, her last one, while we were still in the shop, suckled her and got her up and walking before trading locations for the octagon. She could sit up all night with a sick baby and somehow still be there for everyone else the next day. She collected and saved children's clothes and passed them down till they disintegrated. She acquired the next round of clothing at thrift stores. Thrift stores in America are full of quality clothes and she would pick up good stuff for dimes and quarters always cotton or wool. She sewed and mended. While Bob was manhandling the next unruly bunch of heavy objects, she was thinking ahead as to each child's wants and needs. We encountered a beautiful old treadle at an auction and what she couldn't do on the machine, she did by hand. She knitted innumerable hats and mittens and baby blankets. She would darn a hole closed if that would do or otherwise knit a new one. She took up a hand spindle and spun out yarn from fleece that was free for the asking. Brown, white, gray and black fleece made into yarn and knitted into patterns and designs. Home spun yarn could come off the spindle thick and wooly to make the warmest of all hats and mittens that Bob could put inside leather choppers so as to carry heavy objects on through the coldest weather.

Jo amassed quantities of canning jars and any other jars with sealing lids. Before we went commercial with our apple juice, she would put up 50 gallons for the family year in five gallon batches on the cookstove. She also canned countless jars over time of everything from fruit to pickles. And through it all, she never missed a meal – never did not somehow produce the next one. And sometimes Bob carried the heavy platters to the table. Those who know tend to time their visits to coincide with the noon meal, just coincidentally of course. She thinks to serve balanced nutritious meals and delicious nutritious desserts – apple cakes and pumpkin breads and brownies and oatmeal cookies. I'm sure I could go on detailing more of Jo's heroics but if having the house awash in the smell of warm apple cake when one comes in out of the cold isn't the definition of a hero, I don't know what is.

Building More

    You can't have too many out buildings on a homestead. There is always something else you want to put under cover. However, number one on that list are yourselves. We were under cover from the start but as adventuresome as it was living in the shop, we had grander fantasies of space and warmth. We arrived with a house in mind and were working on it directly or indirectly the whole while. The shop we did and the chickens and goats at least had cover from rain and snow but the other buildings had to wait – sometimes years – until we got other priorities established. The cider mill was just the press with a 10x10 roof; the sap pans were out in the open – if it rained or snowed in them, we just boiled it off; and the equines and bovines acted just like the U.S. Mail. To build a 'real' house with my limited carpentering experience was an intimidating affair and to build it with the'Homesteader's Bible' castigating me every time I would think about buying in something, made it even more interesting. We wanted to build a round house but compromised to an octagon which at least gives you straight walls to deal with. The inspiration for this building came from a painting, which was pictured in the 70's publication 'Shelter', of a Mandan earth lodge. It is one of a series of aquatints done by Karl Bodmer, a German, who accompanied Prince Maxmillian of Wied on his journey through the American west in 1832-34. The setting is the interior of a massive round house in winter. All the people are in there from oldsters to babies, the fires are going and the place is festooned with drying buckskins, hanging corn, bows and blankets. The roof is a whirl of long poles balanced on a circular earth berm at the outer edge and on what looks like a square plate supported by four long posts towards the center. The rafters don't come together in the middle but stop short to leave a square opening at the peak providing ventilation and a smoke hole.

The painting doesn't show you the outside but we can assume that it wasn't called an 'earth' lodge for nothing. It was well insulated with that earthen berm around the walls which extended up onto the roof. I was enamored of that building and stared at that picture trying to decode its secrets. Or better yet, I spent hours pondering how to make one just like it but 'better'

I realize that you are on shaky ground when you are trying to balance on the word 'better'. Let's just say that we didn't particularly want to live like the Mandans did in 1830. We could do without a dirt floor or an open fire pit or a sod roof but the essence of the dwelling I thought could be preserved and I hoped it could be built using the same whole tree construction methods we have already discussed. Now I had been fantasizing round houses for quite some years before this and had built one with a Peace Corps friend in a small village on the Mosquito Coast of Nicaragua named Tasbapaunie. I have talked about this place already in another context but while I was there we worked up a 30ft diameter house out of bamboo. This was not an indigenous style. We materialized it out of our heads. In fact, years later, I happened to be reading a book called The Caribbean Edge, written after my time there, in which the anthropologist author talked about this "upper Amazon" house incongruously situated in the village among the traditional gable end cottages. To build it, we harvested these amazing 6" thick, 40 ft long bamboos. They were jammed into the sand at an angle like flying buttresses and rested on a circular wall frame 30ft in diameter until they all met more or less at the peak in the center. There they were tied together with a jungle vine called 'wit'. On top of those rafters went palm frond thatching that was also tied on with wit. We began to sing our own song – 'you've got to have wit, miles and miles and miles of wit'. The old boys would come by to watch and kibitz and tell us how the first "water spout" to hit the shore would certainly carry this thing away. So, feeding off the Mandans and the upper Amazonians, we were able to come up with a plan for our own house to balance the rafters on two concentric octagonal plates thereby allowing the rafter ends to float at the peak giving us the freedom to put in a sky light at the top. That gave us three concentric octagons: the outside wall, 12ft high and 40ft across; the inside plate, 20ft high and 16ft across and the sky light, 5ft across and 25ft up there. This is a 'hip roof' – an eight sided hip. I am saying this to point out the one superiority of a hip roof to a more common gable end. What keeps a gable end roof from collapsing are those so-called 'collar ties' on which an attic floor is often laid. However there is relentless pressure over time to 'pancake' that roof and heavy snow loads are very worrisome as a result. A hip roof, especially a round one, is held together by a dynamic tension. All the rafters would have to go at the same time pushing out and since they are strapped together round and around by nailed boards and/or purlins, that scenario is well-nigh impossible. Over time we have had some mighty snowscapes on this roof and I have never been tempted to shovel it off. The tonnage of four feet of snow lying on 1500 square feet of roof that is then rained on during a thaw might surely be calculated by somebody but I'm at a loss to give you a figure that must be astronomical.

After writing that sentence, I wandered off to do something useful and began thinking: wait a minute Bob, why be so lazy, surely there is a way to come up with some numbers around this snow load. A reference says that fresh snow weighs 10 lbs per cubic foot and packed snow weighs 30 lbs. Let's split the difference and multiply by 20. That yields 120,000 lbs, or 60 tons! That seems more than astronomical. So let's say that after being rained on, the snow subsided to only three feet deep – now there are only 45 tons on the roof. I'm in disbelief myself but mathematics is the purest science!

Snow or no snow, we could get the look of the Mandan roof from the inside and we could get the 'smoke hole' at the peak but the 'earth lodge' part seemed somewhat dubious. That is until we looked at the steep bank just north of the two old

maples and decided we could cut into that and have half an earth house with four of the octagon's sides facing out to the south. This was the only time in the process of setting up the homestead when we hired in heavy equipment and the man and his dozer came and carved a forty foot circle into the ledge. The back three walls are under ground along with a rectangular root cellar which needed some help from a charge of dynamite set off by a wizened and deaf old dwarf who just kept grinning at me as he pushed the plunger while I was asking him to let me know so I could plug my ears   The idea to not put the house on a traditional foundation or a slab or on top of a cellar was formulated in the spirit of doing as much for yourself as possible as well as to save money. We brought in the cement truck to pour the 8ft back walls but the rest of the base, we cobbled together ourselves.

U EFF OHNO

Upon submerging himself into any story, the reader invariably wonders as to the truth being conveyed there. Can I really believe what I'm reading? How much of this wordage is sheer fabrication? And invariably the true test comes down to whether or not there lurks a UFO somewhere in the tale. If indeed the author can't resist, one rolls one's eyes and prepares for a bout of lunacy, or an acid trip, or a long, twisted tunnel into paranoia concerning the U.S. government, the N.S.A. and the dark side of the moon. If this author insists on regaling me with his very own UFO, might I not conclude that he is a lost cause and bail out right now? Well, you might but don't, because this one belongs to the tale of the octagon house and is intriguing, mysterious and unidentifiable.

I was standing just outside the door to the shop looking out over the octagon. It was in a late-summer, early-fall evening surrounded by fireflies when I called out Jo to witness. We had been camping out in the shop for a year while working on the construction and by this point, the scooping into the hillside of a circular indent and the placing of concrete and stone outline walls were the only evidence of things to come. We weren't advertising and expected no visitors but who or what did come was beyond reckoning. Looking out over the foundation walls from the high point by the shop door, you would see a bare earthen space 40 feet across defined by eight clearly visible walls. Looking down at it from a vantage point straight and high above, I mused later, the octagon, placed naked on a flat, bare stage, might seem like a clue, a message, a target or perhaps a play about to happen.

It had been another in a long series of hard days. I was tired. Not drowsy but relaxing and about to go inside for the night when a light appeared in the air above the octagon. A shimmer; diffuse, not sharp but seeming to hover very close. It seemed the size of a pie plate but given its fairy-light quality, it might have actually been the size of an alien flying saucer hovering a thousand feet above. Now before you get too excited, my disclaimer here is that I do not believe in outer space aliens visiting the earth or in flying saucers, however this little saucer of a character then began to circle slowly right around following the boundaries of the octagonal foundation. Slowly around and around glimmering right in front of me. I quietly called out to Jo who was inside putting the children to bed. She watched it circle. I had a witness. Don't believe me – ask Jo.

We watched together in silence for a while until the pressure to do something or say something became undeniable and given my penchant for irony, I came out with a phrase long-forgotten but something like: "do you think we should invite it for dinner?" The light immediately blinked out – disappeared in an instant – no noise, no smoke and we never saw it again.

Okay, its up to you. This visitation was not a drone so eliminate that possibility. We are now in the year 1978 long before drones became a household word if not a plaything. So …what was it? Where did it come from? Where did it go? I have no idea, no explanation. Foxfire? Swamp gas? St. Elmo's fire? Some unknown natural phenomenon? Or a paranormal happening? A visitation from another dimension, another universe, another time, another place? Whatever the explanation, we felt elated and strangely honored or chosen but all we could say in the end is that it was an Unidentifiable Flying Object.

The octagonal frames went together the same way as the rectangular frames described above. The only difference is that the half-lapped joints on these beams are cut to 45o instead of 90o. We were still using peeled whole trees with only the ends being carpentered. The eight walls were each 16ft long, so the 8"-10" beams were lapped on top of the corner posts and pegged there with 1" maple 'trunnels'. Those 'tree nails' were made by sawing rough cut maple into 1" strips and then chamfering the edges with a draw knife. The posts were 12ft high at the front of the house and 4ft at the back. This meant that the upstairs rooms would start with a knee wall but with the rafter overhang bringing the roof close to the ground in the back, the northwest wind could sail over and around that house without hardly noticing it. All the beams and posts were done out of balsam fir except for four thick 8ft trunks of red oak which I bartered some M&M work for, given that there is no oak growing anywhere nearby. These oak posts were placed on concrete pads in the center 16ft apart in a square as the support for the inside octagonal frame and the upstairs floor. If you will picture a tic-tac-toe of beams laid on top of these posts and extended and mortised into the wall posts, you will get to all eight corners. On top of the tic-tac-toe were set eight posts octagonally to be lap-jointed together 20ft up. Now the entire frame is up. There are two octagonal plates – one at 12ft, diameter of 40ft; and one at 20ft, diameter of 16ft; and only the rafters are left to do. How to get them up there, was the question. The answer was – a gin pole. A gin pole 30ft high set on the exact center point of the octagon, with a block and tackle at the top and guyed off with heavy rope in four directions. The rafters were 25ft long narrowing to 5" or 6" at the top and we could pull them up from off of the upper bank and hold them while we maneuvered and worked them. With the gin pole holding them balanced on the two octagonal plates, we could push them around east and then west until all 32 were in position. It's possible that just spiking the rafters into the plates would have been good enough but not to take any chances, we cut mirror image 'bird's mouths' into both timbers until they locked together and then spiked them. Now when all 45 tons are sitting on those rafters, I comfort myself knowing that they are all exerting equal and opposite force on each other and they are not going anywhere. Holding each rafter in turn with a rope gave us the freedom to mark them, roll them, cut the bird's mouth with the chain saw, roll them back, check the fit, roll them back again etc., etc. I'm sure there would be other ways of accomplishing that task but the gin pole allows you to refuse the offer of a crane for $100 an hour.

All right now! There's the skeleton of the house. It looks pretty good. It even looked like it might work. But the challenge has just started. How to proceed with everything else that has long ago been worked out in putting together a regular stick frame house, which for this house, where things are definitely not regular, would require some inspiration. That was the question which we faced at each juncture. Roof? Floor? Walls? Doors? Windows? Plumbing? Stairs? Bedrooms? What was where and how to do it and stay loyal to the Homesteaders Bible? We will try to stay with the inspiration and away from the perspiration while we discuss the things that worked and those that didn't. You have to start with the roof. Once that is on, you feel that God is on your side. You can start stacking material under cover, leave your tools lying about, set up a table saw (make your own table saw – p184) and worry not about the weather.

We covered the rafters with pine boards so that is what you see looking up from inside, then covered the pine with one massive sheet of black plastic as a vapor barrier. An elderly gent who used to be a scout master, came by just as we were hopelessly dealing with this unwieldy beast and gave us a lifesaving tip: Pick up a collection of round stones, or golf balls if you have them, wrap the plastic around them at the edge and slip knot a cord around each, cinch and tie off. That plastic needed to stay put for a while until the next layer held it down and those cinched stones did the trick through all sorts of weather. On top of that went rough 2X8s on edge every two feet; the cavities filled with cellulose; popple boards nailed vertically; tar paper, and by that time, the winter was upon us and we left off the final cover of cedar shingles till the following spring. That popple was the last of our stash sawn from the regrowth around the house site. There was one glaring piece of evidence of my amateur status in that roof and that was my, what I thought was, fantastic skylight. This was not the center dome but a solid, heavy sheet of plate glass 5'x3' that came out of an antique funeral wagon which I inserted into the north side roof just as if it were an enormous shingle. With hindsight I can say that this was a terrible idea. In fact, I will stick my neck out and say that any skylight set into the slope of a roof is just trouble waiting to happen. This one didn't leak directly rather it condensed in-house moisture continuously and ran it down out of sight into the roof below. As it turned out, that was a problem that fixed itself – you will find out why a little later. The central theme of this pole construction and the one fact that continuously demands your attention is that poles are neither perfectly straight nor flat. Adjustments must be made.

For instance, on these rafters which become level across both plates because you measure and carve, but swerve and dip elsewhere, the ¾ pine accommodates but the 2X8s lying across five rafters might need a hunk cut out here and there or a shim underneath from time to time. However the whole roof ties together and has its integrity but if you stand at a distance from the house and sight along the ridge lines, you will notice the roofscape has its idiosyncrasies

The same method for siding used in the outbuildings was employed on the house. Rough pine boards nailed top and bottom on plate and sill backed up by a second layer covering the cracks. Reverse board and batten. The difference here was that the doors and windows were framed out first with 2X6 and the boards were cut to fit. Now I'm starting to get the impression that the amount of lumber being used here is really piling up. But let's figure that, for instance, the entire pine outside wall might have taken around 800 board feet of lumber and that amount could be sawn out of five or six nice pines so we could load up Two-Ton Tony with 10 logs and come back from the saw mill with enough to keep going for a while. And the winter provided us with plenty of catch-up time to pile up logs with M&M humping them to a landing.

I have said that we did not start with a concrete slab. Instead we took a page out of the Nearing's book and slip-formed stone base walls around the front. These were three feet high and cemented in with rocks and rubble collected from the tumble-down wall along the lane. I like these stone walls at the base because they eliminate the perpetual problem of rotting sills. The splash of the rain off the eaves doesn't hit any wood except for the front door. This situation is also helped by running the rafters 4ft out from the walls to provide a large rain shadow plus providing dry space to stash miscellaneous stuff against the walls. So far we have two inches of pine along with windows and doors between us and the elements and when we moved into that house after living in the shop for three years, we felt really snug. I did have a plan to insulate and then panel the walls which involved yet more wood. If you cross cut wood, you create sawdust, but if you saw with the grain, you create long strands that used to be known as excelsior. Shingle mills, by the very nature of their work, create mountains of excelsior They saw back and forth, back and forth through a 16 inch block spitting off shingles and leaving behind almost an equal amount of cedar on the floor. I figured that this stuff would make good insulation since, being cedar, it wouldn't rot and insects don't prefer to hang out around it. Shingle makers are dying to have you come and clean out this excelsior for them so that's what I did and both of us were happy. I began stuffing used 100lb grain bags with it and affixing them side by side on the pine wall, feeling warmer bag by bag.

One of the single most expensive items to buy for a new house are insulated windows, and doors are close behind. The reason why windows are so expensive is that they are required to perform two separate functions – admit light and provide ventilation. If you separate these functions, you can make your own for the merest fraction of the cost. To start, it requires getting sheets of glass cut to the size of your proposed windows, or as in our case, framing the openings to the size of the glass that you already have. We had sealed, double paned windows taken out of a Holiday Inn because the desiccant between the panes was absorbing instead of banishing moisture and starting to obscure the view. We cut them open, scrubbed them clean and put them into the wall separated by a ½ inch spacer – an insulated window. It took a while to get the second pane on some and we had visual evidence of the efficacy of a double pane – after a below zero night, the single pane would be covered with ice, condensed and frozen from the inside air, whereas the double pane might just show a 1/2 inch band of ice along the bottom. We learned along the way that these double panes have to be vented to the outside or they will fog and not want to defog. It works to seal the inside one air tight and just leave the outside pane in loose. O.K. That's the light part; what about the ventilation? That becomes a separate, screened mini-door set in between the panes that can be opened as needed. Ours are hinged at the top and opened with ropes and pulleys but I can envision other ways of doing it. This vent door can be paneled and decorated and insulated as thick as the wall. Ours are six inches thick and stuffed with cellulose.

Our actual doors were made the same way as the vents. These are the exterior doors not whatever you need inside. Inside doors can be as simple as ship lapped or tongue and groove pine held together with a couple of backboards but outside doors can be framed like a wall and insulated like a wall. Door knobs? Anything is possible but you would probably have to manufacture your own. Our doors just friction fit and you put your shoulder into one to enter.

It seems that one cannot make a house and escape the eternal debate over whether doors should open in or out. They should open out so that the wind could not blow them in but they should open in so that when your arms are full of baggage, you can force entry with your shoulder. We chose to honor the wind and push the way into our house. We didn't have to buy the friction or the door sweeps which would undoubtedly be plastic. Old woolen coats found in thrift stores work pretty well cut and folded over or better yet a sheepskin cut into strips and stapled to the door so that it shuts so tight you have to barge to get in.

So far we have walls, windows and doors but we can't move in until we do something to cover the large hole in the center of the roof and since we are not really going to live like the Mandans in their earth house, we also need to do something about the dirt floor. The four great oaks holding up the middle of the house are already sitting on concrete pads and the slip-formed walls around the front rely on hand-dug trenches, so we know that we are standing right on ledge. The dozer had

Door knobs, pulls, and latches

scraped us down to the essence and making those pads hardly required any digging so the idea surfaced – why not float the entire floor on small concrete pads. We made up a bunch of forms 8" square and shoveled the pads in parallel rows six feet apart. Then we set 2x6 stringers along the rows and nailed in the joists every 20 inches until the whole place looked like a spider's web. I had an idea of how to keep this floor dry and warm. That was to put ventilation registers around the outside next to the walls and have the stoves take their air from underneath the floor which would in theory suck warm air from the house between the floor and the ground. This floor was only about one foot off the ground so before the subfloor went on, the earth was covered with plastic sheeting to help keep the moisture down, and the 'coup de grace' was to fill the spaces between the joists with random rocks. We trucked in Buster loads of stone and dumped them on top of the plastic before boarding it over. The rocks would extract heat from the incoming air and reradiate giving you a gloriously warm floor. Did this work? Well, 'glorious' it is not but neither is it frigid and it does have the added benefit of sweeping the moisture out of the tight space underneath the floor.

O.K. The hole in the roof being temporarily plasticized and the floor down, warm or not so warm, I could work out a skylight now on the flat and out of the weather. I thought – "How about geodesic?" If it works on a circle, wouldn't it also work on an octagon? So I sliced up a whole passel of 1x1s and started screwing together triangles. It was miraculous. You have eight triangles to start and when you connect their apexes, you have 16 and on those cross members , you build eight more, and then they become 16 and you keep going like that with the triangles getting smaller until – why did this surprise me so? – You end up with a tiny octagon in the very center. It was the last of the concentric octagons. The whole thing we carried onto the roof and bolted it over a frame. It was bulbous so we called it the 'dome' and underneath the geodesic were four hinged and screened vents opened and closed from inside by a 20ft pole ending in a hook. The warm floor escapade may have been a little dubious but this system of cooling and ventilating the house was and is truly terrific. The wall vents are opened and the dome vents are opened and the warm air rises and escapes out the top while cool, fresh air comes in at the bottom. If we are in the middle of our annual quota of four summer days in the 90s, we will only open the vents at night to cool the house for the following day. Or if we are canning syrup on the cook stove and unattended it boils over and frazzles across the hot steel sending smoke pouring into the house, we open a dome vent and watch the smoke being sucked out and away.

Homestead Solutions #4

A spiral staircase is not necessarily just the thing for the house you are planning or building. A straight staircase may be called for or a 90° bend with a landing in the middle. However if you're looking at a spiral staircase, here's one that we built that is handsome to look at and an interesting challenge to build.   Start with a 12" pine log that seems more knot-free than most and cut it square top and bottom at 11 feet. That's 8ft between floors and 3ft more to extend to waist height so you can hang on to it coming down. The steps are 30" long and are supported by hardwood 2"x4"s – in this case, we used white ash. The hardwood is to be mortised into the log. A good 4" in should be enough. I use a 2" drill bit and a chisel to make these mortises but there are other methods and tools you might use yourself.   The pine is soft so that helps the process. The mathematics involved here are of course critical. How to plot out in advance exactly where these mortises are to go? O.K. There are 12 steps 8" apart vertically. They occupy ¾ of the circumference of the pole. Measure the circumference; divide by ¾; then divide by 12 – in this case, the steps are 2.25" apart horizontally. So start from the floor and go up 8" and across 2.25' all the way up and if it doesn't work out right, start again and refigure it. You can even use a framing square set on the top of each step to mark the next one – despite the roundness of the log. The steps then are 2"x12"s of any wood you wish or can find. If you are going for 100 year stairs, you would want to find some kind of hardwood to use, however we just used balsam fir because that is what we had and so far they have lasted 30 years and at the rate they are wearing, they look to last at least another 30. The risers here are merely cosmetic and could be whatever wood would look pretty.

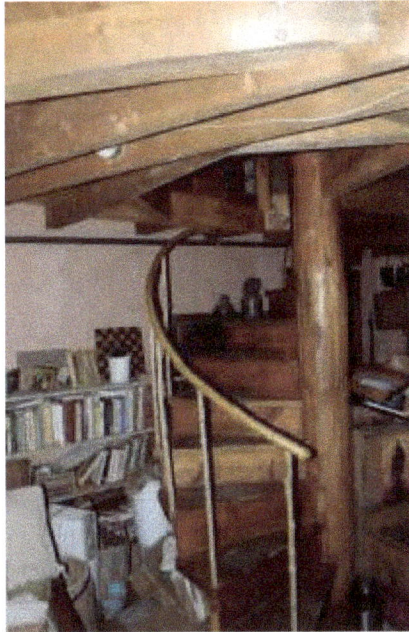

The funnest part of doing these stairs was making the handrail. I searched out an ash sapling, tall, straight and skinny. This is in the spring when the sap is up but before the leaves show. About 3" thick seems about right. Cut it the correct length for your handrail and then ... keep looking until you find three trees together in the necessary alignment as in the diagram to jam your ash pole into just the right curvature to fit your spiral and leave it there months into the summer until it is dry and will forever stay in that shape. You will see that by moving the rail either more horizontal or more vertical while clamped, will yield a more or less sharp curve. Our rail sits on 30" high maple treelings that whittle to fit in one inch holes bored into the steps. These could be found in stands of maple regeneration so thick that these gnarled treelings though quite old are stunted.

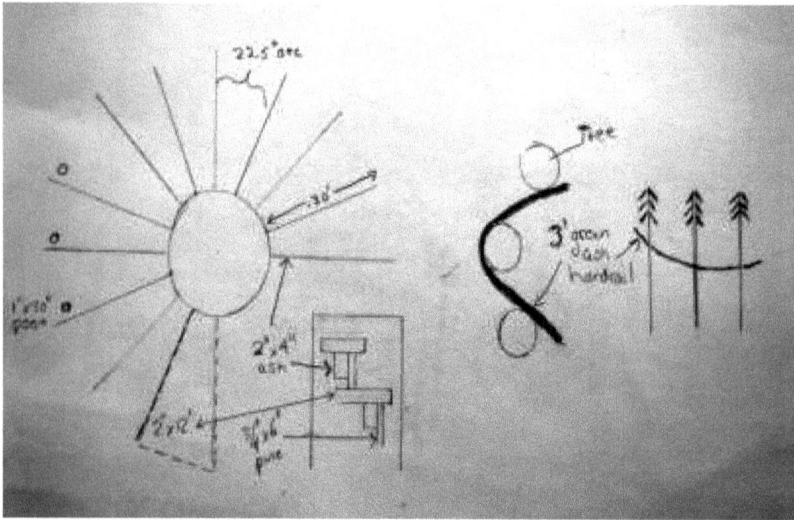

Often when I have read advice about building your own and it comes down to plumbing and electric, they recommend hiring professionals. If you don't know what you're doing and you are fumbling and guessing, the consequences could be either soggy or grave. Well, I thought; how hard could it really be? One thing connects to another whether it's beams, pipes or wires, so let's read a book, talk to somebody and do it. First of all, the wide open house lends itself to wide open systems. It makes things considerably simpler if you are not hiding either pipes or wires inside of walls or floors. So I decided to expose both systems either on the walls or along the second floor beams. You can buy plastic covers made to go on top of exposed electric wires but I copied the design and made them out of lengths of 1x1 pine and fit those into wooden houses surrounding the plugs and switches. You go to an electrical supply place and the man tells you what you need. Take these boxes, these switches, these 15 amp breakers, this number wire for this application and that number for that one etc. and after that it's black to black, white to white and screw in the ground wires. Of course it takes you five times what it would take an electrician to accomplish the task but time is what you've got. I find that the most irritating and time consuming part of the job is actually connecting those pesky wires to the tiny screws on the fixtures. Plumbing would seem to be more of the same. The water needs to get from here to there so you chart a path, measure out a diagram and go off to the hardware store. It becomes relatively foolproof if you do it all in plastic pipe. You cut it, fit it and glue it and you're done. However, if you prefer copper pipe, which didn't used to be so expensive that thieves wrangle it out of unoccupied houses, you will have to learn how to 'sweat' them together. That would be soldering, but look at it as if soldering, as well as welding and brazing, is one of those homestead skills you will be glad to acquire and will use over and again.

When we moved into that house in 1982, we immediately had the feeling of being hermetic. It was so quiet. We missed the sounds of the wind and rain and the branches thrashing against the side of the shop. But we didn't miss the snow blowing in through the cracks or the constant battle to keep from freezing. We slept on the floor (the subfloor) in our sleeping bags arrayed around the barrel stove while I gradually worked the upstairs inhabitable. If you visualize the tic-tac-toe frame of main beams that was supported by the oaks, you see that it divides the space into four rectangles and four triangles. If you start hanging joists two feet apart parallel to the outside walls in one of the triangles and proceed all the way around, you begin to get dizzy contemplating all the concentric octagons. These joists were also balsam fir with tenons cut on the ends and let into mortises in the main beams. The joist hanging included some to the inside of the four posts which turned the center square into another octagon. The idea there was to provide for a walkway around the center open space from which you could the access the upstairs rooms. Things were progressing one space of upstairs floor at a time; one bag of excelsior at a time; a staircase; a bathroom tub; an accumulating stack of various hardwood boards atop the joists in one of the upstairs rectangles, when we headed out on new year's day 1985 to a sledding party and on the way home, we fell in behind a fire engine lights flashing, blasting up the snowy roads one turn after another still going our way until we knew – the octagon house was on fire.

FIRE

If for some perverse reason you wanted to create a house design that would provide you with the most spectacular fire possible, then that octagon full of wood with a five foot hole at the peak of the roof would be just the thing. When we got there, that fire was shooting up through the hole like a roman candle full bore 30ft straight into the night sky and there was a crowd of awe-struck spectators circled around enjoying the show. It must be something like the bush telegraph – how they all heard and where they all came from so quickly. I do not know. But in the moment, watching our work and dreams turn to ashes, the crowd who should have been home tending to their own stoves, did not tenderize my feelings toward the human race. However there was one strange little man who sidled up beside me and began to talk, and while I was feeling so sick, angry and desperate, I almost pushed him away and told him to mind his own business. He was a saint and a savior. It turned out that he represented the American Red Cross and was to play an enormous role in our lives for the next year.

By that time, we had constructed a long, narrow woodshed which connected the shop to the octagon and the fire fighters were concentrating on preventing the fire from eating that up and getting to the shop. They poured zillions of gallons of water onto the house but there was never really any hope for it but they did save half of the woodshed and the shop. I thought at the time that they should have foregone the water and just let the octagon house completely burn up. It would have saved us a ton of cleanup but later, I thought better of it and realized that they probably saved us more importantly, the three back walls and the root cellar. The scene the following morning revealed a jumbled mass of charred beams and wet and now frozen ashes but also a minor miracle in that the contents of the root cellar were intact. The underground location had protected it from the fire but not from the smoke. The last harvest's bounty was contained in dozens of canning jars that were still sealed but covered in black, greasy soot. They would freeze soon if left there so we rescued what we could and transferred them to a neighbor's cellar. As I write this, it is almost thirty years later and there shows up still an occasional jar as I wash the evening's dishes that has remnant streaks of soot on it.

Everything was gone. The fire had taken it all. We lived with neighbors and friends and the surrounding community deluged us with old clothes, dishes, kid's games and pots and pans. Mr. Red Cross, whose name was Art, while proposing a long range plan, set us up the next morning with indispensable items like toothbrushes, sleeping bags and futons. Art presented us with hope and he presented us with a future at a time when all hope was gone. If we wanted to stay at Gingerbrook and maintain our lifestyle, the Red Cross would grant us money to buy materials to rebuild the house and we would supply the labor. The grant was for $10,000 which to us sounded like a million. He also arranged to replace construction tools that had been parked in the house like a Skil saw which had been made of aluminum and now sits on our mantel as a museum piece of melt sculpture.

If there were ever an organization that deserves unending support, it is the Red Cross. Art worked with us all winter drawing up plans and traveling with me to lumber yards twisting arms and ordering in advance and at a discount.

We took Mickey and Maud and Bossy and moved in with a friend who had room in his house and in his barn and spent the rest of the winter either collaborating with Art or working the shop back into shape to house the family again. We reinhabited the shop on the 1st of May and moved back under an octagon roof the following January. The second octagon went up in a breeze. This time I knew what I was doing and the entire fame was 2x6 and plywood so that volunteer framing parties could easily help. The dimensions are the same and the plan is still there to look up at the roof and be reminded of the Mandan earth lodge. We resurrected the gin pole and hoisted those rafters again but having lost the supporting oaks, we set up eight 20 footers instead to support the inside plate. The dome is no longer geodesic but now mimics the octagonal roof that it sits on. Under the old dome, after a cold night, it would rain an octagonal pattern on the floor. It would frost up with condensation during the night and rain down when the sun hit it. We needed a double paned dome and it seemed too crazy to double pane all those little triangles. This one is a good house, though it's still not finished yet - it's good to keep something inside to work on during a vicious winter day. This house does what it's supposed to and it's attractive enough but that first house was really my baby and I grieve for it now and again. The twin maples in front of the house, our totem trees, miraculously survived the fire. The nearest, some 30 ft away, lost one of its multiple trunks and the bark along a high arcing branch which manifests today as a healing scar, the lips of which are thick and slowly pulling together.

150year old maple next to house 30 years after the fire

I'm sure you are talking to yourself now asking but what caused that fire? We never knew, but the top priority for the new house was a real chimney. We had two fires going in the first house; one on either side of the center sporting metal stove pipe all the way up to the high roof and out. One fire was a cook stove and the other a heating barrel stove. It is possible that one of these pipes was somehow involved or more likely a wood fired hot water heater that I had geniused together, but he who dies by fire may once again live by fire. We still heat and cook with wood and the real chimney sometimes supports three fires at once. The backside has a fireplace and the front flue carries two thimbles – one for a heater and one for a cook stove.

So many houses and barns in this region disappear in fire over the decades and centuries of wood-fired heating that the buildings which remain from the 19th and even the 18th century stand out as living miracles. The dreaded chimney fire is often responsible. It surprises you like a rabid dog. You suspect nothing. You just keep on firing that stove day after day and then one morning you hear the low moaning of a distant train accelerating that begins to sound like it's going to blast right through the side of the house. The whole inside of the chimney is on fire. All the creosote that has built up in there has ignited and it's sucking air up through the chimney like a tornado. If you're lucky, just the chimney will be destroyed and if you're not, the entire house will go up with it. Needless to say, a chimney fire inside a metal stove pipe is bound for disaster.

The only way to prevent chimney fires is to always have a clean chimney. If there is no creosote, there is no fire. How is it possible to always have a clean chimney? One way is to keep a chimney sweep's brush and use it often. Unlikely proposition that is, so another method is to burn it out every day. When you start the fire in the morning, load the stove full and then open up any and all draft possibilities and let it rip. The idea is to create a mini-chimney fire every morning, burning out

157

yesterday's deposits. If you are fearful or tentative, you become part of the problem not the solution. Another safeguard against this rabid beast involves the choice of stoves. Chimney fires happen – that could be a bumper sticker, but I suspect the incidence of same has increased considerably since the advent of airtight stoves. If you load one of these, close the draft and go out for the day, you are inviting it to practically distill that wood into its constituent chemical compounds, one of which is creosote. One of these stoves could leave your chimney literally dripping with black goo. Before the advent of petrochemicals, there was an entire industry based on distilling wood to obtain a wealth of carcinogenic compounds like paint thinners, methyl alcohol and creosote. Two rules of thumb for fire are: the more air a fire gets, the cleaner it burns; and the warmer the chimney, the cleaner it stays. A bare metal pipe always remains too cold and consequently invites those gaseous hydrocarbons to condense inside. A masonry chimney with packing around the flue will warm up and stay warm all winter especially if it has a top-closing damper. This device is one of my candidates for the best invention of the 20th century. Especially in conjunction with a masonry stove which is fired and then shut down, the top damper stops all airflow, turning your chimney into part of your radiant heater. Needless to say, a masonry chimney built on the outside of the house, which you often see, would be no help in this case.

The stove that is designed to allow the fire to burn consistently at maximum intensity with full access to air is a masonry stove. Made from brick or stone and clay, this type of stove has a long history around the world but not in the U.S. until recently. There are many regional styles but all send the fire through circuitous channels of masonry to extract as much heat as possible before heading out the chimney. They are quite efficient and leave no creosote. I had heard about these stoves and hoped to build one someday but bricks are not cheap and we were staying plenty warm in the second octagon using that barrel stove and a cast iron cook stove we picked up at a farm auction. That leaky old barrel stove actually burned hot and clean, and could put out impressive amounts of heat in short order but it was a hungry monster gobbling up firewood by the cord. The breakthrough came when we responded to an ad for used insulation and I noticed a large mound covered in weeds next to the house. Curious, I dug into it – bricks! Hundreds of bricks piled up from a torn down chimney and left to age gracefully for a couple of decades. Take them away if you want them, she said. That was the start of one of my sub-careers as a mason. Take your trowel; slap down a slug of mortar; set a brick on it; tap it down with a hammer; put a level on it for both level and plumb; and then clean up the joint with a pointer. That's it – do it over and again a few hundred times and you have an edifice, be it a building or a stove. First we took out the iron cook stove, removed the steel plates from the top and used them to finish off a masonry cook stove in the same place. Then, a few years later, we built a heater with the rest of the bricks. Now there is quite a conglomeration of brick set just to one side of center in the house, all of them acting as a massive heat sink after the stoves get going in the fall. A massive heat sink and a massive amount of weight but since the floor sits right on the ground, there was no problem supporting it.

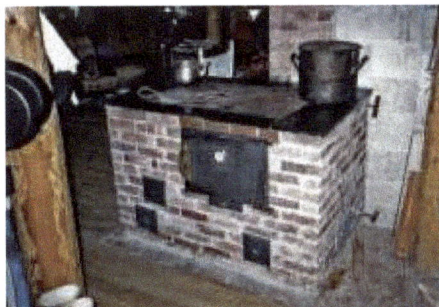

Cookstove newly bricked. Stainless pot turned black surviving fire in the root cellar.

I didn't materialize these stoves off the top of my head. There are available designs to follow.

The cookstove is especially complicated. It incorporates a metal oven which you can either buy or weld up yourself and it incorporates three separate baffles which direct the heat in various directions. The masonry heater which we built is a design which comes from Finland. I once heard or read, and I will repeat it without knowing whether it is true or not, that it is law in Finland that every new house must be built with one of these heaters in it. One thing they surely have in Finland is infinite quantities of wood and its all softwood which ups the creosote factor considerably – a factor which these stoves are made to handle. Our stove will burn anything you choose to put in there and the evidence of its functionality is to be seen by looking at the chimney top ten minutes after starting a fire - there is no smoke to be seen – just a sheen of heat waves. I have a magazine out of Finland which has nothing but separate designs for masonry heaters. There are fifty different designs in there and each design shows where each and every brick in that heater is located. It's all in Finnish but it is so plain that even a rank amateur could follow directions and build one.

Having a wood fired cookstove in your kitchen is an unknown luxury in America today. While you're home during the day, you throw in another chunk of hardwood every so often and it offers you a constant hot surface 3ft x 2ft and a constant hot oven. We keep a kettle over the firebox so that there is always boiling water to make a cup of tea and a five gallon pot toward the back so there is always hot water for doing dishes or some other chore. The oven cruises along at 300o and if you need to get it to 450o to bake a loaf of bread, then you put it two more pieces of wood and wait 15 minutes. If you feel like a piece of toast, you can just drop a slice of bread on the right spot, not too cold, not too hot. It's a friendly presence in the house with the constant reassuring sound of the kettle tootling in the background and it heats the house by itself in the fall and spring when the outside temperature is not consistently below freezing. Reproducing the classic iron cook stove in brick also has the effect of turning it into a heat multiplier. The longer you run it, the more heat it soaks up and the more heat it retains during the night with the baffles shut and the chimney damper closed. If you are seriously firing it to feed 50 people pancakes for instance, the oven will spin the gauge past itself and get to 800°!

Perhaps I've lived enough and learned enough that I've tamed the vicious fire beast but he will never be a dependable pet or slave. We know that without fire there is no civilization. There is no human race without fire and we've got him pretty well harnessed and contained but he's always yearning to bust free and blow out into a wild romp. He will always capitalize on a dram of ignorance if given the chance. Just while I was writing this, a chimney fire broke out in a neighbor's house down the road. I got the call and raced down there and when I arrived, I literally watched the upstairs pine floorboards, separated from the superheated chimney by two inches, blossom into flame. We dowsed that and the fire brigade arrived to save the house but not the chimney. I cringe to reflect upon my own ignorance in this category. I'll share with you some of the truly insane trials by fire I have initiated. One took place in that house in Austin. You don't get much of a winter there but what you do get warrants some heat in the house so I picked up a small tinny pink painted wood stove at a yard sale. It had been used by people smarter than me as a flower pot. This was my first wood stove. I set it up on top of a stump with some pipe going out the window. It fit nicely on that stump - just right and up off the floor. I fired it with 2x4 ends discarded at construction sites until one night, the house filled up with smoke and guess what? The stump was on fire! I picked it up and threw it out the door. I assume you are cringing too. Another famous display of fire ignorance happened when I decided to burn off the paint from the outside of a 50 gallon drum preparatory to making it into a stove. I figured that the most efficient method of accomplishing this task was to pour a bunch of gasoline into the drum and throw in a match. Do you want to know what happens when you do that? Your ears start ringing, your face is black, your beard is singed and you are wondering why you are lying on your back 10ft from the barrel. It's embarrassing to be so thoughtless. However, if embarrassment is the only price you pay for your thoughtless fire practices, then you are merely lucky. If your house burns down and there was no earthquake or lightning involved, then you can't blame it on God. The burning of the octagon was no act of God, it was inevitably an act of Bob. It happened as a result of something I did or didn't do even if I don't know what it was. If you start like a babe in the woods playing with fire, you will undoubtedly get burned but with luck, not so badly that you don't come to know the nature of fire; its intense desire to bust out of bounds and consume all that it can reach. Fire fuels our existence here at Gingerbrook. Firewood is free for the working. We don't need oil or gas or nuclear power but fire is a serious partner that requires that you play by serious rules.

Freshly built no inkling of its fate

Two summers gone by, rebuilt house and woodshed

AQUA VITAE

Aqua – vitae. The water of life. This piece of Latin has long been used to name distilled drinking alcohol. White lightning. Brandy. Vodka. Grain alcohol. I suggest that, given that alcohol is a disinfectant, - a dealer of death – that term should be aqua-mortis and let's use 'aqua-vitae' to describe pure water as the only 'water of life'. There is no life without water. Water is the staff of life. Say what you will about bread or beer or chocolate cake, clean, pure, fresh water is the gift from God. Well water, pond water, aquifer water, distilled sea water, municipal main – it's all H2O but given the choice, wouldn't you rather drink from a spring running out from beneath a stone outcropping somewhere lost in the woods?

This was our thinking when deciding whether Gingerbrook would be a suitable location to set up homesteading. We first looked for the water. As we discussed earlier, we knew that a gravity fed water supply to a future house and garden was indispensable. We discovered the ancient stoned-in spring with a wooden pipe right away but that was located down along the brook and only slightly uphill from the old cellar holes along the road. We weren't going to put a house along the road. We wanted it at a higher spot up against the lane close to the northern boundary. Could we find water uphill from there? It turned out that there were wet spots, seeps and springs aplenty arrayed along the base of the western hill, some of them big enough to send tiny streams into the marsh. They were all about the same elevation above the house site, high enough but not so to blast you right out of the shower, so it seemed a gamble, a try at the lottery to pick one as our water source. But choose you must and the winning candidate has turned out to be a good one. In 35 years it has gone dry once. It is extremely rare in Vermont to experience anything that could be called a drought. It is out of the ordinary in the summer to go for more than a week without rain. This is why it has always been touch and go trying to make hay here. But that summer there was no rain for three weeks and then a month and the spring dried up. You could see the well-drilling trucks making the rounds during that time, but we waited it out and with the next rain, the spring revived. However, we know from that experience that our spring is not deep water but water collected in uphill hollows and bogs and channeled underground. That spring was flowing from underneath a foot-high piece of granite ledge and I mortared in a brick box to catch and collect the water. Digging down in front of the ledge and leveling the dirt and gravel, I set the three sided box 3ft high, 3ft wide and 4ft long right on it and up against the stone outcropping. We know how far from the house the spring is located because we laid in 900ft of black plastic 1" pipe to span the distance. I cleared a six foot wide swath through the woods and hired a cowboy with a backhoe and he did the job in a few hours including hoeing right through a goat fence without slowing down. The books say that at this latitude and this climate you should bury your water line 4ft down. There was nowhere along that entire distance that he could have gone that deep even if he had tried. The average depth is two feet and some place the pipe runs over stone ledge that is only one foot below the surface. The water in this pipe has never frozen although the water temperature at the kitchen sink in February is usually in the mid-30s. Water is not comfortable about being contained and has a way of escaping to follow its urge to the sea and just setting the bottom layer of brick on the ground didn't work to hold back 200 gallons for very long. The solution was to dig out several buckets of pure clay from a nearby bank and plaster the bottom and sides of the box. From the hillside physicists the word is that every foot of elevation yields another pound of water pressure. Our spring is not high on the hill so you do get wet in the shower but it's a comedown it you're used to the standard 40lb blast. It feels like 20 – 25 lbs but by the time you stretch a hose 200ft out and 20ft down to the cider mill, you get what feels like normal push-back from the nozzle.

Funny things happen occasionally with this system. There is no check valve between house and spring and although the end of pipe which shows in the box is covered with a screen, strange things circumvent now and again. One such was what I personally have named a glassworm but which officially goes by 'horsehair worm'. This one appeared in a glass of water just drawn from the tap. It shows as a wriggling transparent six inch long piece of thread and is quite disconcerting if you are contemplating your glass about to quench an August afternoon thirst. He is so thin that he can be sucked right through the mesh of the screen. Another critter which traveled the 900ft to the house somehow eliminated the screen altogether. One of the house faucets suddenly stopped running so figuring that something was clogged in there, I sent compressed air into the plugged one while leaving another open Whump! I was horrified to see protruding from the faucet a hand with five fingers attached to an arm the skin of which was mottled green and brown like a dead man's might be. It could have been a scene from the Creature from the Black Lagoon but so miniaturized that I soon recovered enough to identify a frog. Now before you get too excited, let me say that the spring box is covered by a little house which to close inspection, is frog and salamander tight but somehow they occasionally get in anyway and after that incident, I beefed up the underwater screen with a stainless clamp. It's a mystery analogous to the mice which get into your house. How and where do they get in? Who knows? But somehow they always do. Not to get the wrong idea however about this water. It comes through bright, fresh and clean, these two incidents notwithstanding.

During the one summer of the drought, our spring was dry for perhaps three weeks, however there was still water otherwise on the homestead. The gingerbrook would recover at night, trickle for a while in the morning and disappear by noon. But there was yet another spring that I'd noticed bubbling up through the peat on the flat inside the marsh. Our 'marsh', which might technically be a 'fen', is characterized by a layer one foot thick of organic outwash (peat) from the forest. Beneath this is impervious clay through which this spring had gnawed an opening creating a constant upwelling in which danced and swirled particles of peat. It was August with temperatures every day in the 80s and I put a thermometer in that water. It read 50° and it was apparent that this was deep water from far away. How to get this water to the house was the question? I cut the bottom out of a 50 gallon plastic barrel, set it over the up-swell and pushed it down through the peat to ground on the clay. Then I right-angled a ½" plastic pipe into the barrel and ran it down to the absolute lowest point on the property along the southern edge and started a siphon. The peat cleared quickly and it started sucking air so I put a valve on the end to slow down the flow and was rewarded with a constant stream of cold, clear water. We survived the drought by running that water into a sap tank on the back of Two Ton Tony, parking him on the rise in back of the house and gravity feeding through a garden hose to hookup to the household plumbing. That siphon pipe which extends some 200ft across the surface of the marsh has been running continuously ever since. That would be ten years and we haven't ever needed it again, but the pipe has gradually sunk itself out of sight – subsided into the cattails and sedge and since the water is always at 50o, it never freezes.

Due to the topography of the homestead, any water that arrives ends up in the marsh and eventually in the gingerbrook itself before it disappears under the road to join the unnamed valley stream on its way to the ocean. What about the water piped in to the house? It too has no choice but to migrate to the marsh. When we were camped out in the shop in the pre-octagon days the outflow was through a 2" pipe from the sink curved down and out beneath the lower wall to empty on the ground below.

167

Many hundreds of gallons went out through that pipe to just disappear into the ground. That was a temporary solution; so what about the waste water coming out of the octagon? It would just be 'gray' water – outflows from the sinks and shower. There would be no flush toilet. We wanted to avoid the expense and hassle of a septic tank and preserve the fertility offered by the 'humanure'. A leach field one shovel-width wide and gravel bottomed running down and away from the house has taken care of the zillions of gallons poured into it and leached them surely into the marsh where their destiny awaited them anyway had they not been temporarily diverted through the house. This trench offers the opportunity for unlimited extension for you and your shovel if it begins to show wet at the surface.

What about a pond, you might ask? There is certainly a perfect spot for one at the lower edge where the marsh meets the pasture along the road. It's all cattails and it's where the gingerbrook emerges from the percolating marsh to re-establish itself as a brook. A one acre pond would sit in there nicely and perhaps you could make one like Scott Nearing with a shovel and a bucket. He visited the pond site every day to dig and remove one bucketful of dirt. The mathematics of it are irrefutable – if you dig out one bucket load of muck every day, at some point you will have yourself a pond. The trouble with this logic is that you would need the chutzpah of a Scott Nearing to command the necessary willpower to pull off such a miracle. Somehow I knew that option was out of the question and so was paying someone with a large machine so we've left the site to the cattails, the red-winged blackbirds, the frogs and the encroaching tamaracks

When it comes to living a life that will not be "nasty, brutish and short", I would opine that the prime antidote would be hot water. Life without hot water, not just to make tea, but to bathe in, loses a good deal of its allure. And it would seem that if you have fire and you have water, you should be able to combine the two and come out with hot water. Simple to conjure and not so difficult to accomplish but this was to become a major ongoing theme through many iterations, some sheer genius and others the height of all folly. We have tried it all. It's a long and winding path this quest for a hot shower and it will be difficult but I'll attempt to spare you the minutiae of the tale. There are basically two ways to heat water with firewood. One is direct batch heating and the other is often referred to as 'cogeneration'. The former involves setting some sort of container directly over a fire and conveying the hot water somehow to its destination. The latter would be making hot water as a byproduct of heating your house usually by inserting some sort of coil or manifold into the firebox that will 'thermo siphon' the water into a separate tank often called a 'range boiler'. Range boilers were common when everybody used wood cookstoves and are usually slim 30 gallon copper or galvanized tanks that differ from other hot water tanks by having two ¾" threaded openings welded top and bottom onto the side for the purpose of accommodating the thermosiphon.

Thinking about our necessities before we moved onto the land and into the shop, we had picked up a 'Home Comfort' wood cookstove at an auction for which we were the only bidder, and once the new building had a floor, we placed it in a corner. On this stove surface there was always a 5 gallon pot simmering water. We arrived with a one year old and later had a new-born in that building and its remarkable how well a kid can be washed in a five gallon bucket and how big a kid will still fit in the same bucket. Years of cloth diapers and dirty dishes and dirty hands and dirty faces and dirty clothes all depended on that stove-top hot water to get clean. Jo was constantly heating pots of water and carrying them about to their various destinations. In the summer time, as the song goes, when the living was easy, the cookstove would still be cooking but hot water was made to order outside. We started with a 4'x4' sap pan set over a fire pit dug into the sidehill above the shop and hooked to a garden hose running into the house or flipped over a handy branch to provide a shower. Now that was hot water! And piped to right where you wanted it, but even better we graduated to a 55 gallon drum with water in through the big bung and out the small one. These fires were kid-tended. The two boys loved being given the chance to fool around with fire and the responsibility of keeping that hot water coming. Twigs, leaves, dead branches, hunks of bark from the wood pile – it was a challenge which they happily took on.

If we were majoring in the production of hot water, that was HW 101. For the next course, things got more sophisticated. This was for winter time hot water when the barrel stove was being fired. That barrel put out such vast quantities of heat I figured that we could steal some of it to heat water and not notice the difference. As I explained previously, the stove set-up in that building involved a barrel set on the ground connected to a stove pipe going up into a second barrel on the living floor connected to another pipe going up through the roof. The idea was to thermosiphon cold water from the bottom of a range boiler through the fire and back into the top. The thermosiphon keeps the water moving as long as the tank is placed above the fire. I put the range boiler in a far corner and ran ½" copper from the bottom under the floor into the first barrel and up through the stacks and the second barrel to exit the stove pipe above my head height and back over to the top of the tank. Most thermosiphon systems place the tank as close to the fire as possible but this one had ten feet to travel back and forth and fifteen feet to travel vertically, so how did it work? That was a while ago and since then I've set up two or three other thermosiphon systems and several batch systems and I will now state unequivocally that this crazy, cobbled up hot water fantasy produced more hot water faster than any other I've attempted.

That system required soldering the requisite copper piping and in my hubris I thought what could be easier? That is until late one night when I was called awake by my nose alarm. While living in that shop building, we slept in sleeping bags on the floor and in an attempt to baffle the cold and yet stay in contact, I would bundle and enclose all except the tip of my nose. As I was programmed to awaken every night around 3am in order to refill the stove, I could judge instantly by the state of my nose just how things were going with the fire. This night the nose knew that something was amiss and I clumped down the outside stairs and was greeted by the surreal sight of water pouring out of the door of the barrel stove. Pouring out and gouging an arroyo in the dirt on its way out and under the back wall. I had to deal with it right then and there otherwise the sirens' alternative of diving back into the bag and waiting till tomorrow would have led to everything becoming frozen. The lesson learned? In designing your system, don't put a soldered joint right in the hottest zone in the stove – the intense heat will overwhelm the buffering temperature of the water and melt the solder.

Once installed in the octagon house, we continued our heroic quest for yet more hot water. The summer outdoor showers with their fire pits were abandoned and the cookstove, the range boiler, the barrel stove, and the copper piping were all transferred to the new house – and subsequently destroyed in the fire but for our purposes here we will lump everything together in one octagon house.

At that time in the early eighties, we caught wind of a novel unit of a water heater. It was made in Mexico and was comprised of a vertical tank set on a tiny all-metal firebox. The idea was that in the desert areas of Mexico there might not be any real wood to speak of so this rig was designed to burn grass or cactus spines or cucarachas. It could be plumbed to your supply, cold in at the bottom and hot out at the top and it was designed to provide ten or fifteen gallons of hot very quickly. This was a good summer time rig when the barrel stove wasn't in play and the kids could keep it fired for baths or showers. This one worked for a while until one quiet evening I heard a hiss and a trickle like some small child was peeing on the floor only to discover the Mexican heater had sprung a pinhole leak and was squirting a stream across the room. A toothpick was perfect to stop the flood but after another month or two, the tank had accumulated 5 or 6 more toothpicks and we named it the porcupine and sent it to the dump. T'was a good idea though, I thought. Perhaps I could make my own version. I hunted down a galvanized 30 gallon tank and put it on top of a base made from brick. The tank was originally from a gas-fired heater and featured an exhaust pipe welded up through the center. The fire box was just a cubic brick space larger than the Mexican in order to accommodate a real fire and the door was cast iron salvaged off a junk cookstove. This rig really made hot water, so much so that one day I opened the cold faucet at the kitchen and watched in awe as it began blowing and spitting *steam*. It would have been extraordinary enough to find hot water coming out of your cold faucet but this was steam. The steam continued to blast for another minute followed by hot for a while before re-establishing itself as a cold water tap. Meanwhile of course, the hot side was working on a full 30 gallons of super-hot water. The explanation? These systems were never encumbered by temperature/pressure relief valves so in this case, as the water began to boil in the tank, the steam pressured its path through the least resistance up the pipe toward the spring; that is until I opened the cold faucet allowing the steam to escape that way.

These batch heaters were necessarily 'on demand'. If you wanted a shower, you needed to rustle up some newspaper, find some kindling, bring in some firewood and tend the fire not until it was blowing steam but until by feeling the metal tank, you knew you had enough hot water for a good one. This yielded ornery kids sometimes but in general was beneficial for character building.

That hot water maker was a beauty but had a short-lived career disappearing in the house fire, so it was back to the factory to produce replacements. The first was a brilliant idea but like many brilliant ideas, didn't fly very far. It involved spiraling ¾" flexible copper and inserting it into an 8" pipe and putting the whole thing on top of a fire. That had no choice but to make hot water but so slowly that I was compelled to come up with another. These batch heaters were all about summertime hot water. Winter water always came out of a barrel stove that was equipped with a manifold made of 10ft of ¾" galvanized pipe. This thermosiphoned and since the range boiler was already sitting there, why not use it for summer water also? Hitting on all cylinders and revving along, I cut another tank in half, welded a pipe into the middle, put it on a brick firebox and attached thermosiphon pipes into that same range boiler. We survived on that one for a couple of years but it was not too efficient and everything went by the by once the masonry stoves were built. Feeling no twinges of nostalgia, I tore it all out and installed a soldered copper manifold alongside the fire box of the masonry cook stove. The old range boiler began showing rust spots through the galvanize and when I investigated buying a new one (hard to find), I discovered that it was cheaper to buy a brand new electric hot water heater, take out the element and use it as a thermosiphon tank. Something to keep in mind concerning messing with ½"copper pipe is that it is forever reusable. If you can find some as 'scrap', you can always cut it, clean it and resolder it

Today the thermosiphoned water collects in that new tank which acts as the cold feed into an electric hot water heater. In high winter when the cookstove is fired all day every day, the electric heater rarely turns on and in the summer, the cold water from the spring gets time to warm somewhat first before going from one tank to the next. However, after all our hot water trials, which although I have tried to summarize, may have seemed interminable, now no matter which fire is or is not burning, we participate in the modern miracle of merely turning the handle knowing that the hot water will flow. It's the height of luxury.

Turkey Talk

Your regular commercial turkey – that is; your Thanksgiving or Christmas turkey – is a man-made creation. Most of them are white and would never be mistaken for a real (ie wild) turkey. Even those that look the same; aren't. The original genotype has been tinkered with over the centuries in the eternal quest for yet more white meat. The bird with the largest breast is the one we want to breed the next generation. To accomplish this, all modern commercial turkeys are bred by artificial insemination. Why? Because the magnificent breastiness of the tom; the imposing width and breadth of his great chest gets in his way and prevents him from actually copulating with the hen. He stutters and shudders and dances and prances all around her dragging his wing feathers on the ground and will mount her as she squats to receive him, but he can't physically accomplish the task. The hens, however, are fertile, lay large spotted eggs, and will set and hatch a clutch of 8 or 10. How do I know this if they aren't able to produce fertile eggs when left to themselves? The answer is that we were able to encourage fertilization in a couple of ways.

As part of our desire to experience animal husbandry to its extremes, we figured that raising some turkeys would be entertaining and ultimately filling. We purchased some poults from a hatchery – straight run – male or female however they came. They were called "Broad breasted bronze". They are colored just like wild turkeys. There is one slight difference – if you look at the tips of their long tail feathers, the horizontal stripes there are white whereas the stripes are bronze on the wild turkey. At least they seemed more like real turkeys than the ghastly and ghostly whites. I learned later that the reason white turkeys are preferred by the Thanksgiving industry is that the white feathers pluck without leaving dark remnants in the skin. Turkeys are full grown and fit for breeding at 5 or 6 months of age. I couldn't figure out why we weren't getting fertile eggs when the time came until one day as I watched a pair mating, I noticed the Tom trying but missing. So I picked up the hen by her ankles, held her upside down, noticed a glob of semen on her feathers, scooped it with my middle finger and pushed it into her vent. Quasi – artificial insemination! Believe it or not, it actually worked. That hen set a clutch and hatched 3 or 4 poults. I didn't really want to cultivate that skill or turn it into a lifelong profession, so fortunately another option presented. We learned of a man who kept a passel of turkeys in a barn-sized structure enclosed by wire netting. He was breeding back into them an increasing share of wild genes. They were wary and excitable. If you surprised them they would fluster en-masse and ricochet along the wire. We brought home one of his half-wild Toms to match with our hens and relieve me of my inseminatory duties. When left to free range, turkeys will go a long way towards feeding themselves. Especially later in the summer when the fields are alive with the cricket hatch, they will snap them up along with grasshoppers by the zillions. The hens will find a hidden place, usually under some brush, to set their nests. If you watch while keeping yourself hidden, as the hen goes off to lay, you can locate the nest. The chances of her being picked off by some wandering carnivore are somewhat high, so you can get her protected after she starts to set by picking her up in the dark and closing her in with her eggs in a box or barrel for 48 hours before opening the door into a fenced area.

At this time in Vermont and the rest of New England, there was a big push to re-introduce wild turkeys into the ecosystem. With the felling of the forest in Vermont and the transformation from woods to field, came the disappearance of the larger native animals such as catamount, wolf, deer, moose and turkey. However, by the 1970s, the forest had reestablished to the extent that the majority of the state was again wooded and some of the animals were coming back on their own but the wild life managers felt that the turkeys needed help. They brought wild turkeys in from Pennsylvania and other places where they were already thriving and seeded small flocks around the state. At the same time, they instituted a public information campaign and especially warned people about polluting the wild by letting domestics escape or otherwise intermingle. Therefore what this guy of ours was doing hybridizing turkeys was severely frowned upon and our own Tom was also pavo non grata. However any objections were soon overruled by the resounding success of the program, such that today you can't ride the back roads of Vermont without seeing turkeys everywhere.

At that time in the 1970s, any literature you might have read about raising turkeys for meat recommended keeping them on a wire floor up off the ground and feeding them antibiotic laced mash. This was extremely unappealing and we decided to just follow our druthers, let them free range about the farm and feed them only whole grain - that would be corn, barley, wheat and oats. Antibiotics were out of the question and I didn't trust mash then and I still don't today. Grind the grain into powder and add various minerals and vitamins and supplemental proteinacious stuff, and you have the perfect, scientifically formulated feed. Well maybe, or maybe not. Maybe you don't actually know what fell into or was put into the mixing vat. Ground up chicken parts seem to make their way insidiously throughout the food chain. Anyhow, the turkey has got himself a powerful gizzard that yearns to do its own grinding and the bird is healthier and happier when it can go to roost at night with its crop full of hard nuts to crack.

The offspring of our domestic hen and the half-wild Tom seemed to be lured more by the call of the wild than the easy living provided by homestead handouts. They could elevate themselves effortlessly and the first winter we spent at Gingerbrook, there were two adolescents that roosted every night at the peak of the octagonal roof. The unfinished house had been put to sleep for the winter with a cover of black paper on the roof except for the five foot wide hole at the peak 25ft up. These two would fly up to the hole and spend the long, cold winter night perching on the edge and shitting down through the opening. However, come spring, these young turks came down from the roof and disappeared. That is, until two days later, when driving down the road to Chelsea village, we spotted them high, high in a dead snag of a pine. Then a few days after that, we began to hear excited reports of a pair of turkeys that were roosting on various rooftops right in the village. They were uncatchable and we accepted the news with a mixture of wonderment and whimsy just as if we were innocent of all turkey shenanigans.

First winter roost for adolescent turkeys

Having a Tom turkey roaming about the homestead adds a wildcard central character to the cast of your play. They are big, tend to show off and hog the limelight, and in season, get to be downright pugnacious. This boy that we kept, even though half wild, still had plenty of chest to him and weighed around 20 lbs. He had his territory and his hens, and he would put up with no rival, including his own reflection. The front three sides of the octagon were well windowed down to the level of his neck and he would patrol around and back, gobbling, puffing, wing dragging and attacking those interlopers in the windows. But those saucy rivals weren't easily scared off: pesky devils; they were always there waiting to challenge him again. Perhaps his frustration led him to seek other targets, like children. He never bothered adults but he would size up children and determine them to be within his kingdom. When our oldest boy, Adam, was seven, the Tom would be hiding, waiting for him to get off the school bus. Adam adapted rapidly, using evasive tactics like leaping out of the bus and running for his life to the house. Ben and Will, manifesting the warrior in all us humans, decided to gird themselves for battle with the turkey. They constructed shields out of plywood and leather straps, and swords out of two pieces of wood and bravely set forth to St. George that dragon. Still feeling somewhat intimidated, Ben, the general of the army, one day took the extra precaution of wielding an old handle that had broken off a splitting maul. He burst in through the door with tears streaming, crying that he had killed Tom. Ben had cracked him upside the head with the handle and the turkey had gone down like he'd been shot. However, he did revive and got up woozy but alive and Ben was much relieved. Tom, though, apparently had learned a lesson, or maybe he had received a lobotomy, because never after did he attack anybody, large or small.

One gobbler tends to attract another – a fact that is employed by turkey hunters with their specialized callers – so we would often hear wild Toms in the woods responding to ours. One day, while listening to an exchange, I saw a wild gobbler come out of the woods and head for our Tom who had gone out halfway in the pasture to meet him. Male turkeys fight just like gamecocks. They jump at each other feet first and try to spur each other in the head and the battles can go on for quite a while but because of their bulk, they tire faster than roosters. Wild turkeys are famous for their elusiveness but while engaged in a cock fight, they lose sight of anything around, so that you can creep up on them and dive in to snag one by the ankle before they even know you're there. The two boys and I tried that once when we noticed a battle in progress as we drove by a hayfield. We commandoed toward them low and fast and got within 15ft before one of them noticed, the surprise of his life and they were gone like jackrabbits. However, this day I hung back and just watched. The wild one was trim and fast but our boy had bulk and he used his chest to consistently bowl over the other guy. After about 5 minutes, the challenger was beaten. He gave up and retreated back into the woods; but what did I see next? Another turkey coming out to our Tom. However, this one was slim and svelte. A hen! Our shining knight had just won himself a lady. She was beautiful. She had the grace and poise of a Chinese courtesan that you might see in one of those old black and white movies, so Jo named her Mai Ling.

Over a period of days, she gradually became less wary of us and moved closer to the buildings until she was spending nights in a big popple right next to the house. Come evening, she would move close to the trunk and then, as if pulled by a string, she would fly straight up 40ft to her nighttime perch. For such heavy birds, they are remarkable flyers. They prefer to run and can move amazingly fast on the ground but when pushed, they take to the air. Perhaps you have had the same experience as I, scaring one up on a lonely forested road with the dark trees close along both sides and have that turkey sail in front of your automobile, speedometer saying 40 mph, for a couple of hundred yards before finding an opening towards which to tilt and veer away into the woods. Mai Ling came out of the woods in the fall of the year to tantalize us with her beauty and give us the gift of a sense of wonder in the unexpected and the unforeseeable. She left the first of January when the new octagon house burned down and we never saw her again.

You Could Do Without but You'd Rather Have the Right Tool

Occasionally someone asks me what manner of tools do you need especially in order to homestead? I reply – "You need them all". However, start with a scythe. In fact, two scythes – one grass and one bush blade. Keep it razor sharp – this is easier to do with a European blade – and you will use it all the time. The scythe is the quintessential homestead tool and you will be happy not to be holding onto one of those nasty little whizzer machines that have conspired to turn suburbia into an illustration out of Better Homes and Gardens. Beyond your scythe, there are a few more tools that you'll need. You will need hammers – a 16oz claw hammer, a 20oz framing hammer, a ball peen, a cross peen, a two pounder and an 8lb sledge. You'll need a splitting maul and 2 or 3 splitting wedges. You'll need a felling ax, a limbing ax, a hatchet. a broad ax, an adze, log dogs and a peavey. You'll need a pick, a digging mattock and a garden mattock. You'll need two round pointed shovels, a straight edged spade, a narrow transplanting spade. a couple of garden trowels, two snow shovels and a long handled square shovel for muck, slush and ice. You'll need 2 or 3 garden hoes, 2 sharp hand hoes, a large mason's hoe and a wheel hoe. You'll need two garden rakes, a leaf rake, a potato rake, a 3 tine pitch fork, a six tine manure fork, a ten tine compost fork and two digging forks. You'll need cloppers and loppers and nippers and clippers. You'll need two watering cans and several hundred feet of garden hose. You'll need three sizes of mason's trowels, a mason's float, a pointer, a mixing trough. a 4ft level, a 2ft level, a torpedo level, a chalk line, and a plumb bob. You'll need a 16" bow saw, a 36" bow saw, a pruning saw, a crosscut saw, a jig saw, a back saw, a hacksaw, a skil saw, a table saw and a chain saw. You'll need carpenter's squares, tape measures and rulers. You'll need rasps, files, chisels, screwdrivers, nail sets, pliers, vice grips, clamps, a plane, a bench vice, a propane torch, an oxy-acetylene torch, a fire extinguisher, wrenches and spanners, two sets of sockets 3/8" and ½". You'll need a machete, a drawknife, a froe, a Swiss army knife and a utility knife. You'll need snow shoes, a wheelbarrow, a garden cart, an air pump, a battery charger, a voltmeter, jumper cables, 2 or 3 heavy chains, various 25ft ropes, pulley blocks, a come-along, a post-hole digger, bolt cutters, hoof nippers, a 5ft iron bar, 2 gooseneck crowbars, a cat's paw, a bit brace, a power driver and wood bits up to 1 1/2" and metal bits up to ¼"

And of course you will need nails and screws and nuts and bolts of all sizes and descriptions. Now is that all? I doubt it. We are not even going to cross the line into the house where the list multiplies into frying pans, 5 gallon pots, strainers, funnels, garlic squeezers, potato peelers and wooden spoons, and inevitably the next job that comes along will have you studying this list and saying Damn! – I could use another tool for this one, but you finish the chore without it and sometime later, that very tool will jump out at you from a table at a yard sale. Inevitably you will have to buy a new tool at some point but with some luck and perseverance, most of these tools can come from auctions or garage sales or farm liquidations or family friends who need them no longer.

Homestead Solutions #5

A Table Saw

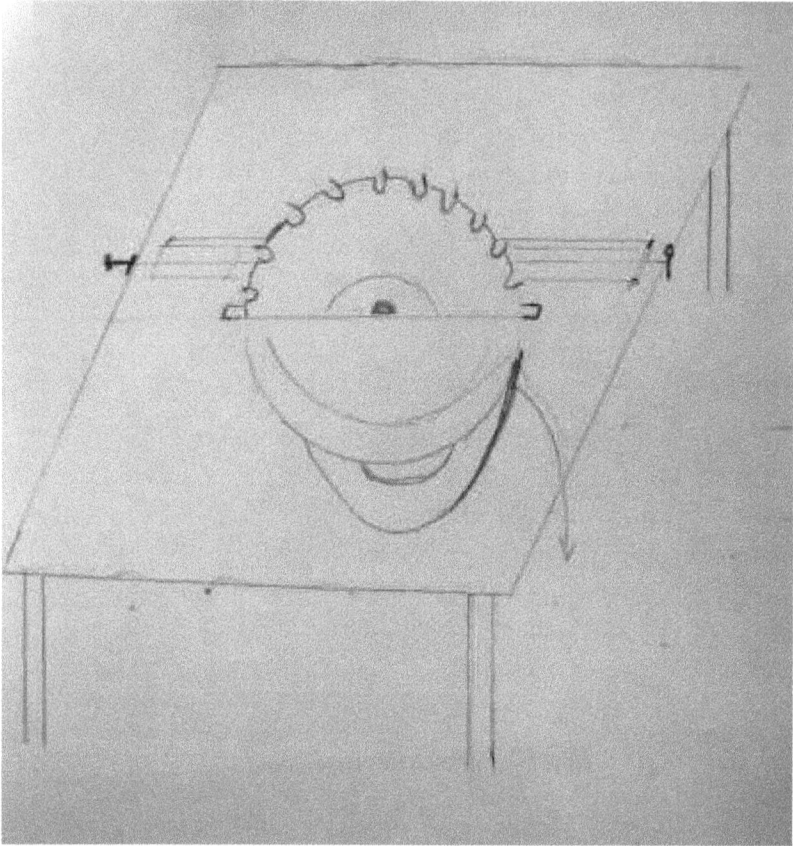

A table saw is really an indispensable tool. You can of course do it all with a skil saw and a variety of hand saws but if you are doing a lot of carpentry, like putting together a house, when it comes to making trim, you will love your table saw. However such an item would cost you plenty so here is a tip for engineering a table saw on the cheap. This plan requires already having an old skil saw or acquiring one that still works.

Start with a perfectly flat piece of ¾"plywood measuring at least 3'x3' and cut a slot in the middle slightly longer than the diameter of the skil saw blade. Set the saw on the plywood with the blade through the slot and either use the holes that are already in the plate or drill four of them and screw the saw down tight. A ¾" screw, given the thickness of the plate, will probably not protrude the other side. Now flip the rig upside down and manufacture a set of legs for the whole thing to sit on and you've got yourself a table saw. It's helpful to have a fence for the table and you can make one using a 3 1/2' bar clamp. A pipe clamp will also work. It's just a little harder to drill to accommodate the screws which will hold a 2x4 onto the clamp. The 2x4 will sit facing the blade and the clamp will hold it tight and straight.

Those Human Beings, Part 3

BARRY

He came singing the song of myself so eloquent and persuasive that he was impossible to resist. Although he presented as an amalgamation of a hundred stories featuring himself, he was amusing, informative and instructive. A poet, a master of wordology, talking and writing, he might have been considered a latter day Walt Whitman except that it is rumored that Whitman never left his room while Barry lives beyond the walls. If he ever sleeps under a roof, it would be that of a barn, shed or porch and it would be with his head next to an open door. Preferable however would be to set up in a carefully chosen location in relation to where he finds himself, under a tarp or if the night promises to be clear, under the starry sky. He will often show up for breakfast in the mornings after he sees smoke begin to rise from the chimney and report on the doings of the night: the changes in the weather; the snortings of the deer below the garden; the squeakings of the mice in the cider mill; the rummagings and scratchings of a skunk around the bee hives. He will make fiercer noises than they in the night to scare off the deer.

Where he finds himself defines Barry's life. He owns no property, no house, no car and claims no home except wherever he happens to be at the moment. Don't get the idea that he is one of the poor hopeless and bedraggled homeless. He comes and goes as he chooses but to and from a network of people who are happy to accommodate him when he shows. This network comprises what might be considered as the Barry appreciation society which extends across the entire country. He has an astounding knack of arriving in a rural location or a small country town for the first time and immediately connecting with someone who 'adopts' him and allows him to establish a base often including using the house to make tea or eat meals. He travels with his own mug – an enameled metal cup that holds an entire pint of tea which he keeps full for most of the day. I do not think that most of us would be so welcomed showing up at a house or farm and presenting oneself hoping to be trusted and treated accordingly but Barry projects a vision of himself that quickly breaks down barriers. He is so practiced singing his own song that he doesn't seem egotistical or suspicious but comes on rather like a pilgrim or monk. Many of the connections Barry makes either live alone or are elderly and they rapidly assimilate into what I call Barry's extended family. He is a powerful worker, strongly motivated to accomplish necessary tasks and he quickly becomes indispensable. He will cleanup, re-arrange, move heavy objects, do garden work, trim trees or bushes, split and stack firewood and keep company with his unquenchable story tellings. This is a tremendous boon for the elderly many of whom come to depend on him. Once established, these relationships often continue for years with Barry coming and going according to his own calendar. Several times, he has followed an old one into creeping dementia when he would show up to deal with piled up bills, throw out tons of junk mail, identify possible targeted scams and drive them to doctor's appointments or the grocery store.

Although we have met hardly any, Barry's extended 'family' is known to us in intimate detail as I suppose we are to them. When he arrives for one of his sojourns, he first fills us in on where he has been since last time and who he's stayed with and what is their state of health, state of family, state of farm or ranch, state of weather and condition of harvest or business. We know these people only by hearsay but as presented and portrayed by Barry, ongoing over the years as he comes and goes, they seem to be our lifelong friends, part of our dramatis personae. We have followed some of these families through children and into grandchildren, learning each generation's quirks and foibles, their work habits and their educational attainments without ever either seeing or talking to any of them. There are several dozen people involved in this family held together by Barry glue and given the infinite detail of his description, I imagine that many of them could tell me more about my own life on the homestead than I. These days, most of his travels take him between Vermont and Oregon. How he decides when and where is perhaps somewhat mystical but if any of his people wish to have him housesit or if some crisis presents which he feels would be helped by his presence, or if a certain geography beckons, then he will go. Vermont became one of his home bases as a result of doing alternate service as a C.O. in a Vermont hospital during the Vietnam war and he stayed on to accumulate an ever widening circle of friends and geographies. Barry is a master of culture – the culture of humans to be sure but above all that of silvi, agri and horticulture. He has his people but he identifies strongly with favored landscapes.

He stayed attached to one slice of landscape in Vermont throughout three ownership changes. He apparently came with the land as he introduced himself to each succeeding set of owners and was accepted as if he were some glacial erratic come to rest there or a permanent inhabitant of the accompanying woodland. The last of the three had decided to get into the maple syrup business figuring that's what you do if you own maple trees in Vermont. There are various methods to set up a pipeline system for collecting maple sap and one of them, which could be considered criminal, involves stringing wire ratcheted tight between every tapped tree and on to the mainline. The wire is wrapped around or spiked to each tree; the plastic tubing is then tied to the wire and the whole thing is then left there for eternity. Eternity in this case came along sooner than expected and the erstwhile syrup maker absconded leaving Barry as the sole inhabitant. He looked upon the unholy mess of wire and plastic and couldn't stand the sight. There were no future property buyers in the offing and he felt that he had to take care of this on his own. The wire had already begun to bite into the bark and it presented an evil rat's nest that most people would have walked away from unless they were being paid a hefty wage. Barry was not being paid and it took him weeks but he cleaned up that entire mess on his own, cutting the wire, unwrapping it from each tree, coiling it into hundreds of sections and disposing of it all. The reward for him was the same reward he gets from much of his labor and that is the artist's satisfaction in the creation or, in this case, the restoration of sanctuary.

Creating sanctuary is often his gift to his various hosts. If he is not splitting firewood or digging and weeding garden, he might select a site that has grown in and with a bow saw, a sickle, a mattock and a shovel, he will clear the brush and pile it strategically to create an inviting space and offer the wee creatures nesting and hiding hostels. Then he might rearrange some large stones, transplant some favored shrubs or wildflowers and perhaps set up a place for sitting and contemplation. This same aesthetic is reflected in his choice of sleeping and/or camp sites. He'll camp beside streams or, in our case, on top of the little plank bridge over the gingerbrook where he can lull to its ripplings and watch the light sparkle on the water. Other times he will set up in the middle of the woods expressly to commune with the hermit thrush in the early morning and late into the evening. He is a musician and a musicologist and would play extempore on the piano sounding quite like the song of the thrush.

It was the summer after the fire when Barry first came and he came accompanied with the moniker of Butternut Barry. This was because he was a great champion of the butternut tree and a cracker and purveyor of its nuts. He had been tracking down select trees, harvesting nuts, cracking nuts, planting nuts and tending young trees for years. He did the same for black walnuts and hickories but the alliteration of it was irresistible and Butternut Barry he had become. He traveled with a grain sack of butternuts, a special light cracking hammer and an old boy-scout knife that featured just the right nut-meat extractor. He traveled to Oregon on the train with a full sack of nuts in order to trade and barter when he arrived. He likes to crack in just the right place and sets up a hefty cracking stone and will show you just how to position the iron-clad nut and how to tap, tap, tap to break the shell so that the meat might come out whole – not easy to accomplish. Sometimes he would go to cracking and settle into a meditative state for hours and emerge to present an entire jar of nut-meats. As the years passed, he could show us butternuts that he had planted here and there which were now robust nut-bearing adolescents.

Barry walks everywhere. He walks on bare feet. He says his feet don't appreciate being stuffed into shoes. He avoids mechanical transportation and machines in general as much as he can. He cleans his teeth with a black birch branching, or a yellow birch if black is not available. They both taste of wintergreen and he chews the ends to a fray and works that through his teeth. He knows the character and characteristics of every tree and harvests bark, twig and leaf of such like sassafras and slippery elm. He will strip the bark of slippery elm just in the spring when it is loose and carry a stash with him to offer upon arrival. He knows the medicinal herbs and shrubs and will mail an occasional box of perhaps sage from the dry side of the mountains in Oregon. He transports and transplants certain trees and shrubs that he feels will be appreciated. Oh, you have red currants and black but no white. I'll bring you a white currant that I know of. Or; there is a special and spectacular black walnut tree that I visit from time to time. I'll bring you some of those nuts to plant here. He listened to my plan to scatter lime in the sugarbush and insisted on coming to help. The idea involved walking up and down the steep western hillside innumerable times carrying frontpacks of limestone and scattering as we went. He had been worried about the effects of acid rain on maple trees and really took on the project as if it were his own.

He holds no love for large, powerful or fast machines not necessarily as a philosophical position but rather as a witness to their heedlessness and destructive potential. The prejudice is based on innumerable personal run-ins and disappointments. He will choose to 'rescue' a shadow of a cherry tree or a baby butternut and lavish attention on it sickling grass and gathering forest leaves to mulch around it while cutting away and digging out any competition, only to have the land owner, enjoying his new riding mower, run right over it. Or he will put days or recurring weeks into transporting rich muck soil and autumn leaves and surround a stately and ancient maple with a deep reviving mulch only to see the man oblivious on his tractor scrape the bucket right through it, having decided this is just the place for a road. One winter of abundant snow, Barry had dug himself a snow cave in the middle of an open field in which he kept his things and spent the nights in his sleeping bag. He returned to it late one afternoon to discover that some snow machines had driven right over it, once again heedless and oblivious. He concludes that the ease of power at a fingertip and the intoxication of speed puts people at such a remove from their surroundings that things get destroyed willy-nilly. Using hand tools forces one to stop, look, and listen before chopping, digging or hacking.

Barry studies maps and reads U.S. Forest Service publications and U.S. Geological surveys looking for likely places to explore and hang out. He wasn't enthusiastic about formal education but is in fact formidably educated. He doesn't read fiction but reads extensively in geology, natural history, philosophy and general history. He is capable of conversing with the learned on any of these topics but when he frequents libraries looking at geological surveys, it's because he wants to find either accessible hot springs or wild, lonely and beautiful terrain in which to spend time. For instance, he was attracted to Hell's Canyon and realized he could walk from the end of the road down through the hot, dry side canyons into Hell's Canyon through which the Snake River divides Oregon from Idaho. It's wild and it's lonely and he'll stay there wandering for weeks and he has had close encounters with golden eagles and mountain lions. He tells the story of staring into the yellow eyes of a lion at a distance of 20 feet for an eternity before the cougar blinked, turned away and disappeared. During one map quest, he spotted a hot spring in Eastern Oregon, went there and was immediately adopted by the old couple who had inherited the spring, it being but a remnant of a high class spa and hotel popular during the great age of the railroads. His circle of acquaintances soon spiraled out from the hot spring to include many other old-timers. One couple managed a general store in a neighboring ghost town, the remains of a once booming timber enterprise. Back in the day, there had been cut so much Douglas fir and Ponderosa Pine that, besides the meager sales at the store, the owners lived for decades by mining the residual sawdust piles for sale as mulch. Barry would camp nearby out in the sagebrush and mind the store for them if they wished to escape for a while. This man also kept an ancient fire engine – a tanker full of water – at the ready in case of a range fire. Grass fires are not that uncommon in the dry summers of Eastern Oregon and one day he got the call and took Barry with him and as they rocketed over the crest of a hill in sight of the smoke, they noticed a road crew shoveling a trench at the bottom. "No brakes" he shouted and frantically flapped his hand out the window semaphoring his distress to the crew. The men looked up, got the message, scrambled for their lives and gaped in awe as that beast loaded with 2,000 gallons of water hit the trench at terminal velocity so that Barry said their heads hit the roof but the truck cleared the trench and rolled on to the grass fire.

He is full of stories like this. He has acquired an unlimited supply as a result of his constant traveling – much of it in isolated or unusual locations. His stories constitute chapter and verse in his constantly evolving song of myself. Whereas we might have to think hard to even come up with today's date, Barry is able to place at least a year number on just about all his wheres and whens. Perhaps it's a result of not staying in the same place where time and repetitive chores and projects tend to blend and blur and become indistinguishable. These days he seems to alternate between Oregon and Vermont. When he heads out, he might be going also to Western Oregon where he has established connections on the coast and he camps on the headlands jutting into the mighty Pacific or he tramps into the wilderness of the Siskiyous. He connects with artists and writers and writes his own long prodigious letters laced with quotes and poems often in the shape of numerous post cards showing off local scenery. He rarely stays in one place longer than a few weeks and works himself into a boyish enthusiasm building up to the next move. In other times he has harvested oranges and cut sugar cane with the Jamaicans in Florida and passed a goodly chunk of time in West Virginia. There he was entrusted with caretaking an exclusive men's club. This was located in the depths of a steep-sided river canyon cutting through the Alleghanys and the only way in or out was by train, the rail-bed of which had been chopped out of the cliff next to the river by slaves. The track was so precarious that the train was limited to 10 miles per hour and Barry jumped the engine to bring in supplies for the members and take out their garbage.

His arrivals bring with him news of the natural world. What was the character of the time and place from which he had just come? The weather that tracked him? The unending storms off the ocean. The lack of rain. The unexpected blizzard. The winds that bring the hot dry air. The trees and shrubs in flower. Birds in transit, in place, in song. Mosquitoes, flies, ants, chiggers, ticks, rabbits, coyotes, house cats and dogs. We get detailed reports on all of it. All of it, especially the weather, being his constant concern and companion. If he comes in early spring, he begins a daily or hourly report on who's following him in. He hears a magnolia warbler, then a few days later, a wood thrush; then he is ecstatic because they are coming in fast – the tree swallows, the bluebirds; a cardinal sings his arrival for a morning; a trio of rose-breasted grosbeaks put on a tremendous show competing for the loudest and the most melodic. The catbird joins the conversation carrying on from the cover of the hemlock hedge. The catbird is Barry's totem. They seem to have a long-standing special relationship. He will come out and sit exposed in a bush nearby as Barry works in the garden. He is effusive and loquacious in the same way as Barry. Barry copies the bird's squeaks and trills and then adds a whistle of his own which the catbird, a supreme mimic, then will incorporate into his own repertoire. Barry reports in from the wild while he is around. In case we are missing something, he will fill us in. Not only bird sightings and songs, but the first trout lily flower on the hillside or the pussy willows showing or the ginseng and golden seal population in relation to last time he checked.

Barry may be an itinerant monk or man of the spirit but he is no saint. He does not aspire to be a St. Francis. He has his dislikes and compulsions. He makes enemies – two of which are blue jays and squirrels. Blue jays he just dislikes on principle as do many others who maintain sunflower seed feeders. They scare away 'nicer' birds and hog all the seeds. And they eat fruit in season often stripping your berries before you get to them. He is unrelenting in his persecution of blue jays. He doesn't shoot them but yowls and hisses and terrorizes them into fleeing the premises. He reserves a special enmity for squirrels. He is a hoarder of nuts and squirrels are rapacious pillagers of nuts. This is like a fight over gold nuggets. He trains friendly dogs to go bananas at the very sound of "squirrel" until you can't mention the word in a conversation without the dog racing to the nearest tree and barking insanely up the trunk. He cuts limbs away from houses so that they can't reach the roofs. He's the most canny trapper of squirrels inventing sure-fire methods and transporting them many miles away preferably to the other side of a major river.

His obsessions are not limited to just animals however. He will attack certain invasive plants that other people walk away from in despair such as Japanese knot weed and gout weed (Bishops weed). If he feels that such and such a place needs to be liberated or sanctified, he will immerse for hours, days or come back for years to eventually dig out every last shred of root capable of repopulating the site. He performs these obsessions not with detachment but with vengeance. Barry is not dispassionate. He gets worked up over the perfidy of plants claiming more than their respectable amount of territory as well as certain people that have somehow broken 'trust' with him - people who were once part of his 'family' but with whom he has now severed connections. He will hold a grudge but at the same time is often thoughtful and generous. He will give time, gift or money to a perceived need. Money? He has money saved because he works for cash now and again and hardly spends any of it. He calls himself an American peasant in that he will do any kind of manual labor for short periods taking on necessary but unpleasant jobs for money. He will also work for the U. S. Forest Service planting trees in Oregon. After a clearcut, the Forest Service hires bodies to replant the lodgepole or ponderosa pine or sitka spruce and Barry makes a good wage doing that because one gets paid by the piece and he plants more trees faster than anyone else. He supports art work and artists by using his money to buy their works which he then gives away to those with houses to keep and display such things of beauty.

It is a subject of conjecture among anthropologists and evolutionists whether it is not mankind's natural inclination to travel. Whether we do not have a primary need for movement and that the act of journeying gives one a sense of physical and mental well-being. Babies will usually cease fussing or crying once taken outside and walked. Mankind started its long journey just looking for food, staying in one place long enough to exhaust the edible possibilities and then moving on. It was the agricultural revolution that stuck people in place to tend their crops. Not everyone succumbed to the security and slavery of the farm however. Many evolved into nomads dependant on their animals; the root of the word being nomas, a Greek term meaning pasture. These people moved with their flocks or herds in a seasonal cycle and universally conceived a deep disdain for the farmer who they saw as stuck in the mud. The farmer trades his freedom for security and begins to accumulate wealth whereas people on the move tend to be lighter, freer of possessions and pared down to the essentials. Barry leads a nomadic life but would not be thought of as a 'nomad'. He is able to accumulate a certain amount of 'stuff' by caching things here and there at his friends and he does not seem to hold himself above the common run of humanity. But he does delight in his freedom and always anticipates his next move with mounting ebullience. Not being claimed by the mundane having to deal with leaky plumbing or broken fences allows him more space for affairs of the spirit and exploration of the mysteries of the natural world. His true calling is to translate these into words – that is to say, poetry. He is really and actually a poet and has filled many a notebook with those words and who knows, perhaps someday they might escape into the world and do some traveling on their own.

The Forest and the Trees

If the wealth of the homestead is to be located – if the foundation, the underpinning of the life could be isolated and identified, then we would have to look to the forest. The forest provides the trees and the trees provide us inestimable value. A stand of trees as an adjunct to a farm would be called a woodlot but the approximately 35 acres of trees circumscribed by the arbitrary boundaries of Gingerbrook feel themselves to be part of a much larger community which extends out for many miles and could be called a forest. The north-western boundary along the top of the ridge is unmarked and invisible to the inexperienced, and if you crossed it and just kept walking, I think that you could stay in the forest all the 100 miles to the Canadian border. You would have to choose your path judiciously, cross many a road, climb many a forsaken stone wall and some embedded barbed wire but I'm sure that you could stay under the trees the whole way. I find this amazing given that the whole state was basically treeless in the 19th century.

The forest community advertises itself by communicating and acting simultaneously. These trees in the Northern forest all flower and fruit (i.e. seed) to reproduce but not every year. Often several seasons will pass without flower on certain species but, for instance, when the sugar maples flower at Gingerbrook, the maples everywhere flower at the same time and the pollen is flying in the springtime wind. The same can be said for all the species – when the beech produces nuts here, it produces nuts over wide swaths of territory. How does this happen? The only possible explanation is that the trees cross-communicate in order to cross-pollinate. The word goes out and they all sap up – who can refuse an invite to an orgy? I said that the Northwest boundary would be invisible to the inexperienced, meaning that if you knew what you were looking at you could just about pinpoint the line. There is no fence or stonewall but there is an abrupt species change. You would walk out of mature maples and ash and into a mix of younger trees dominated by many large white birch which are now corroding and beginning to implode. It's all continuous woods now but the historical land use has stamped a pattern there. White birch comes in on open land in full sunlight but it is not long lived and will die out when crowded by competing growth. We know that the land was all cleared of trees in order to pasture sheep by the mid-1800's so there must have been a fence along that line at some time and it's just that our side was abandoned as pasture and allowed to grow back before the other and given enough time, the two sides would conspire to blur the invisible line even further. There is another invisible line below that ridge at the bottom of the hill which also has a tale to tell of historical land use. Where the terrain flattens there is a straight line of tall, arching maples which comprise what we have come to call "the gallery" Above the gallery lies the "sugarbush"; individual maples densely spaced all the way to the top of the ridge. Below the gallery are more large maples but which quickly give way to softwood – balsam fir, red spruce, tamarack and occasional bull pines. However, the maples below the line, though large, have grown as multiple trunks – this would only happen because they were browsed as babies and responded with 3 or 4 sprouts. We can conclude that the gallery was a fence line and that cattle (by that time sheep were gone) were excluded from the hillside but allowed to roam the bottomlands until sometime in the 1930's or 40's. There is no evidence of wire along the gallery which only means that they didn't use barbed. Barbed wire has been around since the 1880's and when some cattle enclosing soul would staple it to a line of trees, it stayed there long after he was gone. Long after. There are still remnants of barbed wire fence along the rubble walls at the edge of the property along the lane that go right through the middle of 20" maple trees. I can't imagine how long ago they were hung. Thinking about the average growth rings on a maple and calculating backward leads us to assume that the wire has been hanging there for at least 80 years. Now what kind of steel was that wire made of? Why hasn't it rusted away by now? I once climbed onto a six foot section embedded in neighboring trees, used a branch to balance and jumped up and down on it – the wire did not break! However, I wouldn't be surprised if there isn't an insulator or two swallowed inside those gallery trees. Electric fence has been around longer than you might think. The idea dates back to the 1930's. I once cut a beautiful tall and straight beech located on a boundary line and took the bottom log to the mill for sawing. Halfway through, the saw blade destructed and the sawyer commenced to curse me for I knew not why. He had run into a porcelain insulator smack in the center of that 16" log. Porcelain is harder than the hardened steel teeth of the saw blade and every one of them was ruined. Part of his cursing had to do with someone stupid enough to bring him a fence line tree to saw. I considered that the time would not be ripe for breaking out the dictionary and discussing the finer points differentiating stupidity from ignorance.

The maple that comprises the sugar bush on the hillside and the white ash with it accompanied by an occasional beech and yellow birch, were cored by a forester to determine their age and are now in the range of 100 years old. It is an even aged stand, although in their competition for light and nutrients, there are winners and loser trees. The winners measure at 20"-25" diameter and the others range on down to a mere 8". Scattered throughout are several 'wolf trees' – all maples – that are hoary, ancient and massive relics that were never cut. We can surmise that they were left perhaps to provide shade for the sheep pasturing the hillside. One of them came down in a storm and I took the bottom 6 ½ ft to saw into planks for a trestle table. Because it was so hefty, I needed to borrow a neighbor's tractor in order to move it but before I did that, I counted the growth rings at the cut and arrived at 200. One of these trees, still standing, is at the very top where the ridge flattens and it measures out at 40"diameter. Monarch; king and queen all in one, surveying the distances, slowly and patiently waiting and watching as its offspring and fellows have filled in the vista until all to be seen to the distant ridgelines are tree tops. A domain returned – in maple time – in this case, measured in centuries.

The evidence seems to fit with the generally accepted historical timeline. By the 1860's, the sheep were on their way out and people were leaving Vermont for greener (or flatter) pastures. The people who would feel like leaving foremost would have been those who were farming in the hills – thin, bony soil and nary a flat place to plow a straight line. Gingerbrook would have been one of those places with a regrowth starting during those last decades of the 1800s. Some of the earliest and fastest wood went down in the famous hurricane of 1938 as evidenced by the few hump-and-hollows still evident on the hill, and more of those came out with an old friend of ours who told us that he selectively logged there with a crawler tractor in the 1950s. That would leave pretty much what we see today.

There is a ton of wealth represented by the maple and ash in that sugar bush. If we were to cut every last one, and sell them for lumber, we would be wallowing in cash. We would also be wallowing in despair. Pockets full of cash and hearts full of despair. Given that choice, I think we will pass on the cash. I raise this (hypothetical) point in order to talk about the real, living wealth that accrues to us from our maples and also from the rest of our woodland. Some cash in your pocket and no despair would seem a worthy goal and we accomplish that one by tapping the maples. One tap in each maple each year yields approximately 1/5 gallon every year. In today's dollars, that nets about $10. Multiply that by hundreds and you've got something to keep your pocket occupied for a piece – and meanwhile, the tree keeps growing, leafing, flowering and being part of a forest that provides food and shelter for many a being – animal, vegetable and mineral. To stay on the subject of trees and cash for one more round, it's real that you can cut and sell for lumber maple, ash, yellow birch, cherry and white pine logs but you will realize much more value if you harvest and saw them up one at a time and sell the wood directly to cabinet makers and fine carpenters. In the living and dying forest, there is always another tree that you might want to take out and use part of it for a saw log. Perhaps you are just thinning trees that are growing into each other; or you notice that a major branch has snapped off in a storm and the tree will begin to rot down into the stem; or a tree is showing signs of dying for some inexplicable reason and if you cut it soon, it will still yield some fine boards. There are several black cherry trees on the property – few enough that I know where each one is. I keep an eye on them because the wood is so beautiful and so valuable, however, one beauty, located not far from that monarch maple at the height of land, went unnoticed for some years before I realized that it had died. It was standing dead and the branches were starting to fall off but when I had it sawed up, that cherry was the most striking, luxuriant, dark red wood I had ever seen. Cherry sapwood (the living) comes out a light brown when dried but the heartwood (the dead) becomes much darker and progresses to red as the tree ages. This tree was solid heartwood and had aged and weathered on the stump to this amazing color.

Actually, selling hardwood boards has not been something I have done often. The wealth of the forest doesn't necessarily show up as cash in your pocket if your main goal is the homesteading goal of doing for yourselves. That cherry is now in our house transformed into cabinet doors, furniture and a heartwood surround for the staircase. Each hardwood, when planed, sanded and oiled, displays its own beauty of color and grain. Ash has an obvious and outstanding grain pattern; yellow birch shows no grain but has a soft honey color; maple shines with an inner translucence; butternut yields a glowing tan color, a nirvana for fine carpenters; and beech looks similar to oak but is lighter in color. These distinctive hardwoods create visual and artistic relief, much like you might use paint, when used throughout the house for different applications like window trim, door design or partition walls. Each pie-shaped bedroom upstairs in the octagon highlights a different wood. This reflects a remnant desire of mine to wall the first octagon completely with wood – each of the eight sides a different species of hardwood. It seemed a splendid idea at the time, born of the commitment to do as much as possible without buying in material, but in retrospect, I'm glad that's one dream that went the way of fire. It would have surrounded us with too much woodiness without the relief provided by plaster walls. I had accumulated quite a pile of diverse hardwoods stacked on the unfloored upstairs joists and was still adding to it when the greedy fire snacked on them before heating up the main course.

As you move north along the hillside out of the sugarbush and into the drainage of the gingerbrook, the cast of woodland characters begins to change. There grow still ash and maple but other hardwoods (that is to say, deciduous - some 'hardwood' is softer than some 'softwood' –ie. basswood vs tamarack) are scattered about into the mix. Red maple and brown ash are rare but grow in the damper locations. There are some very large basswoods and a bunch of hop-hornbeam and an occasional remnant popple or white birch and/or gray birch getting slowly crowded out. Red maple is scarce at Gingerbrook and I rarely interact with it except to marvel at the brilliant red flowers that supply the first action of the new year for the honeybees. In the spring, it comes as a surprise, there might be a red carpet thrown down for you beneath a red maple. Brown ash is even scarcer than red maple. It is a relatively small tree found in wet places that is weak limbed but has found fame as "basket ash". If you beat upon it with wooden clubs after soaking a section in water, the wood will delaminate along the growth ring lines.

These thin and pliable slabs can then be sliced to the required width and woven to create a strong and long -lived basket.

You would find it a quite difficult proposition to climb a skinny white birch to a point high enough in order to induce it to bend you softly back to the ground. Robert Frost may have actually tried it but I rather feel that he watched a series of wet, heavy snows do it for him and imagined what fun to be a boy swinging down a white birch. Besides being a famous subject for poesy, white birch has acquired fame for other reasons. It becomes 'canoe birch' when the trunk is smooth and limbless and you may cut off with your knife whole intact canoe sized sections of bark. It is 'paper birch' when the bark disengages of its own accord and flutters in thin sheets from the trunk in the wind. These sheets are often such that you might scissor one to size and post a letter on it. It is plain old 'white birch' when the tree is branchy up and down and the branches often show black near the trunk. These three versions of white birch can all grow quite sizable as opposed to 'gray birch' which, although sometimes close to indistinguishable, is really a different tree. It is a "trash tree", short-lived, small sized with very weak wood. There are hardly any of these left now in the Gingerbrook woods and any that you do see, look like Robert Frost has been at them. White birch is notorious for rotting quickly, trapped inside its watertight skin. Sometimes a tree with its top snapped off, will stand there rotting until the trunk becomes just a barky husk filled with punk. The bark is impregnated with some kind of resin that makes it not only water resistant but a sure fire starter. Even in the rain, it will burn lustily. This quality will allow you to throw absolutely fresh-cut white birch into your stove to produce enough heat to keep the ice crystals out of your water glass during the night. The burning bark dries out the first inch of wood to allow that to burn which in turn dries out the next inch etcetera until the whole wet, green chunk is gone. Perhaps this is common knowledge, but I learned it directly the first winter we survived at Gingerbrook. We had spent the summer building the shop, uninsulated and somewhat breezy, and were heating with a homemade barrel stove. As noted previously, it was a 55 gal drum underneath the floor with its pipe coming up through to another drum in the living area and then out through the roof. To this day, I love barrel stoves because you can load them with a mess of heavy, long pieces and when things are getting serious and it's 25 below and the wind is howling down from the north pole, you can open wide the draft and turn that drum cherry red, the pipe cherry and the upstairs drum cherry too and keep that frost at bay no matter what. But not with green white birch you won't. We burned that all winter long to beat back the less than serious weather. I would cut it from the future garden sites during the day, pull it up to the house in one of those plastic kid's sleds, burn it that night and repeat the process the next day. It required two full barrel loads to get through the night so I would wake sometime around 2 or 3a.m., poke my nose out of the sleeping bag to assess the heat level in the house, hop into my trusty boots, go outside and down the stairs, reload the barrel with that white birch, leave the draft wide open and quickly get back into the bag hoping it was still warm and hoping that the live coal had enough chutzpah to motivate the birch bark and warm us through till morning. One last note about white birch is a wonderful and perhaps little known characteristic which is when you bring its limb wood into the house, it not only does not rot but as it dries, the bark tightens and sticks to the wood seemingly forever. I have used it for railings, banisters and door handles, and the more it gets handled, the shinier and more beautiful it becomes. It becomes burnished often with reddish tones among the white and black.

Recently, in late October when the leaves are all down and you can see the forest through the trees, I was walking through the woods on the eastern end above the source of the gingerbrook and I noticed a big tree on the ground in the distance. I couldn't figure what it was even when I approached until it dawned on me that it was a monster popple that had uprooted and blown over in a summer storm. The thought occurred to me then – this was the last popple on the hillside. A survivor that had sprouted in the open and hung in there through the years of regrowth of maple, ash, beech and birch and had grown so big that initially I didn't recognize it as such. The Fall of the Last Popple – or The Quake of the Last Aspen. It sounds plaintive and tragic but weep not for the popple because there are plenty more just over the horizon. Popple and its kin balsam poplar/balm of gilead are members of the Cottonwood family. They are called so because their tiny seeds release in the wind and float encased in cotton fluff to anywhere and everywhere. But they will only grow in full sunlight and so will populate abandoned fields and hillsides. They are ridiculously fast growing and send out roots unfathomable distances. If you cut down a big popple, the resident root system will send up sprouts all over the place, sometimes up to 100ft away. A lot of popple is harvested for pulp and this trait would allow you to repeatedly harvest a field planted with popple every certain number of years without replanting. The old-time Vermont Yankees around here have great disdain for popple and would refuse to use it for anything but pulp. They wouldn't consider burning it for stove wood or sawing it for lumber; I suppose because there are more and better choices all around thus relegating it to junk status. However, I have chopped it and sawed it and burned countless cords for sugarwood, framed the first building with whole popple logs and nailed popple boards onto the roof of the first octagon. It is true that it rots almost instantly when left outside but when kept dry it is very tough and resilient and presents you with a very white and shiny board when planed. The truth be told though, today I wouldn't go out of my way to especially find popple for any of these applications – it's just that we had such an array of beautiful, tall and straight popple growing in what is today, our front yard, that I felt that we should use what the land had offered. The land also offered balm of gilead but that is a different story. I write /balsam poplar because apparently it is hard to tell the difference between the two trees – if indeed there is a difference. Some say that balsam poplar is the native and gilead's balm has been introduced and spread from cultivation. Others say gilead's balm is sterile and can only reproduce through cloning. Whatever the case, we have always called the tree gilead and the balm is yours for the taking and making if you harvest the resin-sticky and odiferous buds in the early spring. The wood from this tree is neither strong nor attractive. When you saw into it, you are reminded of slicing into a rotten cabbage – it's wet and almost black. It does dry into a somewhat reasonable board and I have used some in non-critical situations like the reverse battens for the cider mill. But most of that gilead's balm went back into the earth as bottom logs defining the terraces of the garden and the branches disappeared into the sap fire.

That pretty much sums up the inventory of deciduous trees to be found within our Gingerbrook boundaries. There are a few other bit players in the scene like choke cherries, alders and pussy willows in the marsh and an occasional moose maple (striped maple) and there is exactly one very big elm surviving on its own on the top of the ridge. Elm flowers and seeds very early in the spring and its seeds whirl in the wind and consequently there continue to appear saplings here and there whose future will be defined by their battle with the disease. There is no sign of chestnut ever having grown in this vicinity and if it did, it is long gone and there are no living stumps still striving to hang on by sending up sprouts. There are also no oaks of any kind either on the property or nearby. It is elevation related because as you move down the waterways to the west towards the White river and east toward the Connecticut, the oaks begin to show up and become a major part of the canopy on the slopes along the rivers. These are exclusively red oaks which are the most cold tolerant of the species. It's not that they won't grow here – I have planted some and they have thrived from the very beginning putting on 12 to 18 inches a year, and now there are even babies coming up in unexpected places. I have also planted black walnut, black birch, weeping willow, black and honey locust, hybrid chestnuts, mulberry, butternut and heartnut trees. All these except the heartnuts, have done fine. None of them, except butternut, grow here in the wild. Black birch is a spectacular tree whose twigs and buds are a source of wintergreen. Wintergreen used to be distilled commercially from black birch but you can get it now by chewing on a twiglet or steeping buds for tea or putting it in your sap beer for flavoring. As they go from white to black, the birches get progressively heavier, denser and the wood more beautiful.

If there is one tree worth planting and cultivating on your homestead it's the black locust. This character is a miracle covered in bark and thorns. First of all, it might be the fastest growing tree in temperate climes. Secondly, when you plant one, you'll soon have a covey because it quickly begins to root sprout frantically. Third, black locust is not only hard and strong but is the most rot resistant wood east of a redwood. Fourth, it will grow and prosper just about anywhere. It thrives in gravelly locations where other trees would languish. Black locust is worth planting not only because it flowers up tremendously for the honey bees in June but really just as a provider of the best fencepost god could devise – at least in this region. If you order 25 little ones through the mail, you'll soon have 20ft trees and many root sprouts which you may harvest continuously for fence posts that won't rot. My first fence posts were cut from anything handy – usually balsam fir – and they would rot and snap off at ground level in just a few short years. I then tried tamarack – reputed to be quite resistant – and they lasted somewhat longer but not long enough, so I'm now harvesting these black locust sprouts as they get to size one at a time to replace posts that are only still there because the wire is holding them up. Also if you basal prune those saplings as they grow to encourage tall, straight poles, you've got replacement shafts and poles for your horse drawn equipment – none of which you are likely to be storing under cover to prevent them from rotting. If I had had these black locust poles back in the snow roller days, the incident at the road with those lag bolts tearing free and dumping me in the snow, would never have happened, depriving us of the story and the Washington village "frost fighters" of their mule herding rodeo adventure.

These last-mentioned trees are part of the homestead but not part of the forest and we started this section talking about the forest and wealth. The imported, planted trees certainly add to our wealth but the core value comes from firewood. Firewood is the center around which the entire operation revolves and high quality firewood comes from the hardwoods. Ash, maple, beech, yellow birch and hop hornbeam – in descending order of availability – these trees have fueled our existence. We have no automatic back-up heating and we have always cooked on a wood cook-stove. In the early years, we used the cook-stove all year round: now we cook electric during the summer – that is – June, July and August. Now at least, after moving out of the shop and into the octagon, our house is reasonably snug so that we don't have to burn mountainous cordage just to keep from freezing to death as they had to do in those huge, old, thin-walled farm houses. And those were the days before chain saws when you'd better have raised five hefty sons and given then cross-cut saws and splitting mauls on their fifth birthdays to get them feeling right about their inheritance.

I once picked up a random hitch-hiker and he asked me: "What do you people do here during the winter?" And I replied: "We just keep throwing wood in the stove and hope to make it through till summer". Then he asked "What do you do during the summer?" and I replied "Get ready for winter". It was a joke but not completely. You are on shaky ground if you don't have that firewood dry and under cover before the snow begins to fly. It can get to be an obsession – some people I know have 4 or 5 years stashed in advance and they get warm just looking at their firewood. It took me a while to mosey onto firmer ground in this regard: Those perilous years of burning green white birch and fresh-cut maple and ash are now long gone along with the trusty barrel stove and these days I cut, split and stack firewood one winter to be burned the next. The winter time is the right time to work on firewood. The bugs are gone; the dirt is gone; the woods are lovely, dark and deep – O.K. don't get carried away – actually they are lovely but these woods are neither dark nor deep: they are filled with light and they are pristine. The snow covers everything and with a horse and sled you're a happy man.

There are various strategies for getting in firewood. Assuming you don't have a skidder parked in your garage, these strategies range from successful to ludicrous. An example of the latter comes from Ennis who used to navigate his out of the woods in a wheelbarrow – try that if you are looking for an excuse to move back to the city. Another pitiable method involves driving your pick-up into the woods – even a four wheel drive is bound to end stuck up, banged up and hung up at least half the time. A tractor with a trailer is an improvement, but even that limits your range to the roadside. A tractor with a winch goes one better but pulling whole trees through and around other trees is no picnic. You would need a snatch block to pull sideways and you have to cut off the bigger limbs and bundle them with the log to get them out. This last option at least has the merit of getting you into the woods during the winter instead of in sweat and bug time but you don't want a tractor on your homestead anyway. A skid horse is a vast improvement on all these schemes. With him, you can go just about anywhere and navigate back through a welter of forest to your landing without damaging standing timber. Using these last two options, the skidded logs are usually piled together in an open 'landing' where you can reach them with a truck in the summer after the mud has dried. This is what I was doing with Mickey and Maud for a few years before I hit upon a much more satisfying system. The 'pile' of logs, without the use of tractor power, becomes more like a haphazard disarray and the wood, even though skidded through the snow, is usually plastered with dirt. The former condition leads you, with chainsaw in hand, to be balancing on top of said haphazardness slicing off firewood sized chunks and the latter, to spitting sparks off the newly sharpened chain as you saw through the dirt. Besides putting up with these sorts of fun and games, you are once again back to working firewood in the summertime – one of my prime no-nos. So, I decided to build us a sled – the sled you have seen pictured already. A small one that M&M could pull OK – just as wide as they so it would fit between any two trees that they could squeeze through and about as long as they were so that it would maneuver easily. It turned out that it holds close to a half-cord weighing near to 2000lbs so by the time I got to the second one, I built it rugged to withstand the inevitable collisions and subterranean booby traps. Today one heavy horse (Pudgie) pulls that sled, doing the work of two pony mules, and it's his favorite job. Using this sled in the winter woods is a joy. He'll bring the sled right next to where you have dropped the chosen tree and piled the cut-up chunks so that you could still find them if it happened to have snowed a couple of feet the previous night. The biggest rounds could have been split into reasonable halves or quarters, then all loaded into the sled and brought out of the woods right to the door of the wood shed where they are offloaded for further splitting and stacking. The tree is dropped on top of the snow with the branches up in the air right in front of you and the trunk lying out for easy cutting without fear of running your chain into the ground. Everything is clean and you never feel cold working up firewood in the winter woods. I was pleased once we got that system down pat. It is often said that firewood warms you twice, once when you cut it and twice when you burn it, and it's a forever a point of discussion among firewood cutters as to exactly how many times you pick up any given piece of firewood before it settles into the flames, so I am thinking now to count and come up with a number when using the sled..... I arrive at a total of nine from living tree to BTU. Cut the tree down, then cut it up, then pile the chunks – that's one. Split some of them – two. Load the sled – three. Unload the sled – four. Split to cookstove size – five. Stack in woodshed – six. Load into dumb waiter – seven. Carry into house – eight. Put into stove – nine.

Transported and piled, waiting to split and stack

The most outrageous scenario for getting your lumber out of the woods was one I encountered in the famous region of the Darien, past the end of the road in Panama. I had heard that the British army had undertaken a publicity mission for Land Rover by attempting to drive through the legendary Darien gap. I had not heard whether they succeeded or not but with my pie in the sky and my head in a hole-in-the-ground, I cared not and decided to follow the wide and obvious trail that they would have left all the way to Colombia. I heard later that the British army needed a helicopter to get out of there and I needed the luck of the lunatic naïf to escape myself. However, during my wanderings, I bumped into two guys with two chain saws, a couple of ten gallon cans of gasoline and a beat-up 20 gauge shot gun. They were deep in the jungle, miles away from any road and they were cutting mahogany – free lancing, all by themselves as a way to make some money. Mahogany doesn't grow in stands so they would wander around until they found one, cut it down, and then cut it into logs. This was virgin rain forest and these trees were monsters. How did they possibly expect to profit from this venture? They were subsisting off their shot gun and while they shared their fire-charred howler monkey and iguana with me, they explained. They figured that they were operating in the flood plain of the mighty Bayano river so that by the middle of the rainy season, the water would be over our heads right where we were sitting and would thusly lift the mahogany logs, swirl them out of the forest and down the river to the town where they would be watching in their canoe for their marked mahogany lumber to come to daddy. I complemented them on their ingenuity and fortitude and left them, hoping I would have more luck than their logs in escaping the Darien. That was in the 70's and it provided a small clue to the future awaiting the tropical rain forest. It starts with some guys with chain saws looking to cash in and ends, as I'm sure it is today, with the jungle vanished and cattle everywhere.

A chain saw is like a valued sled dog that has done and continues to do so much work for you so that you depend on him and take him for granted until one day when you're not looking, he turns on you and tears you to pieces. It is an incredible tool and a viciously dangerous beast. I have run it into myself several times and just luckily, I still have all my limbs and fingers. Once when we were moving back into the shop after the house burned, I decided to lighten things up a bit by adding a window to a dark corner. That was an easy matter, the wall being only one clapboard thick, to plunge the chain saw through and cut out a rectangle but before I knew what was what, the blade had kicked back, hit me in the face and cut through my upper lip. The rules of conduct are basically the same for any tool – think out first what you are going to do, pay attention while you're doing it and consider all the possible what might go wrongs before you finish. You get to thinking that sled dog won't bite and you become lackadaisical and bam! you get chewed up. I consider the chain saw another version of our ongoing pact with the devil: you get the promise of unlimited power and in exchange, you sell your soul to the machine. I became so disgusted with my first chain saw, which was a heavy, old, used clunker, that I threw it over the bank and made a solemn vow to do all sawing with cross-cut saws and never touch another chain saw. Just a few sorry hours later, I retrieved the clunker from out of the bushes and, humiliated, put myself back in servitude to the diabolical machine. Once you have been there and felt the power, it's not easy going back.

Plenty of other dangers lurk in the woods when it's just you, your chainsaw and the trees. There are "widow makers" just waiting for you out there and trees that have fallen in contorted positions so as to be holding back tremendous tension to be released by some unsuspecting soul with a saw. Cutting up timber safely in the woods is all about riding the line between tension and compression and learning to recognize which one you're into before hitting it with your saw. My first tree with my first chain saw was a big, long-dead elm that a friend was offering to me for firewood   I walked away from the butt as it began to keel over in a line exactly opposite to its direction of fall and as if hit by lightning out of a clear blue sky, I was catapulted 10 ft through the air to land on my face in the pucker brush. First tree I ever put a chainsaw to and it knocked me over. The explanation of this curiousness is that the big tree landed branches first, the elasticity of which caused a recoil sending the butt into my butt causing my brief flight into the brush. The lesson there – walk away at 90o.

Widow makers, as indicated by the name, occasionally kill unsuspecting loggers. They are dead limbs high in the canopy that become disengaged by a falling tree and come down on to your head even if you feel that you are out of the way. My own interaction with one of these was fateful but I'm still here to tell the story. I always look up to check for potential widow makers before starting a cut but this one caught me by surprise.

It was about the size and length of an arrow and it hit me just beside my left eye. The falling tree, as it crashed by a neighbor, bent this branch and after it went by, the branch whipped back, broke off and arrowed into my face, one half-inch from blinding an eye. So, as the old man says: you can't be too careful.

Most of the approximately 35 acres of woodland on the homestead are dominated by hardwoods. That is more than enough to keep us in firewood, cabinet wood, tool handles and equipment poles forever. However to complete the homestead wood supply, you'll need softwood (ie. Conifers) also. You can try to build using just hardwood but it soon gets awful wearisome when you can't even pound a nail into it. You can also fire your syrup arch with just hardwood but it produces too many coals which clog up the grates and not enough flame to reach the backpan. So your homestead needs a supply of softwood. Spruce, fir and pine and perhaps you also have hemlock and tamarack. The most plentiful conifer on the property is the balsam fir. It is ubiquitous but its heavy growth parallels the gingerbrook drainage from northwest to southeast through the land. It doesn't grow so fast, doesn't grow so big and doesn't live so long but it has been a tremendous benefit to life on the homestead. Most balsams seem to max out at about 15" in diameter and 75 years of age when they quit. It is true that they don't like being shaded however it just seems that is their allotted life span. When they grow in tight together, they make beautiful poles. The bottom branches have died off making the trunk easy to skin, especially in the spring when the bark peels off nicely in long strips with a draw knife. I have used these poles in all our buildings, especially for rafters. The larger trees saw up well into good rough-cut boards, useful for all kinds of applications around the farm. As they die or keel over, I send them into the sap fire. The sap fire is a greedy, demanding character and has consumed more balsam than any other wood in our time here. Balsam fir has acquired regional

215

fame as a Christmas tree and as greenery for wreaths. It's that balsam part that smells so good. Quite a few Vermonters cut and sell balsam fir Christmas trees as a sideline to put a little extra money in the bank. Making wreaths is also a thriving little local business. We do both of those things but only one tree and one wreath each season. There is always another pretty little balsam out there wanting to come into the house for Xmas.

Balsam fir is the pointed tree of the north country. Its spire is high and thin and its branches bend down easily without breaking thus making it god's tree in regions of heavy snowfall. Spruce trees are built in a similar manner and march along with balsam all the way to the northern limits along the higher latitudes in Canada. However, the native spruces come in three varieties red, white and black, with the black growing small and stunted to the very tree line and the red being the only spruce we have here. It is only sparsely represented and is scattered among the balsam fir but can be found occasionally in drier, stonier places. If you read through the old-timey forestry books, you will find engineering statistics on every tree. Such factoids as: the weight of a cubic foot of dry wood; the toughness of such wood placed under certain stresses of both tension and compression; and rot resistance in contact with the soil. There are certain indefinables that these figures don't capture however: balsam fir and red spruce read out about the same by the numbers. They are both light and soft but I find that red spruce is considerably stronger than balsam and I try to save it for needier situations. Perhaps because it grows so slowly and the growth rings are so close together explain the difference. Red spruce will hang out as a diminutive underneath a hardwood canopy seemingly forever growing only a few centimeters every year waiting for an opening. It is one such that traps the snow above to form a small cave below into which you will either bucket dive with your snowshoes or lose your heart for a whole minute when a ruffed grouse rockets out from his snug hole right between your feet. Red spruce does not peel without great effort so only when I feel the need for a stronger pole, will I look for one that size.

Monarchs of the forest. We have already seen some of them but as we move into the second century of regrowth out of the sheep clear-all, increasingly the kings and queens, the overlords of the Gingerbrook woods are the white pines. White pine is in a special category in that it is really the only tree in the east to approach the grandeur of the titans of the Rockies and the west coast. Eastern hemlock grows big and lives for hundreds of years but doesn't exhibit the classical lines – the massive column of a trunk and the tremendous height - of a mature white pine. They were the king's trees – the chosen few that bore the king's mark during colonial days that you were forbidden to cut even if they were located on your land. The royal navy was reserving these white pines for use as masts in their massive ships of the line. The pines here have another hundred years to go before the king might come begging but they are well on their way to royal status now. Actually because of soil and climate factors, I don't think the pines here would ever quite qualify for that coveted mark. They are another tree that is sun loving and will only sprout and take off in the open but if they didn't seed in heavily and instead grow widely scattered in an abandoned field, they would never make it into one of the kings ships because they will open up gnarly and branchy, growing horizontally as well as vertically. These pines, however, will give you knotty-pine boards and a lot of sugar wood. Every time you cut a pine for its saw logs, the remnant top leaves you a welter of large branches and upper trunk which require dealing with but which yield quantities of sugar wood. White pine is not built like balsam fir or spruce to withstand heavy snow so it tends to peter out at higher altitudes and latitudes. A wet, heavy snowfall or a round of freezing rain will break branches right off a big pine and leave it looking somewhat bedraggled. But in general it is a beautiful and majestic tree and its wood is a carpenter's delight. Easily sawn, easily carved, shines when sanded, doesn't twist, check, crack or shrink, pine lumber mellows in place to wonderful deep amber. While leaving the most prominent pines in place, we have cut and milled a lot. The entire outside sheathing of the octagon is rough-cut pine and much of the inside trim is pine, planed, sanded and oiled. The eight sides of the house present a quick lesson in how rough-cut pine weathers to different colors. Most of the wet weather comes from the east and that side has turned gray. Moving around to the south, the wood is a pale amber; to the southwest, a dark amber; to the west, brown; to the northwest and north, almost black Exposure to water is what turns untreated wood siding gray.

Except for the hedge, there are more or less only 15 hemlocks within the boundaries of Gingerbrook. Hemlock gets to be a big tree in its maturity and the largest here is getting to be 2ft wide. I have used a couple in the past for the sole purpose of spanning the gingerbrook with a bridge. Hemlock is fairly rot-resistant so I used two 10ft logs as stringers set into the muddy banks to set the bridge on. The logs are already almost in the water so that when we come across with two-ton Tony loaded with slabs to stack in the sugar house, I tell myself – if the bridge collapses now, we will probably survive the fall, but that hemlock is tenacious and hasn't dumped us yet. Hemlock lumber is common in our area and commonly used for rough-cut framing jobs in sheds and other outbuildings. The preference is to nail it in place while green because it will twist and check and shake while drying in a pile. Hemlock is one of the few conifers in Vermont that thrive in the shade so it is often found in the deep ravines that radiate up from the river valleys before opening up into the fields and meadows above. These places are difficult to log so they are often repositories of ancient hemlock trees. We have no such ravine but our hemlocks do stay close to the water as do the tamaracks. Tamarack, also known as American larch or hackmatack, likes the water so that it wants its roots right in it. It is growing in our marsh and gradually taking over the entire wet zone of two or three acres. It is unusual in that it is a conifer but not an evergreen. Its leaves turn a bright yellow in the fall and are shed along with its numerous tiny cones. These don't hesitate to sprout and the tamarack army is moving steadily across the marsh. It is difficult to negotiate any tamarack because the horses flounder in the marsh but I don't want the marsh to become somewhat of an ecological dead zone as I have seen in other tamarack conglomerations, so I dream up possible logging methods and meanwhile, I harvest occasional fence posts as the saplings get to size. Tamarack is actually a handsome tree with light feathery leaves but there are other interesting characters in the marsh that would disappear under the advance of the army such as Joe Pye weed, sundews, spirea, red osier and boneset.

I think that finishes our tour of the forest and the trees. If there are only a 15 hemlocks, there are hundreds of balsam fir. If there are dozens of white pines, there are a thousand maples. If there are only six brown ash, there are hundreds of white ash. If there is only one elm, there are many scattered birches, beechs and black cherries. The woods we have been describing are just a tiny slice of the greater forest which they inhabit, circumscribed by arbitrary lines drawn by men and influenced by the specific history defined by those lines but ultimately free to disregard the lines, jump stone walls and disintegrate old fences. Somebody who once thought I needed to be insulted called me a 'tree hugger' as if that were a hopeless character defect and I acknowledged that was indeed true and that I certainly had been known to hug one once in a while – try it; it's quite satisfying. It's not quite a love affair but the trees are central to our life on this land. Left to itself, this country wants to grow trees and we just share the space with them and profit greatly by the association. Plenty of other beings also profit. When I'm out there cleaning up after sugaring and I'm ankle deep in spring beauties, trout lilies and squirrel corn, and the bumble bees are already at work long before the honeys shake off their winter torpor, it becomes pretty apparent how to define the word 'wealth'.

This Path Must Lead Somewhere

Everybody loves a path. Cows follow the same lines through generations across a sidehill pasture. Horses wear a grass-free groove through their pasture back to the barn. Deer follow habitual trails through the woods. And people fear the 'trackless forests'. If you lose yourself rambling and stumbling through the deep, dark woods and come upon a path, it's a eureka moment. If there is a path, there is hope. A weight lifts off your soul. You have been shown the way. The path offers a way – a way out or a way in - and it promises comfort and safety. Where someone has stepped before is less likely to hold some nasty surprise for yourself as you follow.

Even if you tend to avoid the deep, dark woods, the path is still likely to hold you in thrall. One just automatically tends to the ideal line from place to place and then stick to it. It wouldn't necessarily be a straight line but rather the 'best' line avoiding hazards and likely following a contour. There are no unknown or hidden dangers waiting for you as you walk the 100ft between house and barn twice every day but your innate map sense has laid out a path and you keep to it. You walk it in the mornings before the first snow fall to let the animals out into the field and you walk it in the evening to let them back in. When the snow comes, you shuffle through the first few inches to leave a track. It snows again and you follow the track. As it doesn't snow again for a week, the path gets packed down hard and defines the floor of its own valley. Then you get two more six-inch storms but you remain faithful to your path wading along and packing it down. Now the snow outlining the path brushes your knees as you make the daily rounds. Then inevitably arrives a real snowstorm bringing you 16 more inches. This doesn't render your path invisible however – there still shows a slight indentation to mark the way. It takes a bunch of days to pack that storm into your path and surprisingly the surrounding level is still at your knees. But the high cold usually follows the snow bringing wind from the north and wind from the west swirling the light stuff on the surface and brooming it into your valley of a path. You tromp it down and the floor level rises. You pack down more and the wind delivers more until one day the hardpack path is now at the same level as the surrounding snow and you realize that you are walking or actually balancing on a ridge 12" wide and 3' high. If you perchance step off or more likely slide off track, that knee-high barn boot disappears and snow cascades onto your socks. But you never want to abandon your path and start another. That is your path and you're going to stick with it. However when the sugartime thaws come along, your loyalty or your tolerance for folly finds you performing a circus act for an invisible audience. It's hard to be embarrassed when no one is watching so you slog on wreathed in your own bemusement. There is so much snow packed into the path that it remains perched high above the melting surround and begins to resemble the knife-edged south col leading to the peak of Mt. Everest. That 12" of walking surface begins to disintegrate to 10", then 7", then 3" but you stick with it eventually walking side-straddle in order to stay on top. Slipping and sliding and sloshing into spring, your path to the barn is the last visible remnant of winter so that when the brown and flattened grass emerges all around, it shows like a perfect crescent ridge arcing from house door to barn door and then vanishes beneath your boots.

Critters and Varmints

Part of the deal of living up against the woodlands and growing your own involves cohabiting with wild animals. Wild animals have their own agendas but it seems that on top of the list is finding food and if you happen to be offering easy pickings, they are happy to get that food from you. Therein lies the source of an age-old conflict. "This is my food", you say but they don't seem to share your vision of the rule of law and this difference of opinion leads to psychological problems. You might be the most ardent conservationist and wildlife lover and all of a sudden you find yourself wanting to kill, to eradicate, to eliminate. These sudden emotional gushers are usually directed against what we might call 'varmints'. There is another obvious approach to this situation which could be called 'preventive maintenance' usually involving a fence or many fences, however there is something that does not love a fence so there is pretty much some kind of a varmint hassle every year. It's all about vested interests and protecting what By God Is Yours. We don't like it that ranchers in the West are shooting wolves but I know a dairy farmer who lost a calf to our local version of the wolf, the eastern coyote, and he started shooting them on sight – as many as he could and really, it is hard to blame him. Anyway, I don't own a rifle so I'm not shooting anything which doesn't mean that I'm not allergic to this same syndrome but not all critters are varmints and they are all part of the landscape for us to watch for, feel privileged to see, and endlessly talk about.

There is huge, gnarly old yellow birch located right on the bank of the gingerbrook that when I first noticed it, I realized was a porky tree and had been for years. It is hollowed out from the bottom to a side hole about 8ft up.

Around that hole, the bark was blackened by fire and someone had spray painted an arrow pointing at it. At the base of the hollow, was a large pile of dung gradually cascading into the brook indicating that generations of porcupines had housed in that tree. Some porky hater had fired the den and painted the arrow but I had no idea who. It's known that foresters dislike porcupines but the land had been abandoned so there was no reason for a forester to have been in there. A mystery, but by the time I got there, the porkies were back in residence as evidenced by the fresh pellets on top of the pile. Foresters have a thing about porcupines because they kill trees – slowly but eventually they succumb to being debarked or, in the case of hemlock, having all the leaves chewed off. There was, and is, a circle of dead snags around the yellow birch as evidence of the porkies appetites. They particularly like to eat hemlock. They snip off branch ends so that the ground is littered around the trunk and then proceed to shinny down and eat them at their leisure. They follow the same path all winter back and forth to their gourmet choice of the season. This leaves a sort of rounded half-pipe trail through the snow which I thought would accommodate a wire snare perfectly. I remembered the bent sapling method from reading Jack London and brought the porky in for dinner. Jo made hash out of it, trying her best to make it appetizing, however it was redolent of hemlock resin, the kids refused to eat it and I never did that again. Porcupines are in no hurry and have no fear so they mosey through life not expecting any trouble which means that when you are awakened in the middle of the night by a gnawing and crunching of the wooden siding right below your bedroom window and you go out to tell that porky to get lost, he doesn't necessarily listen to you. So you come back with a flashlight and a long wooden implement to persuade him. This riles him and he starts making clicking sounds with his teeth and whipping his tail into your hockey stick which leaves it impaled with quills. Any fights he might get into usually come to a swift conclusion after one swipe of the tail so he rather quickly abandons the field and mutters off grumping into the night. Aside from the few trees that they might kill, the only real problem you might have with porkies is because of your dog. You might have the most intelligent dog in the universe but when it comes to porcupines, he's as dumb as a stone. We had a dog like that who just kept coming back for another mouthful of quills. Each time cost us $100 at the vets so after the third time, I figured that we had to do something about this ourselves. One of the boys sat on his chest and held his legs down; the other boy held onto a chunk of limb wood which I had crammed between his teeth holding his mouth open and his head against the ground; and I proceeded with pliers to pull out every last quill from his nose, lips, mouth and tongue. I can't really say that he learned anything from it but that was the last time we ever had to do that operation. If you want to catch a porky for some reason, perhaps because he is eating the tires off your pickup, you can do it with a garbage can. Just put it down over him and then scoop and lift and then transport him closer to someone else's pickup.

The porcupines are gone from that yellow birch now. The trunk broke off right above the blackened hole and fell into the gingerbrook, exposing their home to the elements. Around the same time, I began seeing a fisher cat. This was a double hit against the porkies as the fisher is reputedly the only one to deliberately hunt and eat them. Occasionally, if you inspect their scat, you will find a few quills. However, there are still porcupines around. I surprised one recently as I was coming out the top door of the cider mill. He was right there and gave a start, lost his footing and rolled over and over down the steep bank right into the back wall of the ell. A good handful of quills needled into the wood and they are still there. The embarrassed porky righted himself and marched away with all the dignity he could muster.

It is not a nightmare but it might as well be when you wake in the middle of the night to panic, screaming and bloody murder and you realize, because you've been here before, that somebody is in the chicken coop and that somebody will surely be a raccoon. The chicken coop is a magnet for the hunger games. Without it, we wouldn't attract so much wildlife interest. Along with the raccoon, the list includes weasels, foxes, skunks and rats, however none of them present such a challenge as the dastardly coon. He is big, strong, wily, can both dig and climb and has a set of hands that are about as handy as yours. He is also extremely fierce to many a dog's surprise and dismay. He will eat your chickens. He will eat your sweet corn. He will eat your dog and/or cat food if you feed them out of the house. He will rifle your compost pile if you put your fresh goodies out there. He will even eat the grain intended for your animals. I once was about to reach down into a drum of scratch feed only to see two little coons sitting in the bottom looking quite satisfied with themselves. Mr/Mrs Coon will be the scourge of your homestead if they can. They surely would if they could. The meaning of which is that you have to take preventive action. That coon that woke me for the last time was a big, old male who got in through the coop's roof by ripping up a piece of corrugated translucent that I had recycled to give the chickens more light. He left behind a mess of feathers and a bunch of psychotic hens, and dragged out a plump one to enjoy back home. I knew he would be back, so for the first and only time, I set out a leg trap which had come in a box of metal stuff which I had gotten at an auction for $1. He was caught and disposed of but that did not qualify as a preventive measure so the lesson there was - do whatever was necessary to coonproof the chicken coop. And also coonproof any of those other situations that he might make a mess of. That is easier said than done when you are talking about keeping the coons out of the corn patch. The only sure-fire method is to electrify and flexi-net each patch and make sure there are no holes and they are well charged. Actually I take back that statement – there is no sure-fire when it comes to raccoons. However, I have also put a Have-a-Heart trap baited with peanut butter nearby – the biggest one they make – and that gets rid of a few now and then. I once was surprised to peer into the trap and see three little masks looking back at me. Three at once. I put the trap in the back of Buster and took them some miles away to release them in a remote wooded area. That trap sees a lot of action during the summer transporting not only coons, but also skunks and squirrels. Everybody likes the peanut butter. For this purpose, we buy the cheap stuff, super homogenized from the supermarket. Raccoons wake up occasionally during winter thaws and wander sleepily around looking for an easy snack. They are in the same state during sap season. They will climb into your sap pans to lick up the sweet stuff. Sometimes, if you've left off firing just a little too late, the sap in the front pan will evaporate to a sticky goo while waiting for the next sap run, and I have come to the sugar house to find coon prints in the goo, evidence of their pirate's lust for booty.

Back in the days when we were Have-a-Heart beginners wondering how not to catch your house cats (use peanut butter instead of a tasty morsel of meat) or will a skunk spray you from within the trap (No), we caught a handsome, wee might of a skunk and he was so small and so appealing that we brought him into the house to see what kind of a pet he would make. We named him Gonker after what we thought was the Abenaki for skunk – "Segonku". To cut to the chase here, I will tell you right off that he never sprayed anyone during the time he was in the house. He did scare and surprise quite a few though. Jo was pregnant at the time and couldn't see past her belly one night climbing the stairs she felt his furry tail and almost stepped on Gonker. My brother and wife, here on a visit, woke in the night to find him in their room and spent the next several nocturnal hours trying to encourage him through the door so that they could shut it on him. Gonker did not make a satisfying pet. This was because we hardly ever saw him. He, and skunks in general, are nocturnal so he did his skunking while we did our sleeping. We did learn a few things from him though. He operated under a version of the stand-your-ground law. He would take pieces of dry cat food from your hand but if he thought you were getting too close, he would stamp both front feet as a warning and bend his spine in a semi-circle to point his little sphincter right at you. Looking at that sphincter is worse than staring at the evil eye. We soon gave him our blessing and sent him off into the world to fend for himself but we know from him that skunks will only spray if threatened and usually just wander about the world minding their own business. A problem inevitably surfaces however, when his business intersects with yours.

Skunks are not wholesale terrorists like coons. They are just persistent pests. I have probably transported several dozen skunks over the years. Their pestiest behavior besides eating the cat's food, is their insistence on digging up freshly transplanted tomatoes and squash to get at the manure underneath probably in the hope of finding earthworms. Their next pestiest is of course only the next if you happen to have a dog living with you. Unfortunately I have no magic formula to give you that would rid your dog of that tell-tale stench. All our dogs always stayed outside where they could encounter skunks in the night but also where they could gradually wear off the smell - give it back, as it were. The least pestiest is when they come to live with us in their dotage, and, senile and incontinent, they leak their way around the buildings every night fuming through the screens and leaving us in a skunky funk. Skunks are scavengers and omnivores and they will eat a chicken if they can get it. I surprised one in the chicken coop one morning hiding under the laying box. I didn't think much of it until I noticed a hen buried under the litter. He had killed a hen that was roosting on the ground because she was too old to cling to the bar and then excavated a hole and covered her up. They are reputed to eat honey bees by camping out at the entrance to a hive, scratching the wood and snapping them up as they come out to investigate. I have never seen this behavior but I have seen the remnants of yellow jacket nests dug out of the ground and eaten by skunks. The good news about skunks is that for all my interactions with them, I have yet to be sprayed by one. They are not necessarily eager to unload on you. You will only suffer if you show them considerable disrespect.

Woodchucks and rats, mice and bats. Voles and moles, snakes and weasels. Toads and salamanders, frogs and hornets. Chipmunk and squirrel, beaver and fisher. Fox and bear, moose and coyote. Turkeys and owls, hawks and vultures. Deer and deer and deer and deer. Listed like this, it seems a surprising number of wild animals to be encountered for good, bad or ugly on the homestead. Some are innocuous or actually helpful to you like bats, snakes and toads. Some are rarely seen like bear, moose and beaver. Some are cute tricksters like chipmunks. All are our cousins and beautiful in their own way but some like the coon, are major opponents, especially the white tail deer. The deer make life without fences, though highly desirable, impossible - fences around the gardens and fences around the fruit trees and bushes. Foxes, coons and coyotes make for fences around the chickens and moose make for disappearing fences when they take the pasture wire on their chest and just keep walking oblivious until they have pulled 100 yards of insulators and posts along with them. Deer roam at night and will come right up to the house when we are sleeping. One fall we arrayed a harvest of naked-seeded pumpkins along a bench just to the side of our front door and the deer stood out there all night chomping them leaving a disarray of rind and seed all over the stoop. They will eat the hemlock hedge along the lane during the winter unless I douse it with a homemade concoction of whipped up rotten eggs, water and a spreader-sticker. After we pull the kale leaves at the very end of the season, the stalks left behind are nibbled and gnawed down to stumps by them. The deer have an unerring and uncanny sense to find your newest exotic planting and devour it as if it were a tasty special treat put out just for them. Bucks do a surprising amount of damage to young fruit trees by thrashing them with their antlers in order to rub off the velvet. They don't pick substantial trunks to rub – always some promising youngster the size of a broom handle. Of course, you have the option of shooting and eating these pesky marauders. You are permitted to kill as many as you wish on your own land and deer meat is considerably tastier than porcupine. On the other hand, moose are almost never to be seen and except for the occasional fun they have with fence wire, hardly ever bother. They are close by however as evidenced by an occasion when I tied Mickey to a tree in the lower pasture and brought Maud up separately which set Mickey to bawling full blast like a lost donkey. Immediately a moose came galloping out of the woods and hooved it right through the garden to rescue what must have seemed to be a moose damsel in distress.

One of mankind's longest lasting philosophical questions is why do we prefer chipmunks and squirrels to rats? They are all rodents. They are about the same size and they all would rather eat your grain if given the choice. But we hate rats, love chipmunks, and most of us kind of like squirrels. Chipmunks are brash. I've literally had them run over my shoetops with mouths crammed with stolen grain as I stood working at a table saw. They have occasionally gone down a row of newly sprouted corn, digging each one and stuffing a mouthful. They hang out at the cider mill excavating apple seeds out of the pomace pile and then rushing off to stash them and get back for yet another load. They are cheeky (I wonder if that isn't the origin of the word?) but you can't help liking them. Squirrels are handsome, so athletic and natural circus performers. They are fun to watch but they steal all your bird seed, find your stashes of butternuts and cart them all away, and invade your outbuildings, pile up huge leafy middens in the corners and tear out your insulation. In short, they are somewhat less likable and when they begin to chew into your saplines and leave a real mess of masticated plastic on the snow, they become a whole lot less likable. And considerably less likable one season when they climbed to the top of the varmint-enemy list. It was a year of squirrel convergence. It came after an epic growing season for fruit and nuts and a warm, snowless winter and the squirrels converged non-stop to pillage and steal. I must have trapped out at least 25 of them, both red and gray but to no avail as I watched them run off across the pasture carrying whole ears of corn. We were able to save some popcorn by harvesting early and we ate some sweet corn but the rest was ransacked leaving us no seed from that season. That was a one-time occurrence which forever placed the squirrel on our bad list. There is a 'hot room' in the cider mill where we store bottled juice during the winter which at one point seemed less hot than it should so I ripped off part of the inner wall to discover that all the insulation was chewed and fallen into the bottom few inches along with the desiccated body of a red squirrel   Red squirrels are creatures of the north woods. They live in the conifers and pull the seeds out of cones but they will also forage for anything edible including nest-bound baby birds. They are argumentative and feisty and will scold you if you walk beneath their territory. Gray squirrels are bulkier and easier going and are more at home in the oak – hickory forests of farther south but we see more of them every year. Perhaps that is related to the maturing nut trees and oaks that we planted. The reds and grays seem to be continually reenacting their own civil war.

Rats, however, are something else – we just don't like their looks. Their long, thin snouts, beady eyes set on the sides of their heads and that long, naked tail are not so attractive as the bushiness and wide eyes of the others. 'Bright eyed and bushy tailed' just doesn't apply here. Besides, they are just too damned smart and fierce. They are too much like people. They will go anywhere, eat anything and fight to the death. It is someone's theory that long after humans are gone from the earth, the rat descendants will become the dominant species. They would have what it takes to march through time, living in caves, chipping rudimentary tools out of stone to emerge as the masters of the planet. Way out here far from the madding crowd I thought that it was rather extraordinary when I first noticed sign of rats in the chicken coop. Where had they possibly come from? How did they get here? I didn't wonder for long however, before I put out some Warfarin to get rid of them. That was the only time for rats here but I learned that they will take eggs and live chicks from right under a setting hen. There is another animal that people love to hate that is more ratty than a rat and that is a possum. Same physiognomy and same hairless tail, but bigger, uglier and smellier. They have a mouth full of nasty teeth, they hiss at you to warn you away and they will also happily eat your chickens. Thankfully the possum hasn't gotten to S. Washington yet but they are steadily moving north following the warming trend. Once upon a time I cornered one on the flat roof of the house in Austin and just before he went over the edge, he dropped 'dead'. I picked him up by the tail and carried him with one hand out the window of Buster steering with the other and let him off a distance away. As I drove off, I saw him in the rear-view rise from the 'dead' and stroll off into the bushes.

That house in Austin was some kind of temporary dwelling which attracted temporary inhabitants of which we were some and cockroaches were others. They were called 'wood cockroaches' and unlike the New York City kind, did not depend necessarily on humans for their livelihood. They lived outside and just came in for entertainment and dessert – dozens at a time. They were so ubiquitous that one of them might sneak into your gas tank, plug your carburetor and leave you stranded half way up the hill to 7,000ft cool. If you got up for some reason in the middle of the night and snapped on the overhead light, that would occasion a veritable blizzard of roach wings. I tell you this not to talk any more about cockroaches but rather about turtles. I came upon a very handsome painted box turtle and brought him into the house and let him free range so the kids could get to know him. However we soon discovered that he had an insatiable appetite for roaches. If you stepped on one or swatted one off the wall, he would trundle right over and crunch it with such relish that we didn't feel bad about keeping him around for a longer while. There was a two-year–old with us at the time doing her meals in a high chair and merrily either spilling things or throwing them on the floor. The turtle soon learned that when Raney went into the highchair, it was time for him to circle up underneath. It seemed reasonable to Raney to share the bounty with Mr. Turtle. However, Mr. turned into Mrs. when she squeezed out an egg right there on the kitchen floor, and at that point, we figured that she ought to go back into the wild and dig herself a nest.

There are some critters that you would never expect to have direct dealings with but nevertheless surprise you. Take bats for instance. You know they're around. You see them flitting through the evening sky and occasionally one will fly through the open door of the cider mill on a warm fall night chasing the moths around the light bulb, but you don't expect them to wake you out of a deep sleep in the middle of the night. This has happened several times when one squeezes by a vent opening and begins flying round and round the open octagon under the roof. It's a free-fly zone. The bedrooms have no separate ceilings so when he realizes that there is no way out, he finds you sleeping and flutters right above your head. When you wake, wondering why, he comes back from making another circuit and flutters you another signal. It's a special treat to feel a bat helicoptering an inch or two in front of your face in the dark of your bedroom. Then I have gotten up and stood with the door open until I hear him whoosh by in the dark and out into the night he goes. Another critter like that is the white faced or bald faced hornet. They are very big, probably three times the size of a honeybee, and they pack quite a wallop if they come after you, but they are actually quite peaceable, only provoked by uncouth barbarians or by dreamers unaware of where they blunder. This character is responsible for constructing those football sized paper nests hanging under the eaves which, by the way, the bats will use as daytime hangouts after they are abandoned by the hornets. I have watched them collecting raw material for their nests from a wooden door into the woodshed. The boards there are sawn from balm of gilead and are very soft and fibrous and I could watch from an inch or two away as the hornets chiseled up a slice about 1/8" wide and rolled it up like a scroll for an inch to then haul it back to the nest site. They are fly hawks. They will pick off flies in midair and, as I would be milking a cow outside in the summer, the white faces would be cruising around me and the udder like falcons picking off flies.

We could also put bears in this same category. The eastern black bear. Some people are starting to complain that old ursus is eating the seed from the birdfeeders in the early spring but we have only had one spot of trouble with him when he went after our bee hive. He tore it apart and ate a bunch of brood and wax and scattered things around. When he left, he deposited a large shit as a farewell token. He was hungry. I don't blame him. I think it's terrible when some bee keeper complains and the warden comes and shoots the bear. Do something to protect your hives. Don't kill a bear for some lost honey. Another encounter came in the middle of the night when I woke to the crash of the bird feeder, crawled out of bed and flashlighted out the front door to have a conversation with madame ursa. It was early spring and I imagine this bear was a she and was trying to feed some cubs. She squinted into the light in what seemed a calculating fashion but after a heart-stopping moment, gave me a shrug and ambled off into the night leaving a muddy paw mark on the window pane where she had steadied herself to extend the other paw high enough to slam down the feeder. Bears are deceptively athletic. We surprised one on the road down the way and clocked it at 30mph before he veered full speed into the roadside puckerbrush like a cannonball. One fall day we had a hunting hound show up at our front door and lie down as if waiting for Godot and a few hours later a pickup with a cage on the back came trucking along slowly looking for him. They were running bears for practice. You are apparently allowed to do this before the start of the hunting season. The next morning early our own dog was barking himself silly so I went out to investigate just in time to watch a bear shinny up a big pine right below the shop. As I came closer, I realized that there were three cubs above her all the way to the top. I figured that she had been frightened for her cubs by the hounds and had come in looking for relief. She was draped on the first big branch about 15ft up, her cubs like bumps on the log arrayed above her, and I walked toward her to have a conversation. She watched me quietly until I got 10ft close and then she started popping her teeth letting me know that was close enough. They stayed there for three hours and left while we were eating lunch.

Two other animals that I wouldn't classify as varmints but who have done varminty things to friends of ours are beavers and owls. Our friend Al heard his cat mewling outside his door one night and went out to investigate. Suddenly it seemed that the cat was screeching at him from up on the roof but as he looked and listened the meowing got higher and fainter and disappeared off into the night. An owl had carried the cat away. That is the only time I have heard of that but I'm sure it happens more than we know. Cats are always disappearing.

Fishers are usually the prime suspect and the influx of coyotes could account for more. Our local owl is the barred owl, a famous entertainer for its "Who cooks for you..." call and for its frantic, wild and crazy mating exchanges in the late winter. You don't see him very often but occasionally he will ghost up ahead of you in the winter woods. Beavers have never been seen right here during our time but they work close by. Upstream at the head of the valley there is a veritable beaver emporium from which it appears they have come and gone over the decades because the dam is the only other created structure besides the Great Wall of China that you can see from space. I jest – but it does seem an ongoing historical masterpiece standing 6ft high and curving 100ft long in an arc from east to west. They will go to some lengths to get fresh provisions as another friend found out. He had put together a pick-your-own apple orchard along the top of a ridge which gives way to a steep slope down a quarter mile to a swampy bottom. The trees were robust, grown to four or five inches, and well productive when overnight the beavers came up from the bottom and gnawed down six of them, clipping off branches and taking them away. He didn't know the beavers were down there and even if he did, he never would have suspected they would come that far up a very steep incline to chew up his apple trees.

It's a wonderful thing on a clear, cold winter night to hear the barred owl sound off from the hillside and it's equally beautiful to listen to the coyotes. This is a new song heard in the Vermont hills. These guys started moving in a couple of decades ago when people were talking about 'coy dogs' and then figured they were a new species perhaps formed by hybridizing with dogs and/or wolves now known as Eastern Coyote. I don't see one very often but we hear them close by all the time. They are handsome like large German Shepherds with heavy coats but, as I said before, if we still kept goats, I might not appreciate them as much. Our son Ben herds a passel of sheep and he has them surrounded by impenetrable fence as well as keeping two guard donkeys and a specially bred guard dog with the sheep all the time. That part donkey that was in Maud used to chase any dog out of the pasture that dared to encroach.

It seems an immutable law that if you put up some buildings somewhere and plant some crops, you will end up dealing with endless incoming small rodents. Besides those pesky squirrels and an occasional woodchuck, our quotient here is filled by moles and voles and white footed mice. We've had the usual tussles with woodchucks (also known as groundhogs) who will come in and burrow into some place where you don't notice, like the blackberry patch and proceed to eat their way along your rows of beans. We've fought the valiant fights against them pouring water down their holes or stuffing gasoline soaked rags in there and sealing it off or borrowing a neighbor's 22 and never using it, and eventually it seems that they just get tired of being hassled and move out. The moles here are star-nosed moles and the only time we see them is when they are dead and left around by a cat. They must be unsavory because cats will not eat them. They aren't bothersome. Occasionally they will tunnel along a row of carrots searching out earthworms but leaving the carrots high and dry. Voles, however, really are bothersome. These are meadow voles and they burrow around fruit trees and skin the bark off the roots and the trunk under the cover of snow. We have lost well-grown, productive apple trees to girdling by voles during a particular deep-snow winter. They will also roam your garden and gnaw into your beets and carrots. Some orchardists will put out poison inside small lengths of plastic pipe. I just stomp down their tunnels which you can feel inside the drip line and wrap the lower trunk before the snow arrives. You have possible allies in this mini-battle and they would be fox, coyote and weasel. They can all find rodents beneath the snow listening and plunging or in the case of the weasel long and lithe, coursing the sub-nivean tunnels made by the voles themselves. However, these three varmints also will happily dine on your chickens so I don't really rejoice to see them nearby. Weasels are reported to go wild in a chicken coop leaving behind a raft of dead chickens with only their throats opened but this I have never seen. I have once heard the chickens advertising trouble and run to see a weasel in their yard. He was handsome, bright- eyed and showed no fear and quickly demonstrated his litheness by squeezing away through the chicken wire.

WINTER WEASEL (ERMINE) in greenhouse by way of drainpipe.

White footed mice are also known as deer mice and are quite attractive little critters, but of course, there is no end to them and they persist in coming in out of the cold into your buildings and making themselves cozy. Snap traps baited with peanut butter. The better mouse trap has already been invented and that's what we use. They start moving in the beginning of November and keep at it until the snow and cold permanize.

We might snap a couple dozen every season and most of them I feed to the chickens.

The animals that reside in and around Gingerbrook constitute a neighborhood but do not really qualify as company. They don't choose to hang around even within eyeshot when you are working outside, and if you are accompanied by a dog, you will be even less likely to bump into any of them. That is one of the reasons we no longer keep any dogs here. I watched one of our dogs scare a wild hen turkey off her nest. I counted 12 eggs there and when I went back two days later to check, they were all gone. However I do consider as company the neighborhood of songbirds that vibrate the day hours with their movement, their passage or their songs. No matter what you are doing or where you locate, there is the sight or sound of birds to keep you company. Even in the winter, when you shut down the chain saw to get a break from the racket, there is likely a flock of chickadees gamboling through the underbrush nearby. Chickadees, of course, are everyone's favorite companions. Wonderful little hearts, little fluff-budgets who follow you in groups through the woods and who will eat sunflower seeds out of your hand next to the feeder. How they manage to store up enough energy to last the long, windy below zero nights is a marvelous mystery. Each flock is usually accompanied by one or two nuthatches who counterpoint the deedees chatter with their upside-down nasal peent. Most of our birds come and go with the seasons but not the chickadees. We only feed them during the winter months and I will get into a worry if I see the seeds are gone and I haven't noticed. There are others who also stay around including that tyrant, the blue jay. We had a city girl here for a while who told me about this beautiful bird she had seen through the window. What did it look like, I said. It was blue, she said. Did it have a crest on its head, I asked. Yes, she replied. Indeed, I thought, those damn blue jays actually are beautiful if you haven't ever seen one before or you haven't just seen the hundredth scatter all the chickadees and gobble down all the sunflower seeds or had them scream JAY, JAY at you for chasing them out of the blueberries. It seems a law of nature – when there is a lot of something we value it less. During nesting and hatching time, the blue jays magically disappear. For three weeks in May and June, there isn't a jay to be seen or heard but then they bring their newly hatched back with them from the highlands to bedevil you in their bluejay way. An acquaintance once told me how he sits on his front porch and picks off blue jays from out of his corn patch with a 22 rifle loaded with bird shot. I judged him to be a total heathen shooting songbirds until one summer I became sympathetic and wanted to borrow his tool and technique when the jays began scything into our almost ready flint corn and just refused to scare away. In a mere few days, the raucous tribe can do tremendous damage. Another avian character, so unlike the blue jay, and an iconic totem to some, but capable of coming out of the woods to bedevil you is the pileated woodpecker. He is big and handsome with his bright red top-knot and is usually considered secretive. You hear him occasionally hammering into dead wood in the forest or calling loudly his ratcheting rattle but you don't expect him to be eating your fruit right in front of your house. It's the wild grape rampant up and over a walnut tree that he likes. He'll swoop in right over your head on silent wings to settle in and gobble grapes always before they are quite ready to pick. One season, I tied a scare balloon and flash tape to the top of the tree but the pileated paid it no mind and now I just harvest whatever grapes he chooses to leave us.

The winter will usually bring irruptions of various northern birds like siskins, redpolls or evening grosbeaks but really our winter totem is the almighty raven. The raven rules the winter skies. He revels in the cold rush of northern air to speed cross current, to glide, to tumble, to fly upside down and to croak across the sky or announce his presence chiming like a glockenspiel. If you are doing something in the woods and he flies over, you know because you can hear his wingbeats whish, whish, whish two per second and he'll spot you through the canopy and wheel around once to check on what it is you are up to. Ravens are always watching and are intelligent enough to figure things out. They own the winter skies and when once I watched a covey of them collect down in the marsh, I knew something was of interest there. And indeed, they had spotted first and started in on a deer that was lying dead in the snow. The ravens had signaled the find and not far behind came fox, coyote and dog. A friend who lives just down the road had a pair of geese and was hoping to raise some goslings. The goose decided to lay her eggs tucked into the back corner of a small shed underneath a pile of boxes. He noticed that the eggs kept disappearing and couldn't figure it until one day he happened to see a raven fly out of the shed. He kept watch the next time the goose went in to lay. After she finished and walked out, the raven came out of the trees, flew into the shed and came out with a goose egg in its beak. The raven is the largest bird in the sky during the winter. The hawks are gone as are the blue heron and the occasional eagle, vulture, goose or duck. The owl is secretive and is a night flier and the crow flees the cold hill country for the towns and farms in the Connecticut valley. During a thaw, the crows will show up briefly but in advance of the next blue-norther, they fly back to their comfort zone. There are certain high, open, windy hill tops that we regularly cross in our travels where we always see ravens – winter or summer, they love those zones. They create a valley of fuss in late May and into June while they are raising their babies. They build their nests always in the highest white pines and as the next generation gains strength so does their clamor, squalling into crescendos each time a parent approaches with a mouthful. This ravening dominates the audio for about a week every spring until one day you suddenly realize that they are flown.

Chickens will spot soaring birds long before you will and emit their warning screel. You might search fruitlessly until you see a wee dot way up in the center of the sky which the chickens are keeping an eye on – their instinct knows about death from the sky. That dot may be a raven but it's probably going to be a redtail hawk. If you want to see hawks or falcons in action, just invest in a flock of racing pigeons. I have never seen a chicken carried off by a hawk but we have lost whole coops of pigeons. The tribe of accipiters is responsible. I have watched both cooper's hawks and goshawks chase down our pigeons. A pigeon coop can be rigged with a one-way door to which a pigeon can be easily trained so that they can go in but not out unless you let them. However, after a flyaround, they would often choose to loiter on the ridge of the saltboxed shop before entering the coop. You would hear that clatter of pigeon wings as they launched in a paroxysm off the ridge and down the valley with a cooper's rocketing over the shop roof after them. A pigeon is a mighty flyer – fast, strong and maneuverable – but the hawk is faster, albeit less maneuverable. The hawk would zero in on one and lose air on the feints and jukes but gain on the straightaways until inevitably would fall that puff of feathers 1/4 mile down the valley and another pigeon done gone. But such a magnificent display of airpower it was that I couldn't really begrudge them their catch. The first hawk back in the spring and our most consistent raptor neighbor is the broadwing. They often nest in the sugarbush high in one of the maples and will scream at you if you walk anywhere close by them. The broadwings are soaring hawks like the bigger redtail and they are often visible cruising around above us. They seem to be more interested in rodents than pigeons – they are not built to weave and dart and chase like the accipiters

The redtails and the broadwings are a constant visible presence during the summer but without the attraction of the pigeons, we hardly ever catch a glimpse of either the accipiters or any falcons. The exception is the tiny kestral who sits on the telephone wires, then hovers over the open fields and swoops for grasshoppers or if lucky, voles. We were very fortunate one day to hold in our hands a merlin. He crashed into a window chasing purple finches by the feeder. Merlins used to go by the common name of pigeon hawk but they seem somewhat small for that job. They are the sized falcon between the kestral and the peregrine and they are a very beautiful bird. It was a mighty crash but the glass did not break and he was unconscious but still alive. Jo gave him some 'Rescue Remedy' with an eye dropper and I set him outside on a table. He ultimately came to and flew away. Rescue Remedy has been used here quite a few times with birds and animals in distress. It does seem to help. Once a hummingbird somehow got into the house and buzzed around the dome trying to get out until he so tired himself that we thought he was finished. We put the remedy to him and set him in a comfortable place. That one also revived to fly another day. He amazed us by putting his tongue through the hole in the dropper and up into the glass tube. We could see the tongue go up the tube for about an inch.

There is only one hummingbird that hangs out this far east and that is the rubythroat. I don't know how long one may live but at their metabolic rate, I think not long. Given that surmise, it's apparent that we have established a generational memory in the hummingbirds here. Every spring, we know that they are back from their long journey south because the first one back parks himself hovering at the window right where the sugar water feeder always hangs. Hovering, looking through the window, demanding our attention - wake up you knuckleheads; where is the feeder? Knowing that they are going to be here, just like thinking about the honeybees, influences your choice of flowers to plant. The hummers go to red so we put out plants like cardinal flowers, scarlet runner beans and crimson bee balm (monarda) for their pleasure. They are such fun these feisty little stealth bombers, squeaking and chasing each other always at full speed and then appearing in an instant at your shoulder in the garden, humming in your ear and then gone.

Most birds if you bring them inside to safeguard after a crisis, will not appreciate it and not thrive. Even the hummingbirds we haven't kept them in for very long. But one fellow was an exception. This was a scissor-tailed flycatcher which was hit by a motorcycle as I passed on the sidewalk in Austin. I picked him up and brought him home. We babied him and I hung a many-branched limb from the ceiling. Then we gave him free range and he happily began to feed himself, hovering around the house and picking of flying insects, of which there were plenty, this being summer in Texas and there being minimal screening in the place. Especially at night, he would gorge on the moths flocking around the bare bulbs. He was just a youngster and we watched his tails grow from three inches to five before we left the screen door open one day and off he went fat and happy. He was with us for a couple of weeks and used to land on a mobile that was hung above baby Ben's bassinette, the which seemed to keep both of them fascinated.

There are other birds whose comings and goings especially mark the passage of the seasons. There are the geese of course and their leaving you behind to face the winter alone does affect you, but basically they are too distant – too little connected to our everyday. Bluebirds, on the other hand, are often the first to return and the last to leave. They come by when the snow is still on the ground to check up on last year's lodgings, leave for a time for a place where there will be something to eat and then come back for real when the first insects are motivating. Having bluebirds around is all about installing a house for them. If you build it, they will come. You should probably build two so when the inevitable battle with the swallows displaces one or the other, there remains alternative housing. Bluebirds are wonderful company as they chortle and burble throughout the day and seem unafraid of your presence. They also harvest uncountable insects from around your garden to feed their babies. But the real announcer of spring is the red-wing blackbird. When you hear that first scree-onk, you know winter is on the run. They make their nest in the marsh, hanging it from last year's cat tails so they are always close by. The robins are close behind, arriving as soon as there shows a patch of open ground. But the next real landmark arrival is the hermit thrush. They are the state bird of Vermont and one of the world's preeminent singers. If you notice a slug in the woods while taking down sap lines, the next day you will likely hear that otherworldly song drifting down from the hillside. They like those slugs. The birds are piling in by now. Around the feeder are purple finches, goldfinches, rose-breasted grosbeaks, juncos, various sparrows, cowbirds etc. all bullying the chickadees for more than their share. The next marker bird is the phoebe. You walk out the door one morning and you hear it clear as a bell – FEE-BEE - and you know he's there sitting on the clothesline near the spot under the eave where for years they have always stuck a nest. We walk back and forth by that spot often and each time she flies off the nest and perches away on the line waiting until we pass and miraculously, she always fledges her brood. Now the spring is progressing, the trees are leafing out and I'm waiting for the day the oriole shows up. One morning he's here. I don't see him at first but I sure do hear him. He's over there, he's right here, he's everywhere loudly proclaiming his arrival. The strange thing is that I usually never see or hear him again after those first couple of days. Only one year did they build their pendulous nest nearby where you could see it hanging from the tip of a long branch of the front yard maple.

By this time, life is proliferating fast and furious and the swallows do show (tree swallows) and there is a go around with the bluebirds to see who gets which bird house. The bluebirds usually win out but not always. When the swallows claim a box, they are here and gone in a flash. The boxes are in the middle of the garden and while weeding or planting, if we are considered to be too close, they will escape the box or circle overhead but one unusually feisty couple surprised us by deciding that within a certain radius, that territory was theirs and interlopers beware. Kneeling, standing or bent over, they would come at an angle from high in the sky and skim your head so tight the shock wave would ruffle your hair. Dive bombers or strafers, they would also emit a high, thin screeling as they skimmed then ride the curve to the top, bank and drop into another dive to screel you again. This only happened one season but I loved lifting my head from whatever earthy task and watching one of them come at me from the top of the roller coaster, wings locked in a dive seemingly aimed right at my forehead but unerringly skimming and screeching. As soon as those babies fledge, they translate to the lowlands in the valleys along the streams where the flying insects flourish and we never see them again. But really I am waiting for the last marker of the spring after which we had better get to work – and that is the brown thrasher. He sits on the highest twig on the tallest maple along the lane and commences to put on a display of musical virtuosity unrivalled in the bird world. He makes up phrases and sings them twice and as far as I can tell, no two phrases are the same. It's incredible because he goes on all day long. But like the oriole, he stays (or is audible) for no more than one or two days and we don't see him again either until the following year. Now that seems so unlikely but this same routine happens every year – a magical mystery to which I have no answer.

There are of course many other birds both summer and winter that capture your attention for a brief flash or a long study, some like the tribe of warblers are too various and too skittish and others like the catbird, I like to consider secret friends. The catbird is a relative of the thrasher and sings just as beautiful but in phrases sung only once and not as ingenious. Whereas Mr.Thrasher is a brash show-off, the catbird has a secret which he will only occasionally and shyly let you in on. He hangs out in the bushes and thickets so that you have to work a bit to get to see him. To be "in the catbird's seat" is a saying the meaning of which I ponder in relation to the bird himself. Perhaps one so secretive must have good reason to guard his secret and not tell you, and in a curious way, that gives him power and control. Well, maybe but I'm sure Mr. Catbird cares not for what we may think as he blends into the underbrush and meows at your human delusions.

One character who ranks lowest on my avian list is that sapsucker. Yellow-bellied on not, those guys are trouble makers. As I've said before, if you have no vested interests, you have no enemies. If you are not protecting anything, you are care-free. In this case, it's fruit trees. When I hear that first 'scree' of a sapsucker in the spring, I involuntarily start cursing to myself. They will make the rounds to certain trees and puncture a pattern of dozens of tiny holes in the bark and after those dry up, they'll do it again. An apple tree can just die outright from having its bark destroyed or it can die from disease like fireblight introduced through the holes. There isn't much you can do about it if you don't want to shoot songbirds. If you wrap an affected area with say, a burlap bag or coat it with clay, the sapsucker will just move on to an adjacent limb. The sapsucker apparently does more than just suck sap – he eats the insects that are attracted to the oozing sap. I have seen hummingbirds do the same thing – they need insect protein to grow their young.

Some birds, whose songs were so prominent when we first arrived here like that of the white throated sparrow calling out on still, quiet summer days his mournful "old sam peabody, peabody, peabody, or the veery, always in the woods, sliding down a watery scale over and over, are no longer to be heard here. I know not why, whereas some surprising others have appeared like the turkey vulture. It was quite a surprise to see one summer morning a huge, black thing sitting a fence post holding horizontal his long wings, exposing them to the sun and wind, drying them preparatory to launching. A vulture! What's he doing here? Then I learned that the turkey vulture had been following the roadkill north along the interstates to reach the Canadian border and now it's not uncommon to see them floating and kiting the thermals overhead. I wasn't thinking about buzzards when I carried a dead raccoon down to the edge of the marsh and left it there for whoever to take care of. That 'whoever' turned out to be a vulture which I watched glide down into the marsh the very next day. I had seen buzzards dismember a dead horse alongside the road in Peru, starting in on the anus and eye sockets, but I never expected to see one on the savannas in front of our house. The vulture may be the herald of death but he too has become part of our community – a community which the birds, more than anyone, carry with them and share among us all.

SEX AND THE COUNTRY

It's the beginning of the agricultural year. The snow is gone. The maple syrup has been made. The spring beauties have popped and the plowing, disking and digging has begun. The freshly exposed earth quickly warms up and its myriad inhabitants respond. Most of them are invisible but there is one who shows on the surface of the brown earth and catches your eye like a distant fireflash in the dark desert night.

Like a spark in the desert night

It is so tiny but colored the most outrageous scarlet that it flames an irresistible spark in your eye. He is just the size of the head of a finishing nail and the first time I saw him, I thought him to be the vision of the spirit of passion and fertility. As we always do on the freshly tilled soil in the spring, we were making love and he appeared just inches from my nose and he was dancing, waving two of his eight arms or legs and clearly celebrating. Since then, whoever is on top gets to commune with this scarlet messenger from the earth. Scarlet – the color of hearts and roses and passion and fertility. If he is dancing and celebrating to the tune of this copulation, then I figure all his invisible cohorts are too. The nematodes, springtails, ants, beetles, earthworms, grubs, mites, protozoa, rhizobia, mycorrhizae – they are all dancing in a springtime craze and as the old jive goes – the joint is jumping and ready for action.

Ready for action. It's spring and the whole natural world is gearing up for reproduction. Sex! Having sex. The terminology seems somewhat awkward and euphemistic but choose among any of the others – copulation, conjugation, insemination, fertilization, coitus, congress, fucking, mating. All the terms work for what mammals do but not necessarily for all the other creatures of the planet like plants or fish. They don't conjugate, or have coitus or congress, or fuck, but every creature in order to reproduce either fertilizes or gets fertilized or if you choose, has sex. The wee scarlet earth messenger who likes to get happy and dance, it turns out is not unknown to science and has a name – the red velvet mite. I have no idea what their sex life is about but there are many fascinating versions of how plants and animals reproduce and we are discussing it now because life on the farm as well as life in the wild is all about fertility and reproduction. Without it, there are no calves, there is no milk. There are no chicks; there are no eggs. There are no seeds; there are no beans. With no plant sex, there are no apples, tomatoes and no sweet corn The red velvet mite has got it right – jump up and down with glee.

The love bug dancing and celebrating

The more action in your garden soil, the better your harvest is likely to be. And right then and there underneath the dancing scarlet mite, the lowly earthworms are going at it. Lowly to some but the farmer's best ally, they have coitus and congress, and conjugate in a fashion unrivaled by just about anyone. They are hermaphrodites. They join side by side head to tail each male part to each female part and both produce a cocoon which is cast off to produce more earthworms for the gardener's delight. It seems a fact of life that the more organic material there is, the more action there is. The garden underworld may very well celebrate any and all copulations but a wheelbarrow of compost surely would do the same. I have never had the opportunity to check out a teaspoon of garden soil under a microscope but I take it for granted that it would be rife with living critters. I hear now and again the estimation that the total mass of life underground is greater than that which we can see aboveground.

Life is an urgent affair and the most urgent part of it is the production of more life. It seems that procreation up and down the scale of living creatures is an act full of drama and excitement. It's somewhat difficult for us to register the excitement felt by congressing earthworms but I'm sure it's happening. Because all life on our planet is ultimately related, I'm also sure that bacteria, springtails and beetles get excited and feel the overwhelming urge. Imagine how the maple trees must feel in those seasons when they have gotten geared up for sex and the sky is aswarm with pollen. They are also hermaphrodites. That is, each individual tree puts out both male and female flowers (staminate and pistilate). Each tree is both a sender and receiver of sperm. They are having sex in both directions at the same time. Other tree species do it in different ways. The white ash separates its sexes on separate trees. How they determine who is going to be who is a puzzle worthy of some future Nobel winner. The wind-blown trees are profligate with their pollen. Coitus is an uncertain affair left to the vagaries of the springtime breezes and to increase your chances, you must pump out vast quantities of pollen. And the female or pistilate flowers also accommodate by producing extra long stigmas and furnishing them with stickum that will snag and hold onto any passing grain of pollen. Apparently a single beech stamen will release 2000 grains of pollen and for another unbelievable statistic, it has been calculated somehow that the unending coniferous forest of Sweden produces 75,000 tons of pollen in a breeding season.

There are other trees like fruit trees that make 'perfect' flowers. This is what most of us have in mind when we think 'flower' in that they have both stamen and pistil together in one. They usually dress themselves in pretty colors, apply perfume and offer liquor in order to have their sex. They are also giving and receiving simultaneously however, in this case, not directly but through a third party – those happy-go-lucky flying insects. The lipstick and perfume are put on to seduce their unwitting go-betweens who are happy to oblige given the reward of sweet nectar and high protein pollen. This isn't their own sex they are having but it might as well be given how they act. Honey bees, bumble bees, hover flies, mason bees, miner bees, white face hornets, mud daubers, yellow jackets – upon close inspection in the springtime orchard, they are delirious vibrating into the apple, plum, peach, pear, cherry and berry flowers, covering themselves with pollen and doing the sex work for the fruit bearers.

Despite their inclusion in the well-worn metaphor for sexual activity, the 'birds and the bees', most of the above mentioned bees don't engage in sex at all. The social insects, as exemplified by the honey bees, have their sex done by just one female – the Queen – and a bunch of male hopefuls hanging around like the suitors in Odysseus' palace – only one of which will win the race and fertilize a new Queen and die a glorious death in the act. And she will be inseminated only once in a lifetime – a lifetime which will last perhaps several years and produce many thousands of offspring. So curiously, there is less sex happening among the social insects yet more procreation. Bumblebees, yellow jackets and white faced hornets are also social but they mate in the fall and only the newly mated queens survive the winter and go on to start new hives the following spring.

The solitary bees, some of the wasps, and the hover flies don't contract out their sex to a queen but do it 'solitarily' in the spring after hibernating the winter in various hideaways underground or in punky tree trunks or barky cracks and crevasses. There are many characters under this heading each with their own strategy for raising their babies. Some place their eggs on larvae of other insects, some bring home a paralyzed body and seal it into a chamber along with an egg but many rely on pollen. Those tiny mason and mining bees seen darting among the apple flowers each carry a few pollen grains to a tube fashioned in mud or drilled in wood and seal them in with an egg. The apple flowers are not as profligate with their pollen as are the maples and pines but in their contract with the insect world, they promise enough for everyone. The natural world is extravagant in its production of the male fertilizer – of sperm. The female part –the egg – is precious and closely guarded and only needs one sperm to become fertile whereas across the natural board, uncountable sperm are produced and disseminated to track down and find that one egg. In the case of pollen from many plants, it plays a double role in sex and procreation – creating plant babies and feeding animal babies. The average observer isn't likely to see any of these flying insects mating. The only ones that I have ever watched are the hover flies. These are apparent bees that are actually flies in disguise. Upon close inspection, you see that even though they act like it, they are not really honey bees. However you can watch a male hover fly patrol a flowered patch like a predator drone chasing away other males and waiting for a female to show upon whom he will quickly jump and accomplish that sex in a microsecond.

Is it becoming apparent that the homestead is seething with sex? An X rating doesn't begin to cover it. Every square inch will have some critter at it one way or another. We generally walk oblivious through it all because we don't see it or experience anything other than perhaps a case of spring time allergies. Even the secret life of our party-loving red velvet mite is hidden from us. However there is plenty of above-ground sex to be seen coming either from the wild or your domestic animals. The birds are easier to track than the bees and they range from the mighty ravens doing their foreplay raucously cross-current through the sky and the robins thrashing and chasing through the pucker brush to the demure bluebirds who mate on top of their birdhouse. Mr. Bluebird arrives early in the spring before anyone else and claims his house and burbles and charms the neighborhood and when she arrives a week later, they get right to the serious business of making babies. There's no raucous chasing with bluebirds. She's ready and he's ready and she lowers and flattens herself and he hops on and, blink it's over. They will do this every day while she's laying her four or five eggs and that's the sex for the year; the rest is the hard work of hatching and raising their babies. The tree swallows that arrive after the bluebirds and compete for the rights to the boxes also put on a dainty show of coitus. They will perch side by side on a high wire or on the pea fence. She lowers herself and he hops on and hops off. Then he hops on again and off. And again and off. And one more time, and they shake and ruffle their feathers and swoop off in search of blackflies.

It's difficult not to anthropomorphize when judging the behavior of different animals and as a result, you can't help but prefer one animal to another. People tend to admire lions and cheetahs but dislike hyenas. They are all African carnivores who live by running down and killing grass-eaters but some are perceived as noble or courageous or graceful while another is thievish and cowardly. Eagles are exalted while vultures are despised. Squirrels are cute and industrious while rats are sly, treacherous and dirty. One feels that all creatures should live by the golden rule and although we ourselves don't, we prefer ones like bluebirds and swallows who seem to exhibit the right virtues. There are some animals that are so virtuous by are standards that they engender our love and loyalty. The pigeon is one such and is a good fit for life on the homestead. The domesticated pigeon comes in all sizes and colors. Some are fat meat birds and others are high flyers but they are all beautiful and the dove (i.e. white pigeon) has become the international symbol of hope, peace and love. You can quickly have a flock of white pigeons wheeling through your skies by acquiring a mated pair. They will conjugate plenty and waste no time getting to the next hatch after the first has fledged. They mate for life and are famous for their courting rituals. He does puff out his neck feathers and prance and dance for her but usually its billing and cooing and a constant show of tenderness. They share the incubating chore – there are always two eggs – and they share the feeding and their coitus is smooth with no roughness.

Rape is a behavior that only humans and perhaps a few other primates exhibit. There is an old saying which goes: 'The male proposes and the female disposes'. This would seem to be true usually among humans and almost always throughout the animal world. Therein, coitus or insemination cannot happen unless the female actively helps. Even that hover fly that would appear to us to be waiting to ambush a female, could only mate successfully if the female permitted. One of the most beautiful displays of teamwork can be seen in mating dragonflies. Occasionally we will see them coming up from a pond situated below the homestead and they'll advertise as a flash in the sun. Joined at the tail, two sets of wings flashing, they fly together one upside down in perfect tandem symmetry. In general it seems that males pursue, hassle and harry females but only succeed at mating if and when the female decides. Both of these roles are, unlike with humans, determined both biologically and seasonally. Even the rooster, who we will discuss in a while, does not chase down hens if they are 'out of season' – i.e. not laying. This pattern would seem to be paralleled by the roles of sperm and egg. The sperm must pursue and find that precious egg. Metaphorically, even that random flying pollen grain must find his female and beg her to let him in.

The mammals on the homestead, like their wild cousins, have their sexual activity regulated by 'heat' cycles. This means that they only have sex when the female is receptive – i.e. when she's ovulating. So their copulations are timed relative to their respective gestation periods. Generally the rule is; bigger mammals copulate less than smaller ones. Rabbits or guinea pigs will come back in heat every six weeks or two months as they wean their babies whereas horses and cows would have sex only once a year. I assume that humans were once subject to these same constraints as there is still 'heat' involved in the female's ovulation cycle – it can be tracked with a thermometer. However, somehow humans subverted the tyranny of the heat cycle and have evolved a reproduction strategy that has perhaps overpopulated the entire planet. There are downsides to this strategy however and one of them is rape, which leads us to discuss our friend the rooster.

Old Chanticleer. The cock who crows at dawn – and at all other times day and night. He certainly is a sexual powerhouse and has been a symbol of virility for ages. For him, copulation is not a team sport and he certainly doesn't wait for permission. Here is a story, or actually a joke, told to me by a veterinarian: There were two men standing at the edge of a barnyard in which there scratched 20 hens and one cock. They watched him run down and mount 5, 7, 10 hens and one of the men commented: "Wow! This rooster sure is virile." But the cock didn't stop there. He mounted the 13th, the 16th and started to wobble and stumble as he got to 18 then 19 and finally after mounting #20, he collapsed in a heap of feathers and one of the men said – "By God, he's fucked himself to death". But the rooster, hearing this comment, turned his head to look at them, then winked one eye and motioned up in the sky. The two men looked up and saw a hawk that was spiraling down toward the wily cock. Surely just one of a thousand more bawdy than this joke told about roosters over the centuries. His sexual prowess is mythic – mythic to the point of blind stupidity. I have seen a rooster repeatedly mount a dying hen before she was removed from the coop and another attempt to copulate with an already dead hen lying in the litter. It has to be said that the rooster is the exception that proves the rule that rape is not something that animals do. However, with one final word on Mr. Cocksure, I'll point out that we typically keep around 25 hens and just one rooster and when we set eggs to hatch, we have never found one that wasn't fertile.

During the winter the chicken coop is relatively quiet but as the daylight lengthens and the eggs start coming, the excitement level and the noise ramps up as the sex goes on non-stop, but what about other barnyard fowl? Turkeys of course are famous for their pre-coital displays. Prior to and during the hens' fertile period, the toms are at it all day long. They stomp and dance and puff-up and shudder and vibrate their feathers and sound off like a locomotive letting off steam. They become aggressive and prone to fighting so that more than one tom in sight or hearsay will inevitably lead to battle. But perhaps because of their size, copulating turkeys have to practice teamwork. Toms do not run down hens like roosters. When she becomes sufficiently impressed by his blue face and bright red carbuncles and steam-powered vibrations, she lowers herself to the ground and flattens her back so he can step on and balance till the deed is done. Turkeys do not form mated pairs. Toms will copulate with any hen that comes within their sphere of influence but geese, like pigeons, do mate for life. The gander can be a vicious character, willing to inflict damage on any intruder during the mating and rearing season but he is tender with his goose and they copulate the same way as the turkeys but without the accompanying song and dance. She doesn't need to be re-impressed with her mate; she just wants to raise some more goslings. Each time they engage however, the pair does trumpet a clarion to the heavens announcing and celebrating a successful coitus.

Cows come into heat every 21 days and they continue to cycle until they are inseminated. The vast majority of cows in the U.S. are artificially inseminated. This is attractive to dairy and beef producers as it allows them access to high producing genetics without the hassle and danger inherent in keeping their own bull. We used the artificial man here occasionally when we were looking for a Jersey or Guernsey calf but most of the time we kept a Scotch Highland bull. It is often difficult for humans to know when a cow is in heat but not for a bull. He spends most of his year lazing and ruminating about the pasture but days before a cow is actually receptive, he perks up and begins to pay attention. He gathers clues as to her condition by smelling her urine and exhibiting the characteristic 'flehmen' that many ungulates show at this point – a raising of the head and curling of the lips. As she gets closer, he goes into overdrive staying right behind or beside her relentless, hassling her and moaning, slavering and pawing the ground. This might go on for a couple of days before the cow 'stands' for the bull. This is called 'standing heat' by the artificial inseminator who wants to be at the cow just at that time to make certain that she will 'take'. But for the bull, this is the sum of his desires when she stops fleeing and invites him on. He might mount her two or three times while she is standing but that's the sum of their sex for the year. The calf will be born nine months later and she won't come back into heat for another two months after that so they return to grazing, ruminating and cogitating deep, slow bovine day dreams.

This brings us to the hero of our essay on homestead sex – or perhaps you would be more likely to label him the 'antihero' - the outrageous epitome of lascivious, lewd, lustful, libidinous and lecherous. Anthropomorphizing again with a bunch of words and he cares not – he's just doing what comes naturally. Our antihero is the billy goat, more formally known as a buck goat. He lives in languages around the world as an epithet to the randy male – you old goat – you cabron. He appears in mythology and legend as a faun or satyr. The very devil himself is often portrayed with horns and cloven hoofs. Just hearing that his cloven feet are part of the scene leads you along a path fraught with the possibility of lechery. The little goat-footed balloon man whistling far and wee in just spring is advertising what's in the air, not for children.

Let's see why he has acquired such a reputation. Like the bull and other large mammals, his chances for actual copulation are limited by the female's availability which in turn is dictated by her heat cycles. Whereas, on the homestead we would only ever keep two cows along with any bull, we often had five or six female goats (does). They preferred to kid in the early spring so that would put them coming into heat in October or November. That was high tide for the buck. The action is similar to that of bull and cow but exaggerated. As a doe approaches prime time, she urinates more often and he runs behind her to catch it, drinks some and comes up into a flehmen. The flehmen apparently helps to circulate the odors through his olfactory system allowing him to judge her state of readiness. Meanwhile he is perfuming himself presumably to render himself more desirable, by spraying urine all over his face and neck. He arches his neck down, faces back between his front legs and squirts into his face. If you've ever had anybody accuse you of smelling like a billy goat, now you know what kind of insult that is. He's rank all right but more feisty than ever stuttering and bawling and coming after the does with his head lowered like a snake. During this hormonal craze, he seems to sport a continual erection. His penis comes out of its sheath long and thin looking like the front two feet of a pool cue. And here's the part that really seals the deal for a human observer – with that penis running parallel under his stomach, if he is not spraying himself with urine, he is taking it in his mouth and bending himself double as he ejaculates. Therein lies his reputation as the unquenchable sex devil and this goes on for days or weeks depending on how the various does' heat cycles are distributed. When the actual coitus occurs, it seems an anticlimax to all this self-sex lasting no more than five seconds.

There are plenty of sexual mysteries that we have left unexplored that might require a scientist to explain like parthenogenesis which is what aphids do producing ongoing generations without any fertilizing or a laying worker in a honey bee hive that has lost its queen whose unfertilized eggs will hatch but only into drones. We are not talking about any human babies that might have come along to the applause of the scarlet velvet mite. And there are also critters living around the homestead that we didn't consider for fear of becoming tedious like squirrels and turtles and chipmunks and frogs who each strive in this life to create ongoing life but once you have discussed the sex life of goats, anything else would indeed be an anticlimax.

Those Human Beings, Part 4

HANK

I just happened to be standing on the other side of Main Street having emerged from the Country Store watching a couple walking hand in hand along the opposite side walk. They were obviously tourists, probably just arrived at the newly created B&B down the street and out for a look-see at the nice little Vermont village that they had spotted on the map and checked out in the guide books. It featured a large central green with a church at one end and a country store at the other; a handsome turreted brick library and town hall; a collection of large, gabled and porched wooden houses, one of which had been claimed by the B&B; a stream wending through the middle of it in a narrow valley all enclosed by wooded hillsides.

You could tell they were tourists. They looked scrubbed, laundered and coiffed and were walking without purpose gazing about as they walked. A nice, all-American couple come to Vermont for a quiet weekend. As they reached the corner where the green meets the library, they hesitated somewhat as an old man coming down a side street seemed to be focused on them. He was 100ft away and still coming and beginning to yell unintelligible somethings. The couple froze and stared as if magnetized by the man. He had a massive round bowling ball of a head accentuated by his baldness and set off by wayward clumps and tufts of gray hair poking out on the sides. The head sat on a bull neck and a wide chest. He had on a used-to-be white T-shirt which allowed white chest hair to erupt from underneath the collar. On his face were a pair of glasses thicker than the bottoms of Coke bottles held together by layers of masking tape at the bridge and sitting lopsided at an angle askew and magnifying his eyes so that the whites appeared to be the size of the lenses. One eye, half-blind and filmed over as a result of a boyhood accident with an ox whip, seemed to be on its own meandering off to the side.

This was Hank and he was coming right at them. I was already familiar with the man and had an inkling of the possibilities but stood there just as amazed as the luckless couple. He commenced waving his arms all over and hollering at them so that now you could make out some of what he was saying. You goddamn flatlanders always snooping around bringing your flatland money buying up all the good land. What are you people looking for anyway? Don't you have any work to do? What the hell are you doing here? He was getting closer looking like a homicidal maniac just escaped from the asylum and the couple, frozen like deer in the headlights, suddenly broke free and fled, presumably to never come back arriving home to tell their friends to watch out for the lunatics populating Vermont.

That was Hank and I can state that he was not a lunatic but he was perhaps the most unusual and unforgettable human being I have ever known. There are countless Hank stories and herein I will pass on a synopsis – highlights as it were – of his career. His other main characteristic besides his formidable looks, was his excruciatingly loud and unstoppable voice. He poured it at you like the overflow off the dam at flood time. At full volume, not looking for a word in return, he pounded you with verbiage until you found yourself drowning and looking frantically for a lifesaver. I feel that I owe Hank one thing in relation to this topic and that is I learned how to take leave of my middle class manners, my sense of courtesy and politeness in social situations and say goodbye; I've got other things to do beside listen to you. That turned out to be a lesson well learned with many long-winded locals but of course that wouldn't phase Hank in the least – he would still be yammering at you as you got into your vehicle. He would talk at you through the glass so that you felt compelled to lower the window. He would grab the door top with both hands and howl at you through the window, spittle flying in all directions. He would hold on and start walking as you engaged the clutch. He would be trotting and then running holding on and trumpeting into your left ear as you accelerated delirious to escape but hoping that he wouldn't slip under the wheels.

It would be an unforgettable experience your first exposure to Hank. I walked into a chain saw repair shop one day. There were no customers inside but the two proprietors were going on in tones of disbelief: "Who is that guy, do you think? Never seen the like of it. Or heard the like, you mean. Oh yeah, what a loudmouth. Do you think he's nuts? What was he talking about anyway?" I hadn't seen him leave but I just knew it could only be Hank they were discussing. They had stopped their work and were agitated and excited in the aftermath. Until you became acclimatized, the man was quite a shock to the system.

My first Hank encounter involved car parts. One of his cash-making sidelines involved collecting down and out automobiles in a sidehill former pasture and parting them out. I was looking for something for one of my forlorn vehicles and he sent me off to his 'junk yard' to search for myself. I returned empty handed and we, let's just say it was a carburetor I needed, headed upstairs to the 'carburetor room'. To set the stage here, we need to know that Hank owned one of the biggest houses in the village. Situated right on the green, it was a massive wooden structure, three stories tall with attic dormers that had been built 100 years before by someone with high ambitions and deep pockets. Hank had turned it into a repository for car parts. To get to the carburetor room with its fuel pumps and gas tanks, we passed the room loaded with engines, then the transmission room and then the room with rear ends and wheels. Everything was oily or greasy and the house reeked of gasoline and old engines. On top of this, the house had no hot water system. It had no shower, no bathtub and the only available water came in cold from a spigot above the kitchen sink. Any hot water had to come out of a pot off the wood cook stove. As a result of that visit, from which I came home with nothing, I heard from a friend that Hank had proclaimed widely and loudly, referring to myself: " That sonofabitch could steal the tits off a bull." But meanwhile searching for the carburetor I needed, he had reduced me to a formless pulp with blather. Remember that this is the first time I've ever encountered the man and he is machine gunning me with information and the only item I was able to resurrect from that scrum of language was that he said "My wife weren't no Indian." That struck me as mighty strange that out of nowhere to someone who had no idea of local history, personal histories, social connections or anything else about him or the town, he drops this nugget on me completely out of context. After that I heard him say the same thing again as a mantra and eventually assumed it meant that she was indeed an Indian and it was just another head scratcher – So what?

That wife, Indian or no, was long gone by then and Hank lived in the house among the automotive rubble with his two sons. One, who Hank endlessly proclaimed to be "the smartest man in town", did automobile repair and bodywork in a garage behind the house. He may have been that smart but it was hard to tell because he had a verbal tic which manifested as every fucking third word – as in 'That effing asshole, he's such an effing fool, don't effing know nothing, he ought to effing go jump in the effing river' – on and on semi-automatic at 60 effings per minute. The other son was a lost soul perhaps congenitally disabled or otherwise abled, who for a time could have been taken for the town's mascot. He would spend most of his fair-weather time hanging out in front of the Country Store hoping for treats and relaying cryptic messages in a whisper to incoming patrons. Messages like – mary jones, mary jones CR268 or phil smith BF397, BF397. He had learned everyone's names and memorized them along with their license plate numbers and with this information, he would greet you on the sidewalk across from the green. He was harmless and people were friendly with him and nobody minded and he was a village fixture until Hank died and the State took him away.

Hank cut, split and trucked firewood and along with selling car parts somehow accumulated gobs of money which he kept hidden away, cash only. We know this because there had been brewing a low-level range war with the neighbor next door over who exactly owned the alley between them until one day number one son sauntered over there carrying a shoe box containing multithousands of dollars and bought the house outright then and there. Figure that the village green only featured a half-dozen houses and now Hank owned two of them. This led to an interesting confrontation when one winter the movies came to town. It was to be a tale set in pre-industrial New England featuring horse and sleigh trotting through the snowflakes around a classical Vermont village green. There presented only one slight problem. In front of and to the side of Hank's houses very visible from the green were various automotive relics, some usable and others permanently parked. And no, he would not be so kind as to move them so they could shoot the horse and sleigh trotting through the snow, which by the way, they had to create artificially and blow onto the street given that the winter had turned contrary on them along with Hank. That is, he might consider the possibility if they would compensate him for his time and trouble. He had those smartass flatlanders by the short hairs and squeezed them for all they were worth before finally relenting and dragging all evidence of the age of the automobile around to the back.

Despite the wealth and the obvious access to all things automotive, Hank drove around in an ancient bright orange VW beetle. The windshield was cracked and shivered and the muffler never fixed and as he bombed about squinting though those magnifying glass lenses and craning over the steering wheel until his nose was a couple of inches from the glass trying to see something, anything, he seemed the personification of reckless endangerment. But he rarely ran into anything although one day he rammed the bonnet of the beetle under the tail of his own wood truck while trying to catch up with his son driving. He was wedged, the bonnet was stoved and after extricating, he discarded the tortured metal and motored around without it, the engine of course being in the back. Curiously the sheriff never bothered him about silly things like inspection stickers. Curious because there is something about habitual offenders who will never listen to reason and display an aura of power and stubbornness that leads the police to just give up and shrug shoulders like you might with a big old screwball dog that no matter what you do or say, still keeps chasing cars down the road. The game warden didn't seem to want to mess with him either. He was known to hunt down the elusive white-tail using the orange VW as his weapon of choice. Regardless of the season, spotting a deer peacefully grazing in a roadside hay field, he would veer off pounding through the ditch and accelerate across the grass slewing and racketing the old beetle on the chase to bring home the venison.

He couldn't be intimidated; he couldn't be reasoned with; he couldn't be changed; he couldn't be nudged or shoved off of whatever position he was taking – he just stood like a stump and bellowed. These characteristics might possibly form the definition of crazy and in some other circumstance he might have been hauled off to spend his days in an institution. However, rather than crazy, he could be judged as the essence, the distillation of a natural man – all howling ego unencumbered by social convention or public opinion. Damn the torpedoes – full speed ahead and get out of my way. Many locals tried their best to stay out of his way like one whose family when they heard the bleat of that VW coming their way, locked the front door and hid quiet as mice in the back room until he would leave. But, try this episode on for size: As I walked into the foyer of the town gas station one day where there was almost always a posse of worthies hanging out, I heard the unmistakable Hank and there he was wielding his penis like a cudgel and slamming it onto the counter like a butcher with a hunk of sausage. It's a worthless piece of meat. Whap! It died on me. Whap! The goddamn thing is broken. Whap! It don't work no more. Whap! Needless to say – not a performance you are likely to see every day but just one more scene out of Hank's multi-act play. I heard later from someone who skidded in logs for Hank to cut and split, that he came to the landing one morning moaning in pain from a kidney stone lodged in his penis. Perhaps this was related to his performance at the gas station but this man watched Hank take care of the problem with a screwdriver – a slim long-handled screwdriver that was used to adjust carburetor idle and mixture screws. Crying from the pain, he pushed it in, twisted it and popped out the kidney stone along with a drizzle of blood.

Hank was well into his seventies approaching eighty at this time and was still a bull for work and a glutton for punishment. He exuded force and energy and worked all day on the landing sawing, splitting and loading fire wood for sale. Even if it were below zero, he would be there at daybreak with the two sons haranguing the skidder man to godamnit get in gear and bring that first hitch out here or he'd pick up the chain saw and lead the way into the woods to start cutting. He wasn't a monster. He wasn't a fool – he was just a human outrage. He wanted things done just so and demanded compliance not through physical threat but by browbeating into submission. He deferred to the elder son, 'smartest guy in town', but harangued the younger unfortunate constantly into pulling his weight. He gave his customers fair measure and demanded that his pickup be stacked exactly so as to yield the same each delivery. He transacted all his business in cash and was known to be honest. His skidder man said that he didn't ever bother to keep track of logs brought out because he knew that Hank would, and then every Friday peel off 20s and 50s from his wad to pay him off. If you were around the log landing at lunch time when he and the sons would head in with the third or fourth load of the day, he might ask you to lunch, the contents of which never varied. He fired up the cook stove, lifted out a lid and replaced it with a cast iron frying pan, larded the pan till it showed a half inch of bubbling fat and then fried potatoes. The potatoes had to be 'Green Mountains' and the cuts were always French sliced slim and identical every day.

In amongst his perpetual outwash of verbiage came occasional words of wisdom. He used to say that a man "will die just the way he operates" – an inscrutable piece of philosophy – but further that he claimed that a relative would "die by inches" because the damn fool was always diddling and piddling around. And lo and behold it came to pass that the man withered away remorselessly with one of those neurological diseases like Lou Gehrig's. But Hank, bless his soul, went out as he lived, with a bang. Gruesome it was and extraordinary just like the man. In front of his stove, frying those green mountains, he had some kind of a seizure or heart attack and collapsed face first on the hot surface of the cook stove and frazzled to death.

The state relocated the hapless son after Hank's passing but he didn't adjust and soon passed away himself and the remaining son remained the 'smartest man' but the enormous life force and power emanating from Hank like a howling turbine had gone and the lights began to dim and go out.

OCTOBER

CIDER TIME

When contemplating setting up a homesteading life somewhere, one of the questions to ask is what does this land have to offer. Does the area produce some bounty that goes unused or unrecognized? There are black walnuts galore through a large swath of the U.S. There are choke cherries and wild plums in the drier northwest and huckleberries in the wet. There are wild blueberries in Maine. There is wild or 'gone wild' citrus in Florida. There are mushrooms to be had in the more humid zones. In Vermont there are apples. There are wild apples; there are tame apples; there are abandoned apples; there are tended apples; there are backyard apples; there are farmstead apples; there are commercial apples; there are roadside apples and there are hillside apples. In the merry month of May when the apple trees are in flower, it is a revelation to see all the trees that you never suspected were there. They are hidden in the brush along the back roads and scattered throughout the cow pastures. They come one by one or in thickets which dazzle during flower time. There are usually five to ten trees planted beside or behind old farmhouses and an occasional hundred tree orchard long since untended but still putting out fruit, tucked away along some sparsely traveled byway. Those apples would be considered as 'tame' whereas the majority of apples we are describing are 'wild'.

Wild Apple

The definition of a wild apple is straightforward – it's an apple grown from a seed. There; that was easy. However, as you might suspect, we might have to do some wrangling over this question. Some say these apples are 'feral' and then what about apples that have 'gone wild'? O.K. 'Feral' I can see might have some basis to it but 'gone wild' is out. Either an apple is grafted or it is grown from a seed. Either it's wild or it's tame. An ancient tree growing all by itself hidden in a grove of puckerbrush but putting out a recognizable apple such as a Wolf River has not 'gone wild' – it is forever tame. Every variety known and named is a clone of its original and is grafted onto some kind of rootstock. This apple we are calling 'tame' – a grafted, named variety. There are too many of these to count. There are many books dedicated to describing and preserving the memory of all these apple names. People are always bringing apples to me so that I can give them a name. Usually I have no idea. There is an inherent contradiction in what I'm saying in that most of these apple names (ie tame apples) began their careers as wild apples - perhaps even as one of the seeds carried west by Johnny Appleseed himself. There is no telling what manner of apple this particular seed might yield but if it turned out to be a good one and better yet, a big one, then your neighbor would want a scion and so would his neighbor and so would everybody else want a tree of their own of old Bill Cortland's apple. It seems extraordinary a snip of branch could be passed through the hands of thousands of people over hundreds of years keeping one particular apple variety thriving throughout the planet. There are old English apples whose origin is lost in antiquity but which are still propagated today like for instance, Ashmead's Kernel. And I am sure there would be many a lost apple that could have been a contender which was left in solitude loved in someone's back forty but unknown to the rest of the world. Nowadays there have emerged new tame apples that did not start their lives as wildings. These introductions from universities or institutes are products of scientific machinations. Botanists at work selecting varieties to cross pollinate in isolation and then planting out dozens of the resultant seeds hoping that maybe one will make it into the commercial market. The Honeycrisp is one of those supertame apples.

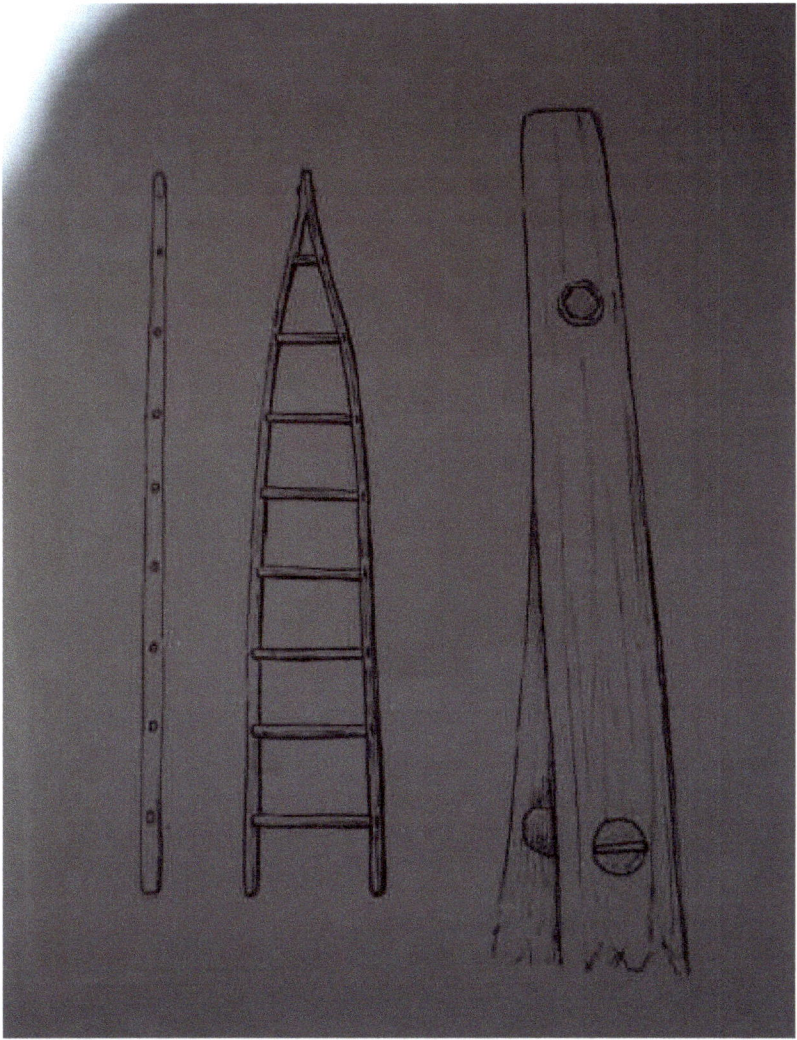

Homestead Solutions #6

An Apple Ladder

Trying to access the fruit on a mature apple tree with a step ladder or a regular extension ladder can become an exercise in frustration or futility. A specially constructed fruit ladder with a pointed top allows you to slide it up through the branches and rest it in a crotch where it will remain stable while you work your way up. You might want two of these ladders to match different sized trees – perhaps one 15ft and another 10ft long. The accompanying drawing shows off a ladder that can be made relatively easily with a chain saw.

Start with a spruce or balsam fir pole about 5" in diameter with relatively little taper for the length you are going for. Skin the bark and drill 1" holes 12" apart (or however far apart you wish your rungs to be) along the length of the pole stopping 12" from the end. Carve a point on the end and run a bolt through 6" from the top. Now chain saw right up the middle and stop before you hit the bolt. The rungs could theoretically be made out of any hardwood – mine are done with ash saplings as close to one inch as I could find so I only needed to pare down the ends to snug fit the holes. Insert the rungs spreading the ladder to fit your own aesthetic. A handy way to insure the rungs stay tight is to split the protruding ends with a chisel and pound in hardwood wedges. Make sure the splits are horizontal to an upright ladder and not vertical so that the pressure of the wedge doesn't split the fir pole.

Apples pack such a wealth of genetic information in its seeds that starting by planting two of them so that they will cross pollinate and continuing to grow them out for several generations and replanting all the resultant seeds, you would have an orchard of dozens of different varieties. These would all be wild apples. They would come in all shapes, sizes, colors and tastes. In my apple wanderings, over the years I have sampled uncountable wild ones and can relate that they can be round, flat or conic; they can be as big as a baseball or as small as a golf ball; they can be yellow, green, russeted, red and/or spotted and striped; and they can be sour, bitter, spicy or sweet. That is to say that you can never tell how a wild apple might taste until you bite into it. Sour definitely predominates but very few are so sour that you won't eat them. Also very rare is an apple that is just tannic or just sweet. Most are combinations of the four characteristics with one or the other predominating. We have one tree growing in front of the chicken coop which produces mountains of apples that taste like mildly sweet water. We have another that tastes like a cup of tea that you mistakenly left three bags in to steep overnight. Every one of them tastes terrific when you encounter it while snowshoeing in January, hanging brown, shriveled, fermented inside its own sack, a frozen mildly alcoholic treat that has somehow avoided the attention of squirrels, bluejays or waxwings.

The idea that all the apples we are here calling 'wild' are actually 'feral' is not without some merit. Apples apparently originated in Eurasia and only arrived in America on the decks of colonists' ships. They would have only brought their favorite varieties with them to plant out in their new home. These apples would already have been 'tame' so we might conclude that the millions of wildings that have established over the centuries are escapees from cultivation or ferals. However, in pursuit of the perfect definition, let's nitpick further and say that feral would only apply to a tame tree that has been left on its own and subsequently swallowed by the surrounding wilderness. The offspring of this feral, from seed deposited here and there by bird or deer or bear or human throwing away an apple core, would then be 'wild'.

There was a well-known cider maker in Vermont that thought so well of wild apples that he applied a penalty surcharge upon his customers if they had any tame apples in their mix brought to press. His name was Herb Ogden and he was not only a cider maker, but a flour miller and a state senator. He was a remarkable man who had been in Normandie during WWII and had returned home with the taste of cidre in his mind, determined to recreate it in Vermont. He built a cider mill/grist mill along the bank of a fast flowing stream and installed a 20ft water wheel to power the whole thing. Now this was well past the age when anybody would ever think of doing such a thing but the result was a dreamscape out of the industrial revolution. Water power ran hydraulic pistons for the cider press; pumps channeling cider this way and that; an elevator evacuating the pomace; a washing tumbler for the cider cloths; the grinder to chew up the apples; a grist mill; and to top it all, a generator which electrified both the mill and his nearby house. The transfer of energy was accomplished with wide belts, some 20ft long, going in all directions spinning drive wheels which he controlled with levers shunting the belts off of one wheel onto the next. It was and is a wonder and should be designated a national historic treasure.

Herb wanted to prove that American wild apples would yield a cidre just as good as the designated cidre apples of France or England. There are classic varieties that have become entrenched in both France and England as 'the' apples for making hard cider. The makers there mix and match to create their own special blends but Herb, although appreciating their product, felt anyone could do the same with American apples. The trucks would line up during cider time loaded with wild apples. Herb would run them over scales and pay by the pound or by the ton. People from all around could make some extra

276

cash in the fall picking up apples to sell to Herb Ogden. That was a big deal in the late 40s and 50s before the modern world intruded and cash was in short supply in backcountry Vermont. He didn't sort them as far as I could see – they just piled into huge wooden bins as they came in where he let them 'sweat' for a time before running them through the mill. He must have figured that each squeeze of a couple of hundred gallons would always represent a wide enough variety of apples so that you wouldn't end up trying to drink excruciatingly sour cider.

I am sure that Herb Ogden did not aspire to sainthood but he has acquired a mythic status among cider people who tend to talk of him in tones of reverence and awe. He was staunch in his opinions about many things and not one to suffer fools. He was re-elected to the state senate many times and if asked if he were going to run again, he would reply "I am not running; I am standing for re-election." If you just happened to show up at the mill with some Macintosh apples in your mix, he would sadly shake his head at the deplorable ignorance of the human race and then charge you extra to squeeze them. It is hard to resist the teachings of such an apple master and we took his lessons to heart. As an example of how savvy he was, I'll tell you we were sitting on a grassy side-bank talking with the kids waiting our turn at the mill, when he walked up to us and with no introduction or small-talk said: "You folks don't have a television do you?"

Before moving to Gingerbrook, we were wandering the back roads picking up apples wherever and getting them squeezed at Ogden's mill. In those days, used bourbon barrels were cheap and available and many hard cider makers used them to age their juice. We put a spigot in the end of one, filled it at the mill and sold fresh cider out of the back of Buster on town greens and farmer's markets. People loved that but certain town cops didn't. You'll need a permit to do that here, boy. Where can I get one? You can't. There ain't no such thing. However we were soon occupied looking for a homestead and it sealed the deal at Gingerbrook when browsing through the thick puckerbrush, I kept bumping into more wild apple trees.

Apple trees enjoy as much sun as they can get and are not happy as these weren't to be surrounded and overshadowed by a rampant young forest. The first step was to liberate them. There were and are approximately 30 wild trees on the homestead and they came out squinting into the sunshine looking mighty forlorn. They seemed all about the same age – I guessed about 50 years old – so they were large trunked but with plenty of dead branches. Step two was to cut those off and feed them to the cook stove. Step three and all succeeding steps was and were feeding those trees. I have mentioned this previously but will repeat it here, that if you are tending apple trees for the purpose of making cider, forget all the fine points that are detailed in hundreds of books of pruning, shaping, opening the canopy to air and light etc, and just feed that tree all it will stand. If you had access to an unlimited supply of classy compost, that would be all you need. You could just stand back and watch your trees boom. Now I'm talking about full grown trees here. Don't get me wrong – if you are starting with babies, there would be plenty of those finer points to consider. However, we don't have that much compost and that which we do have goes into the vegetable garden, so we did things like pasturing meat chickens around the trees and applying judicious amounts of manure in the spring but as I've said before, the real breakthrough was when we started tying our milk cow to the big wild trees.

Pruning is a real concern when applied to commercial eating apples. There the goal is to produce not as many apples as possible but as many perfect apples as possible. Pruning the tree wide open yields many fewer apples but more chance for larger, immaculate apples. If you are making cider, you simply want more total apple. When we are harvesting our wild apples, we cover the ground with tarps and shake the apples down. Picking them up and filling bags is a monotonous affair so I began to think, while on my knees under one of our biggest wild trees, and wonder exactly how many apples were there on this tree. They were countless so I decided to count them. I looked around and counted here and there and decided that there were 10 apples on average in every square foot. These apples averaged about two inches in diameter. Then I measured the extent of the apple fall and came up with a circle having a diameter of 40ft. I will remind you that this one is a very big tree! So πRsquared would get you to around 1200 square feet. Let's deduct 100ft for the area in the center around the multiple trunks and do the math – and the grand total is 11,000 apples! I don't feel this to be an exaggeration given that every square foot could maximize at 36 apples and many in the count featured more than ten. Now it's not my back or knees that I'm featuring here but fertility and what is possible with wild apple trees. That particular tree came out spindly and forsaken 30 years ago from the puckerbrush and without ever being pruned but with twice yearly visitations by the cow, it is producing crops like that every other year.

Tree of 11,000 apples in May

It is a task for a giant to shake free all the apples off such a tree so we resort also to a 'panking pole'. This is apparently a British term which I appropriated from an English friend. It is a fifteen foot pole with a hook on the end with which you reach and shake individual branches. While approaching a certain tree preparatory to shaking, I often fall into reveries like this as I decide what to do: 'To pank or not to pank, that is the question. Whether tis nobler to suffer the scrapes and jabs of outrageous branchings or stay to earth and pank like an Englishman'. Either way, not all the apples come down at once and some trees ripen their fruit over time so it's judicious to shake or pank two or three separate times over perhaps a two week period.

Before and after coming to Gingerbrook, we passed a portion of every autumn searching the highways and byways for miles around looking for apples wild and tame. We negotiated with land owners who often said "Sure, go ahead and pick em"; or "Well, the wife likes to make a pie" and we would pick the apples bringing in a half bushel to the wife and going home with five grain sacks full; or "Can you trade me some cider?" and we would go back a few days later with a gallon jug. We started selling fresh cider in one gallon milk jugs to selected stores. We discovered that the general consuming public believes in 'sweet' cider so we found that tempering the wild flavors with a percentage of friendly tame apples made our customers happier. Our cider offerings were always distinctive however – the zip and zing of the wild made them quite unlike any commercial cider. Some people loved it and one man told me he couldn't tell it from vinegar. We did our apple cruising as a family. The kids were being home-schooled and we combined gathering with mathematics by devising a selection by number system. "There's a tree. Shall we pick it?" How to decide whether to get this tree or wait for the next. Let's do it mathematically. Assign a number from one to ten in each of five categories, add them all together and divide by five. If the number is six or above, we go for it; below that, we don't. 1. Quantity: a whole lot, 10; none. 0. 2. Quality: really yummy, 10; spit it out, 0. 3. Climability: nicely spaced branches. 10; a veritable thicket of twisted, spiny branches, 0. 4. Access: close to the road, no ditch, no fence, 10; barbed wire fence, high on a hillside surrounded by vicious looking bulls. 0. 5. Surface tension: a mowed lawn, 10; a roadside ditch chock full of blackberries, 0. This was amusing and also an exercise in democracy. There would be four or five of us and each had his/her opinion and vote but we had to settle on one number for each category. It led to debate, compromise and apples.

It was in the newspaper. Somebody across the river in New Hampshire was advertising an old cider mill for sale. Herb Ogden was retiring. We already knew that apples were going to play a big part in our homestead economy so why not have our own cider mill? It was a curious little two story house framed around the press, small enough so that a log truck could swing it up and set it down right where we wanted it. That was up against the steep bank cut into the hill by the road which I described earlier, so that the apples could come in high and the juice could go out low.

This press employed a technology that is thousands of years old. I have seen pictures of olive oil presses displayed in Mediterranean museums that show rigs that are essentially identical. The moving parts in those were carved wooden screws whereas ours uses steel screws six foot long and three inches in diameter. They are contained in a square frame of massive timbers that, as big as they are, would still crack under the pressure without the addition of two steel clamps holding it top and bottom. These clamps give a clue as to how old the press is. They are made from 1" steel rod and you can see that they were blacksmith welded. That might put them back into the 19th century when in a place like Vermont, there were cider mills in just about every town and machine shops made cider screws by the hundreds. They mostly disappeared into the maw of the military machine during the two world wars and those that were left retired when faced with hydraulic pumps and pistons. These screws get turned down by manpower and people are always asking me what sort of tonnage is involved here. I say, these are big screws and this is a four foot bar and I am putting into it all the force I can muster, so what do you think? They think all over the place but everybody agrees that the tonnage is undoubtedly immense.

The unit of commerce at the mill is the 100lb grain bag into which fit 70 –80lbs of apples. Each press takes 10 – 12 bags and yields 60 –70 gallons of cider. That is the typical yield but it can vary considerably depending on the apples. Tame apples that are orchard raised with fertilizer and irrigation might on occasion give twice the juice as the same quantity of small, gnarly wild apples. But in this case, more juice just means more water. I often keep a hydrometer at the mill to test the sugar content and the potential alcohol of competing ciders – the average is 6% but some wildings yield up to 8% and that tame just mentioned would test at only 4%. Besides the pressure exerted and the apples presented, there is one more factor determining the ultimate yield of any one squeeze and that is the fineness of the grind. The mill as it was arrived with a grinder powered by an electric motor that was made of a chunk of wood peppered with nails. That seemed like a genius homestead kind of rig but the only way it worked was with you leaning over its mouth putting all your weight onto a persuader.

That was less than satisfactory. You can order a grinder from a cider supply but the Homesteader's Bible does not approve of such so I noticed that those 'real' grinders actually slice the apples rather than beating them to death with nails. So I fabricated one out of a maple round with help from a lathe, embedded with sharpened steel slicers (see diagram) and hooked it up to a three horse motor. This works pretty well. You won't get as much out of your apples as a commercial cider mill which uses a hammer mill but your cider will be prettier. A hammer mill will just about obliterate your apples. It will hammer them down to the cellular level which is the reason commercial ciders are always dark brown and cloudy. But, the finer the grind, the greater the yield. We are not maximizing the quantity by slicing the apples; we're just making nicer cider.

Homestead Solutions #7

Apple Grinder

Start with a chunk of hardwood – preferably apple – but maple is good. The size is arbitrary – size your own to suit yourself but I'll give you the measurements I used by guess and by golly as a possible template. The final round is 6" diameter so start with a chunk of firewood at least 8" by more or less 10" long to put on the lathe. Drill a 1" hole through the middle and insert a 1" steel shaft 16" long. That shaft you have prepared in advance welding a 3" circle of ¼" steel to the 13" mark, grinding it smooth and countersinking four holes to accommodate large wood screws. Put it on the lathe with a couple of light screws to hold it while you cut a circle ¼" deep in the back end to accommodate the drive circle, then pull out the shaft and put it in the other way and screw it in with four big ones this time. When the round is smooth and down to 6", put it on the table saw against the fence so that you'll be cutting into it at an angle to the round – say 30o – and slice a kerf every 2". For the cutters, I used angle iron from an old bed frame which was just the same width as the saw kerf, drilled right through them into the wood and held them in place with stainless screws. Getting the cutting edges sharp and exactly even is a tricky task but you will figure out a method.

You see in the accompanying diagram that there are no additional bearings in the wooden box that the grinder runs in. The sides of the box are made from 2" maple which holds up well with a little help from some added vegetable oil from time

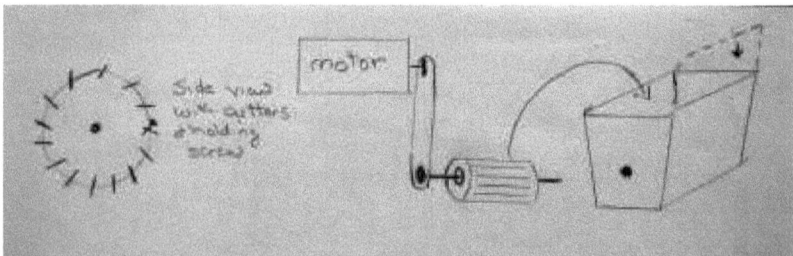

to time. To assure a fine enough grind, I lower a tapered board into the back of the box until it just touches the blades and as that wears away, I reposition it at the beginning of each season.

We had no plans to turn the cider mill into a public institution, but that's what happened. An unconscionable short time after the eccentric little mill building was in place, we got a knock on the door to the shop which surprised us to begin with because, of the few people that we had come to know in the area, none of them would have bothered to knock and standing there was a big man with a slow, deep voice saying that he had heard we had a cider mill. That was our first small town inkling that people out there were actually talking about us. That guy wanted to fill a barrel (50 gals) so to be neighborly, I said why not? He actually wanted to fill two and has been back every year for 30 to fill those barrels and many others. That man just leaned against a stone and started it rolling and it gathered momentum of its own until it seemed like there was no stopping it. We didn't advertise or solicit; we just never said no. We charged a minimal amount and we liked the idea of being a community resource. We had been putting up apple juice for ourselves and once the word got out that this was relatively simple way (more on that later) of providing the real thing for your kids, the back-to-the-landers were lining up to use the cider mill, and the alcohol/barrel boys weren't far behind. There was no shelter for anybody but myself under that tiny roof and as each season progressed, things not only got colder, they got muddier and icier. Vehicles got stuck; children froze and whined and cried; a troop of female lawyers-to- be from the local law school showed up in their skirts and high heels and turned blue and lost their shoes in the mud; an

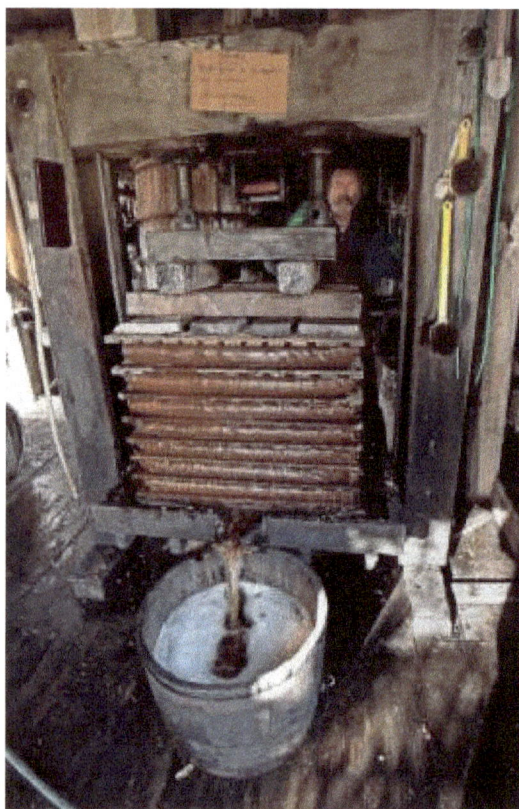

old boy, who wanted to come down from the top of the bank where a ramp was perched for rolling the apples down to the grinder, lost his footing, slipped and bounced down the slope to end up on his back right at my feet where he just lay looking up at me and said very slowly – "Bob, I want you to promise me one thing. What's that Stub? That one day you will put in some stairs here."

He was called Stub and he is now gone but his staircase is there. Stubby's stairs. They are comprised of one section of an iron fire escape that Will picked up in the city. The mill not only needed some stairs; it was obvious that it needed a whole set-up - a whole new building. We reduced the little cider shack to just the frame of the press, left it right where it was and put up the building around it. Once the upper floor joists were in place, the press was winched up hanging to allow a bottom floor to be planked in and then set back down where it sits today. It's still the coldest place in the universe during the first week in November and since there is so much water involved in the cider making process, the floor sometimes resembles a skating rink, but nobody harks back with nostalgia to the good old days of rain, snow and mud. Everything involved with the press except for the four pieces of steel doing the work, is made of wood. This is purposeful so that anything that needs making, I can make and anything that needs repairing, I've got the spare parts. That includes the grinder which has broken apart before under the strain. To replace it requires a chunk of maple firewood, access to a lathe and a day's work.

Barter has always played a big part in our relations with the community. Mostly this takes the shape of a work exchange – you give me a day and I'll give you a day. However, other barters of different sorts happen all the time. People who come by to help often prefer product to cash. Maple syrup seems to exert more attraction than money. It's surprising who will barter no matter how improbable. It undoubtedly helps to be in a place like Vermont where everybody seems to feel that they are a part of the country life but we have bartered with dentists, with doctors, with machinists for shop time; with cabinet makers for shop time, and with heavy equipment operators. At the cider mill, for people who want to stay within the apple economy, we will take apples in trade for a pressing. For instance; if you wish to press out 10 bags, you could leave us two in payment or if it's more suitable, we will accept the equivalent percentage of your cider. We often will trade a pressing with someone who helps us pick up apples. Following the example of Herb Ogden, we also will buy any apples you wish to bring in – as long as they are not orchard apples. This is a stage setting ripe for drama. One hefty youngster who was selling apples to buy gasoline for his car, got it into his mind that he was going to bring in the heaviest bag of apples the world had ever seen. He broke the hanging scale, left triumphant and I never saw him again. There were two old guys in their seventies who through me as the middle man, got into a competition to see who could bring in the most apples. One of them had an egg route and as he drove around making his deliveries in his tiny old car, he would spot a roadside tree, pull over and pick them up. Every bag he brought weighed exactly the same – 25 lbs. We stopped using the scale after a while and by the end of the season which lasted approximately six weeks, he had totaled more than 2000lbs! A ton of apples. He wanted to get to a ton and he wanted even more to beat the other guy. The other guy kept asking me what was the poundage of the first guy and would leave looking determined also in a tiny old car. It was touch and go towards the end but he got so close that I cooked the books and declared, beyond the realm of impossibility, they had ended in an exact tie.

Most everybody loves fresh cider and we now had the means to produce plenty so we thought to make a little homestead business selling to stores. We did that for a while, buying gallon milk jugs in bulk from the local dairy but we didn't appreciate the backtalk – 'Your cider's gone bad. You have to take it back.' After a couple of days, unsold cider would start to ferment. We said – that's not bad, cider never goes 'bad', it just goes better. We weren't going to put preservatives in it and I didn't clean the press with chlorinated cleansers as did commercial cideries – I just scrubbed with a stiff brush and plenty of water – and there were no sprayed apples in the mix, so naturally this cider was going to ferment faster than the other stuff. It never goes bad unless you don't care – it goes first to fizzy, then to hard and then to vinegar – all good. However, we didn't like the interaction so we began to ponder the idea of selling juice instead. We had been making apple juice for the kids and ourselves for quite a while already. We heated it in five gallon pots on the cookstove and preserved it in not only canning jars but any used jar with a sealing lid that we had collected. We were making 50 gallons a year that way before deciding to make it for the public. It is a disarmingly simple procedure: have your jars clean and warm; heat the cider to 180°; fill to the very rim of the jar and screw on the lid. That's it. It now really never goes 'bad'. It will keep in that jar practically forever. It no longer has the exact charm of fresh cider but if you're mixing in wild apples and you're not using commercial orchard apples, that apple juice sure doesn't taste like the stuff you used to get in the supermarket. Now we buy new jars by the pallet load and sticky labels by the thousand and make the juice upstairs at the mill in a maple syrup pan. I am very particular about the mix of apples that go into each batch of juice. I taste all the different types to make sure that the batch will not be too sweet or too sour or tasteless. Every batch is a distinct blend because the apples available are always changing and I make sure that there is a strong percentage of wild apples in each one.

Once you've got cider, it's a short leap to make vinegar. Remember that we are still following the dicta of the Homesteader's Bible which says that anything that is possible

289

to do, you should do for yourself. Vinegar (vin aigre Fr.) easily falls under that heading. It will make itself without any help from you if you merely leave a jar of cider sitting around without a cap. Untainted apples come with their own yeast riders, saddled up and ready to bulldog. Yeast feeds on sugar and will multiply at an extraordinary rate riding that sugar hard till it's all gone, leaving behind a wasteland or a promised land depending upon your viewpoint of alcohol. The alcohol, in what would now qualify as hard cider, does then indeed become a promised land for another creature called acetobacter. Yeast is a fungus, but this one is an animal – a bacteria. Acetobacter, like yeast, happens to be everywhere so that even if you do not intend it, he can find his way into anything mildly alcoholic and turn it into vinegar. He eats alcohol and excretes acetic acid. After your cider becomes vinegar, it has nowhere to go except to become stronger vinegar or, and I'm not sure how this happens, it may transform into weak strange watery liquid if you leave it out in an open container for a goodly length of time.

If you are intent on making your own vinegar, you could just let the cider sit out to collect its own acetobacter and take your chances or you could acquire some 'mother' from an established vinegar with a good reputation. Most commercial vinegars, besides being made from peels and cores left over from the sauce business, have been distilled – that means that there are no longer any live organisms in it. Real vinegar is still alive and to prove it will produce a gelatinous floating layer that is called 'mother'. Mother is fine to eat but most people can't get past the yuk factor and prefer to strain it out. Our own 'house' mother is now long established in our barrels and vats where it reforms continuously and then sinks to the bottom requiring an occasional clean out It has the quality, unknown to most people, of drying out miraculously into translucent paper-thin sheets. Our vinegar vats are four feet in diameter so if you are careful, you can slide out a four foot circular mother, lay it out nicely to dry and have material that can be used like stained glass. It has a wonderful amber color somewhat equivalent to looking through a glass of orange pekoe. One person made a lamp shade out of it which warms up when he turns on the light and perfumes the room with eau de vin aigre.

We use our vinegar for all the usual things – salads, pickles, stir fries and we also drink it in switchels and shrubs as I've mentioned earlier. The idea came up to sell it along with the juice from friends who thought we should share it with the rest of the world. Herb Ogden had a vinegar vat that was as tall as he and which he had been keeping filled with overflows from his pressings for countless years. When he retired, I offered to buy it but he said it went with the mill, so I commissioned two vats 4ft x 4ft built from a local tub maker. This man was in his eighties and had apprenticed with his father making sap buckets and stocktanks and all sorts of containers out of wood. They were doing this either before these products were available made of steel or they were too expensive for the locals to buy. Things going the way they do, he had lately been specializing in hot tubs.

The vinegar vats are made from white pine and they hold about 300 gallons apiece. The cider goes in there straight from the press and becomes vinegary after one year of aging but is really good only after two or three years. It gets transferred from the vat into oak barrels that stay in the house to further age before we bottle it. This would be a considerably different product from commercial vinegar which is made from peels and cores left behind by the slice and sauce industries and transformed under temperature and pressure control in a very short time. It turned out that two vats were not going to be enough. We needed more and after studying the originals, I thought that, with help from a friend with woodworking machines, we could make our own.

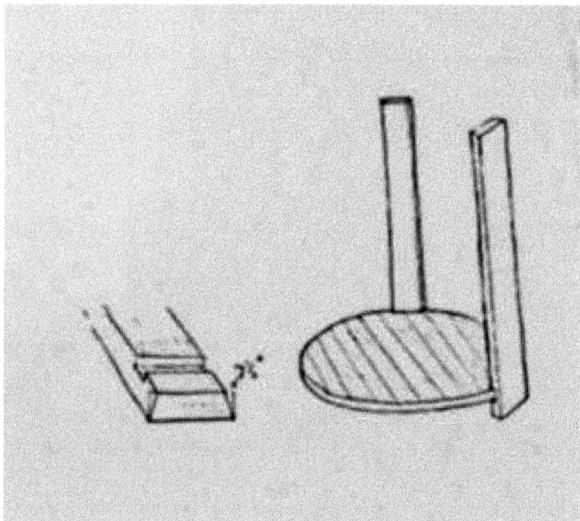

Homestead Solutions #8

Vinegar Vat

Our homestead cider vinegar is aged in wood. It passes a year or two or three in pine vats located in the cider mill where it freezes in the winter and warms in the summer. We hired our first two vats made by an old time cooper but when it became apparent that we needed more, I decided that, with the help of a friend who owned some wood-working machines, it didn't seem too difficult to make our own. They are made from pine 2x6s cut straight and planed smooth. The vat can be any size – the mathematics are just different but the procedure is the same. Figure the number of staves you will need by dividing the width of each into your proposed circumference. A 4ft wide vat has a 12ft circumference which will need 24 six inch staves. The staves need to be beveled. Divide 24 into 360o to get 15o for each joint. Each joint has two sides so the beveled edges on the staves are 7 1/2o. The pieces that form the bottom must be perfectly square and straight. Biscuit or peg them together, draw a four foot circle then cut and bevel and smooth the edges so they will go in snug to a groove you will now cut into the side staves 2" up from the bottom. The groove must be slightly smaller than the thickness of the bottom so that you will have to beat the staves into position with a rubber mallet. Now the whole thing is tightened down until you think its going to implode with four steel bands made from ½" rod bent, threaded and nutted. You can't ever crank these too tight – they just bite into the soft pine staves.

We succeeded in building three more out of our own pine in a futile attempt to keep everybody satisfied. There is a whole population who take vinegar for health reasons and ours qualifies for its beyond-organic essence of the wild. Many of these people have either read or have heard of the famous Dr. Jarvis. He practiced in Barre, Vermontt during the 50's and promulgated the idea that vinegar and honey would keep you healthy, wealthy and wise. One man comes to visit us every year from Maine to refill his empty bottles. One year a film crew from Japan arrived at the cider mill because they were looking for authentic seeming footage to illustrate the life and times of Dr. Jarvis. The theories of the good doctor had apparently spawned a vinegar health craze in Japan. They had come to Barre figuring to find a hotbed of Jarvis enthusiasts in his home town. After they started asking around and received nothing but blank looks and who's that? from the locals, they tracked down somebody who directed them to us.

The vinegar vats are a catchall for wild apples. Anything that doesn't go into apple juice, ends up in the vinegar. The acidity level in commercial vinegar is standardized by adding water but we don't attempt to know what the acidity level is or to standardize it. This makes following pickle recipes more fun than usual, but trial and error will get you in the right place.

Apples are more or less 50% juice so if you grind up 1000lbs of apples in a batch, you will be left with 500lbs of dry apple cake. It is called 'pomace' and it comes off the press on racks squeezed down to one inch thick over an area three feet square. This is a valuable commodity and you have to figure how to do with it. In the good old days when everybody in New England drank nothing but hard cider all the time before the temperance movement caught up with them, they used the pomace to make more cider that was less hard and fed it to their children. That was called 'small cider'. It was made by soaking the pomace overnight in water and then pressing it again to extract the last remnants of apple sugar. This was then fermented and was apparently better than drinking water. Herb Ogden, in his amazing time machine, dumped his racks of pomace into a conveyer/elevator which deposited it upstairs from where it could be shoveled out of a big door down onto a truck. He advertised it as fertilizer and charged by the ton. I pick up the racks, carry them to a Dutch door and flip the pomace out. You can imagine that by the end of the cider season there accumulates quite a pile up against the side of the building. The pile then commences to ferment and gets quite hot. It begins to steam in the cold air and melts off the early winter snow. When Mickey and Maud and whoever else were still spending their winters outside. Maya and I would dig into that warm pile all winter and transport pomace to them in plastic sleds. I can testify that cows, mules, horses and goats will eat it with gusto but give it to a pig, and he will snuffle it, push it around with his snout and then look up at you as if to say – "What is this stuff? Cardboard? Where are the apples?"

Another winter later on when the pile was left to itself, I walked by in late February and noticed what seemed to be the signs of a rodeo having taken place there. Upon closer investigation, I saw a hole like a doorway in the side of the pile. I crawled in. It was like an igloo. The outside layer was frozen and the entire insides had been eaten out through the hole. The culprits were the deer. I could see their hoof prints and a path beaten absolutely straight across the lower pasture and into the woods. Most amazing about this story is when the snow melted and before the grass started to green, you could look across the pasture and see an arrow straight line of black. It was an entire winter's worth of deer pellets deposited on their way back and forth from the pomace pile. Pomace pellets! That was a while ago and now I remove the pomace as soon as it happens. It flips out the door into a garden cart and I wheel it down to the pasture where it gets forked about under apple trees and onto the grass. Horses and cows are stationed there during cider time so they eat whatever they want and the rest fertilizes the environs and radiates apple seeds by the millions.

Every now and again, there happens a season with no apples. One of those years we went searching far off into northern Vermont and encountered an apple wonderland. It was enclosed as part of a cow pasture but there wasn't any grass there because the apple trees grew so thickly together they cut out the light. It was an apple forest! All wild trees, perhaps several hundred, packed together branches intertwined and completely open underneath because the cows had pruned up as far as they could reach. We shouldered out a truckload from that enchanted forest but I bring it up here because I am musing that it would not be difficult to recreate here in that lower pasture. All those seeds. I haven't mowed there in a few years and there are apple trees coming up all over. Horses don't seem to like eating apple leaves but cows certainly do, however there is only one cow wandering around there now and these trees could grow right past her. I like the thought – the Gingerbrook Apple Forest.

Wild apples have no trouble migrating without human intervention. Occasionally I will come upon a large pile of bear shit or a smaller version deposited by a raccoon, both of them packed solid with apple seeds; or I watch a chipmunk load up his cheek pouches from the pomace pile; or I see ten bright green apple sprouts emerging from last fall's horse dung. The existence of the cider mill has set in motion a regional apple explosion. I am leaving the wildings on their own in the lower pasture but otherwise when they pop up here or there, I use them to propagate more tame apples. Wild apples are well and good but we do not disdain all the wonderful offerings that people have tamed over the millennia. There is always another apple that is so sweet or so spicy or so juicy that we want it for our mix, so we often trade scions and graft the new one onto an available wild stock. Now this practice will be frowned upon or downright disdained by pomologists because it does not participate in the science or acquired knowledge of the profession. All the tame apples that you might buy from fruit nurseries have been grafted onto rootstocks that are named and known for specific characteristics. There has been a wealth of scholarship and energy invested in finding or developing these rootstocks and there is much acreage devoted to growing them for the industry. When you graft onto a wild stock, you are making a leap (a small one) into the unknown. However, we are talking about homesteading here not about industrial agriculture so small such leaps add to your entertainment factor. You get to watch and anticipate for years waiting to see how tall this one will be; what shape it will take; how distinct the apples might be from the mother tree etc. We have even 'tamed' our own apple. That is, we named it, grafted it and have given it to others. It's a triple crown winner – you can eat it, juice it or make cidre with it. It has tannin, spice and acid and it's as good as any classic English cider apple. The 'South Washington Chicken Coop". It's bound to be famous one day.

Grafting seems like a highly skilled or even esoteric proposition but really it's something anybody can do. Just be prepared for a goodly number of failures. Even after you know what you are doing, not every graft will take. You can graft onto a stock not much bigger than your pencil sized scion or you can 'top graft' into a large branch or trunk of a tree that you would prefer to sport different apples. I once grafted 26 scions onto a tree that was very vigorous but produced the smallest, gnarliest, sourest apples in creation. I sliced all the major branches at 3" or 4" diameter and put two or three scions into each one. There are plenty of books about grafting so I won't go into details here but there is one tip that when I started doing this, it increased my success rate considerably. That involves making a little cone out of duct tape and stick it to the top of the scion so that it is watertight and then keep it topped off with water until it starts to leave out. If a top graft really takes well, it can grow three feet during its first season and begin producing a few apples in its third season.

Even an orchard of just five or six trees can offer you a complete diversity of apples. One that ripens super early like a Redfree or Yellow Transparent that will satisfy your long summer of apple craving and then quickly turn to mush unless you sauce or turn them into vinegar. Then one that ripens on into September like a Duchess. Then two prime mid-season varieties like Cortland and Liberty which will keep in your root cellar into December. Then finally a genuine keeper like Gold Rush or Rhode Island Greening that won't ripen until it's been in storage for a couple of months and you can still use in May.

I am often asked the question – "Which apples make good cider? My answer is there is no answer. Your 'good' cider might be my swill and vice-versa. If you like the apples going into it, you will undoubtedly like the cider. Taste all the varieties you are picking and mix and match. A blend is usually more interesting than a single apple cider. Most main stream commercial apples all by themselves will yield a very lackluster jug. It pays to be careful. It's very easy to get too sour. Even making hard cider where a bit more acidity is a good thing, one can go too far without realizing it. A fifty gallon batch that I had just squeezed and then thought was too sour for direct consumption, I decided to put into a barrel and go hard with it. But even then, it still puckered more than you'd like so I thought to jack the whole barrel feeling that might solve the problem. Apple jack is something I've done for the same reason the bear went over the mountain however I heartily don't recommend it. It was a direct route to apple palsy back in the day when it provided the easiest way to a cheap drunk. Apple jack is concentrated alcohol by freezing just as whiskey is concentrated by distilling. In both cases, you are removing some of the water but if distilling is done correctly, the bad stuff, the stuff that eventually gives you a palsy, is taken out with the 'heads' and 'tails' and discarded. However, it's all still there in apple jack. My method at the time was to ferment the barrel in the house to keep it warm and move it right along and then in late January or February when an artic high pressure system settled in for two weeks during which time the nighttime temperatures went to $-30°$, I rolled the barrel outside to let it freeze before opening the spigot permitting the alcohol to run out and leaving the water ice behind. From a fifty gallon barrel, depending on how cold it became, you'd get about fifteen gallons of jack. How did that batch turn out? Terrible. Not only had the sour intensified even more but it now smelled like fingernail polish. Fifteen gallons of fingernail polish which I couldn't bear to throw away, so I put it up into miscellaneous juice jars and stashed them in a back corner of the root cellar. They stayed there for years. Every once in a while, we would bring one out to see if we had forgotten what it was like. It remained a man killer and we left it to its fate. The caps started to rust and the jars even rode out the house fire ensconced in the root cellar, which then left them coated with soot. This is leading up to a happy ending of the sad story of the cider which nobody wanted to drink and the hero was an old friend of ours who was a mason and a magician in stone who decided to answer the western call of the wild and move to Montana where, according to what we could decipher, he lived on antelope jerky and whiskey. He showed up years later, looking like his diet agreed with him, and stated that his reputation with the boys in Montana would take quite a hit if he didn't get back there with some Vermont 'hooch' in tow. We were his last hope. Didn't we have something of that description? Umm, well we do have this fingernail polish that we have been avoiding for fifteen years and you could try it just so you know we are not lying. We watched him closely as he tossed down a fingerfull. His eyes lit up and he declared that it was just perfect. He always was on the wild side, but at that point we figured his limited diet actually had sent him over the edge. So I poured myself a teaspoon and whadayaknow but he was right! The bad stuff had transmogrified and that neglected and abandoned apple jack had turned into sherry.

He took it with him and if there was a breakout of apple palsy in Montana, we never heard about it. That was the end of my experimentation with apple jack but it's not quite the end yet of our discussion about apples. There are many other things you can do with apples and cider. You can make cider syrup just like you make maple syrup. Except that cider has a much higher sugar content than maple sap so instead of boiling a ratio of 40 to 1, you only need to boil away seven gallons to get one of cider syrup. Cider syrup, sometimes called 'Boiled Cider', comes out black colored and is I'm betting, the most scrumptious treat you've ever had on vanilla ice cream. If you keep simmering the cider beyond the syrup stage, you will have yourself some cider jelly. It's important to just simmer the whole time so that the pectin in the cider is not destroyed, otherwise instead of jelly, you'll end up with a kind of taffy. You can also make cider champagne. We put it into champagne bottles, wire a cork down and bring it out to blow the cork for festive occasions. This involves pressing a judicious mix of apples, fermenting the cider with some honey in a carboy and bottling it before it has finished completely fermenting. If you bottle it too late, you get no pop: if you bottle it too early, you will explode the bottle or blow the cider all over the room. You can play it safe by waiting until the bubbler is quiet and add a quarter teaspoon of sugar to each bottle or play it more playful and count bubbles. This is underground knowledge – it's time to bottle when the bubble count drops to one every 40 seconds. Or, if you prefer science, bottle when the hydrometer says 1.015. Cider champagne tastes better than Champagne champagne and unless you add more honey or sugar to the ferment, the alcohol level is reasonable at around 6%. This delightful beverage does not ever seem to go off once bottled. In fact it just seems to get better. We have had bottles that were 15 years old and the color had gone from light to dark amber and the flavor had become smooth and rich.

There are infinite variations that come under the heading of 'hard cider'. The above champagne would be one of them however it would be only a distant relative to many a trial to which I have been subjected at the cider mill. Greenhorn and even long time hard cider makers are always bringing a sample of their 'best' for me to try. I don't insult anyone but after they are gone, it is a rare bottle that I don't pour onto the ground. Either it has a funky phenolic flavor or the alcohol level has been pushed too far by adding sugar. One man used to make a 50 gallon barrel each year to which he added 50 pounds of sugar. That's more sweet than the yeast can digest so the consistency was syrupy while the alcohol was as high as the yeast could take it under the circumstances.

Apples don't stop giving at the cider mill. The whole apple lends itself in many ways for your eating pleasure. Of course you can eat them in hand from late August to early May and the more varieties you have, the more interesting that becomes. You can eat them baked – cored with cider syrup in the center. You can eat them stewed in maple syrup. You can eat them sauced – out of the canning jar for early apples and fresh out of the root cellar for later apples. You can eat them dried – slice them like potato chips and spread them on a rack above the cook-stove and keep them forever after in a canning jar. Eat those straight as a snack or stew them in apple juice or make a dried apple pie! Soak them in apple juice and surround them with cider syrup and bake. You can feed apples to your kids as peanut butter boats. You can get into the old recipe books and make apple cake, apple crisp, apple pan dowdy, apple brown betty on and on. And if you made too much sauce, you can convert some of it into apple butter by continuing to simmer until it turns thick and spreadable. And then, you can keep going and make apple leather. You do that by spreading a cookie sheet with sauce and putting it into a warm oven until it dehydrates and you can cut it into squares and give them to your kids for their favorite snack. Lastly, you can always have your horse come running to the pasture fence if she knows you'll have an apple in hand. And don't forget the chickens – they love apples in the winter so they get every apple out of the root cellar once it gets spotty and turns soft. That helps to keep their eggs attractive in the midst of winter.

Let's get back to the subject of pruning once again. I intimated previously that I don't do a lot of pruning. The mainstream message on this seems to come down to – 'If you want to have apples, you have to prune your trees.' This is not true. Apple trees during their prime bearing years want to make apples and only under sad circumstances will they not. They want to make apples just as you, whether you realize it or not, want to make babies. I don't prune the massive wild trees unless one is putting out so many water sprouts that I can't climb through the jungle. However I do prune the tame trees to some extent. If there are two branches rubbing; if there is a diseased branch; if I want to encourage a vertical sprout to become the tree's leader; or if I just have a vision of how a certain tree might look. There is one particular situation where you might want to resort to radical surgery and that could be called restorative pruning. An old tree, having been sitting untended and unloved for years, will go senescent and refuse to produce any more apples. By cutting off its top, you will wake it up and shock it back into awareness. How severely you go about this is your call – you might want to spread it out over several years. Be warned that once you do this, the result will be a hysteria of vertical shootings and you had better make reservations to keep working on those shoots for years to come. Hitting the same tree with a ton of nitrogen fertilizer along with some very scant pruning will also wake it up but without the resultant hysteria. But basically once a tame tree gains some stature and starts to really produce, I just make sure it has plenty of nutrition. A well grown apple tree will produce so many apples that if you

302

are looking for perfect ones for eating or keeping, you will always be able to find enough for that purpose and the rest you can shake down for cider. If you are selling eating apples, it's a whole different ball game. But on the homestead a different mentality reigns. That holds true also for spraying insecticides. Hypothetically if the apple maggot or the codling moth or the plum curculio get to 60% of the apples on a tree and scab gets another 10%, that still leaves you with 30% possible perfect apples. That would probably be more than enough considering that you'll have more than one tree and none of that 70% will go to waste. Although there are certified organic insecticides available and we do keep some of those here just in case, we really never use them on the fruit.

The apple tree is the giving tree and it keeps on giving right to the end. Every year without planning or even particularly trying, I slice up enough apple wood to stoke the fireplace for the winter. Apple wood is very dense and heavy and takes a good while to dry so I leave it out for one year and burn it the next. A branch will shear off under a snow load, or an ancient wilding will finally give up, or after looking crosswise at a particular branch for years, I'll decide to prune it off, so the chunks add up and they are aromatic fruit wood to burn in the fireplace and I always save the biggest piece for Christmas day and I call it the Yule Log.

Sugar Time

It started even before that day at the auction when I watched an old boy drive up in an ancient Ford pickup with a pile of syrup pans in the back. Just living in Vermont it is hard to resist the siren song being broadcast in March when the sun has some real warmth and the snow is starting to melt around the edges - the song being sung that you too can make some maple syrup. Find a maple tree; buy a tap at the local general store; hang some kind of container from it; collect the sap and boil it down.

We were renting the bottom floor of big farm house whose kitchen was all wallpapered with a flowery yellow pattern and we put a two gallon pot on the gas stove and began to boil with the enthusiasm of converts to a new religion. If you're lucky and the sap is very sweet, you might get a cup of syrup from two gallons of sap. That puts the rest of the two gallons into the air as steam into a small wallpapered kitchen and surprise, surprise, the wallpaper will begin to curl up and slough off the wall. It's a hard life being a landlord. Seemingly ordinary tenants will do extraordinary things in your house to your endless dismay and disillusion. We tacked it back up and when it dried, it was stuck to the wall again but looking somewhat rumpled.

Making maple syrup is a seemingly simple process that manifests in endless ramifications and possibilities. However, the first rule is – don't do it in your house. It is definitely an outdoor activity or one that should take place in an unwallpapered shed. Your average gallon of syrup takes 40 gallons of sap to make and some gallons require up to 75 gallons of sap. That's a lot of steam to disappear. However we knew that we were going to get into the disappearing business once we got to Gingerbrook, so when that old boy pulled into the Monday auction with his syrup pans which he said were old but didn't leak, I jumped right in on the bid. They were already 25 seasons used and nobody else wanted them so I became the proud owner of four pans four feet wide and when set end to end, 12 feet long. Maple syrup pans come in an array of sizes and shapes. They seem to start at 16" by 3ft and go to 6ft by 10ft. There was nothing standardized about these pans. Every company had its own designs and sizes. The serious pans sat on arches that ranged from 3ft wide to 3 ½ ft to 4, 5 and 6ft wide, and from 8ft to 10, 12, 14, and 16 ft long. The number of pans used to fill the square footage of each arch also differed between this brand and that. It seems that the old time rigs had more smaller pans and newer ones, no matter what size they are, have just two pans – the front pan or syrup pan which is flat bottomed and the longer back pan, the bottom of which is formed into deep corrugations known as 'flues' A 4X12 was a good sized evaporator for decades but as horse drawn gathering tanks changed to tractor and buckets changed to pipeline, the rigs got bigger to accommodate the increased quantities of sap. Just to flood the pans of a 6X16 before you can light the fire, you would need 150 gallons of sap. Curiously, now the arches are becoming smaller due to the introduction of the reverse osmosis machine. Instead of eliminating the water from the sap by boiling, this machine separates it mechanically allowing you make the same amount of syrup on a smaller rig. Technology has muscled into the maple business in a big way. If you go visiting into the thoroughly modern sugar house today, you couldn't be blamed for thinking that you had just stepped into a nuclear submarine. It's filled with gleaming stainless steel unidentifiable objects, some of them very large, surrounded by pipes, pumps and gauges. Temperature, pressure, level and quantity gauges. This is big business. They are dealing with the sap from many thousands of taps from networks of plastic pipeline extending across the hillsides sometimes for miles. Vacuum pumps used to draw the sap through the lines are now pretty much a standard item. There is a lot of money to be made in maple syrup and there are a lot of people in Vermont involved in the business. For some, the biggest producers, it is their only occupation even though the conditions necessary for the making only last for six weeks in the spring. You could easily sink $100,000 into a new maple enterprise or an all-new upgrade and expect to make back the investment within two or three years.

Needless to say, none of those options are of any interest to me or a lot of other Vermonters who are tapping five trees every spring or five hundred. The back roads that spiderweb the state are generally lined with old maples due to the foresight of past generations who were looking for easy collection paths. During sugar time, you will see buckets hung from those trees and folks collecting into a tank on the bed of their pickup; or there are plenty of people that like to collect sap with a team of horses; and there are others who only tap two hundred but run the sap into their holding tank with pipeline and a vacuum pump. Back in the day of course everybody collected with horses because just about everybody was a farmer and their horses did it all. An amazing fact is that last year (2013) syrup production was only about one half of what it was in 1860. 3.25 million gals vs. 6.6 million. The key difference was the number of producers involved. Back then every single little farm made some sugar principally because it fit into their calendar cycle. Winter work in the woods was over and spring work in the fields had yet to begin and sugar time overlapped with mud time so you couldn't go anywhere and instead of hunkering down to wait it out, why not make some maple sugar?

If you are following the precepts of the Homesteader's Bible, you do not go out there and plunk down $100,000 to get started making maple syrup. We worked our way up reinvesting earnings to purchase used equipment or scrounging and finding abandoned stuff and over the seasons we put together an operation that is surely not the envy of the maple world but has sufficed to yield us many hundreds of gallons. After steaming off the wallpaper in the rental kitchen, we moved on to Gingerbrook where the first spring we set one of the auction pans on top of some cinder blocks in the center of the octagon which was then only defined by its foundation walls. Those four pans were made from 'english tin' which is actually formed steel with a tinned surface. In this case, the tinned surface was invisible because one, it had been burned off, and two, it was covered with 'niter'. Niter is the catchall term for the mainly calcium and potassium precipitate which leaves the syrup as it boils and collects in the filter or hardens on the surfaces of your pans. It's the same phenomenon that happens in your kettle if you have 'hard' water. Pans like these are now no longer made in favor of stainless steel because they contained lead solder. We didn't consider that at the time but so that you will feel better about this, I will tell you that later on we had lead tests done and they came back negative, the explanation being that the persistent niter covers and seals the solder. The recommendation is to never use the typical acid cleanser on a pan like this in order to preserve the niter. The design of those pans was such that the backmost pan was 4'x4' with drop flues, the next pan was 4'x4' with small 2" raised flues and the last two were 2'x4' flat pans set cross ways. They were all divided into channels so that the sap, having entered in the back had to wend its way along 40 feet of channel losing water and gaining density before becoming syrup in the front half of the front-most pan. This particular design was just one of many possibilities that manufacturers had devised over the years and I modified and discarded and substituted by and by as pans came apart or as I thought of some better combination with other pans that became available.

We made a few gallons that first spring despite being surprised by the melting snow creating a pond inside the octagonal foundation so that I had to raise the grates a few bricks higher in order to keep the fire above water. The next spring we were able to set up the entire 12ft of pans in a cutout down by the road. I had discovered or uncovered an arch in the vicinity that was lying upside down in some brush, resurrected it and installed it along with the pans. Its cast iron doors were buried in the earth alongside and were still good but the arch measured only 3' wide so we boiled for a few seasons with 6" of pan hanging over each side. I also found a 500 gallon round-bottomed holding tank in a sugar house that was long abandoned and just about caved in. So add to that a bunch of old buckets and covers, and a bucket full of cast steel taps, the like of which you could pick up easily at sales and auctions, and we were ready to get into maple syrup production. Those cast taps, or spouts, or spiles were produced by the thousands in dozens of individual designs. Many of the designs were patented because of some idiosyncratic quirk and today they are searched for by collectors who buy, sell and trade to stock personal museums. The oldest sap buckets were made of tinned steel rolled at the top around a wire rim. They were all rusty brown on the outside and shiny tin on the inside and usually came crammed into each other in piles of 25 or 30. Historically the next round of buckets were galvanized and again, each manufacturer had his own style. We acquired more hundreds of those of different styles each stacked on top of its fellows. We hung the buckets along the road and around the corner onto the lane and as we acquired more buckets, we just extended farther up the hill. The lane goes over the ridge and down the other side for about a mile and it is lined with maples the whole way but we never went quite that far. Mickey and Maud provided the motive power to bring the sap to the evaporator. To start with I strapped a 75 gallon cider barrel to the sled and they pulled that but as soon as I could find a metal gathering tank that held 120 gallons, we abandoned the barrel and those little mule warriors pounded that load up and down, back and forth, empty and full.

It doesn't get any better gathering sap buckets than it does with horses, mules or oxen. Once they get the idea, they will follow you along while you forage ahead with your five gallon pail. They might stand where they last stopped and once your pails are full and you click your tongue, they will come along on their own. It sure beats using a tractor which either requires its own driver or you jumping on and off while you put up with the noise and the fumes. From what I've already told you about M&M, you might be feeling a little skeptical about these claims right now and you would have good reason because we would never be quite sure that they would stop and wait. The closer we got to home, the more they just wanted to go the whole way. We usually pre-empted them by staying ahead and stepping in front of them at a stopping place. If occasionally they decided not to come when you clicked, one of the kids would run back and urge them forward. It also doesn't get any better than doing it with kids. It was always an adventure for them as well as hard work – lugging pails through the snow with however much sap they wanted to handle; gathering their favorite trees and commenting how this one never has any sap and that one is overflowing today; working around M&M making sure they were steady and feeling that the job they were doing was important. The children also devised jobs for themselves when we were firing. They would skim the scum off the boiling sap in the back pan and feed the 'underfire'. The underfire was their own creation. It was started on the live coals that fell through the grate and maintained with great fervor with scraps and twigs and loose bark which littered the landscape while I charged the overfire with the big stuff. It was all about red faces and a sense of helping to boil down that sap.

Jo adding last drips, Ben holding siphon; Maya keeping M&M quiet

That operation down by the road went on for several years but there was never any structure built for it. If it rained or snowed into the pans, it hardly mattered adding only a quarter or half an inch of water to the many inches that needed to be boiled off. The location had its advantages however as one year an acquaintance mentioned that he had gotten a job tearing down an ancient house in Chelsea but that he was going to have to pay the dump to get rid of it. We brain-stormed and he trucked back and forth all winter depositing the entire house next to the road just below the sugar rig. That season, the whole house went in through the front doors of the arch and out through the grates and smokestack. From the cedar shingles to the pine flooring and from the doors to the windows and from the posts to the beams and the soffits to the clapboards, it all fed the voracious sap fire. When that sap season was finished and the pans were off the arch, I looked down at the grates to discover that they were fused together with a mass of melted nails. These were 'cut nails' or 'wrought nails' which dated the house to the era before mass produced round nails were available. Wrought nails were blacksmith made out of iron rods that were heated, pointed, cut off and headed in a 'nail header' all with a heavy hammer. A skilled smith could turn out hundreds of these in a day and judging from the evidence on the grates, this house that we turned into maple syrup used up a lot of them. Round nails, better known as wire nails didn't arrive on the scene until around 1900 and cut nails, which were machine made, didn't happen until about 1820 and the village of Chelsea started up in the 1780's so it's possible that this house was an 18th century creation.

It was not something you could count on, having a house to burn every year and besides, once was enough. It was messy and ugly and required a lot of smashing and bashing with an axe but you did need something to fire the evaporator every year and as the operation expanded, you also needed ever more. It takes a lot of wood to keep the sap fire howling. That is why sugar makers are obsessed with efficiency and why they have taken to reverse osmosis machines with such delight. Before RO, the conversation was always about finding a bigger rig, or better pans, or a higher stack or forcing air to the fire with a fan. One man has set up two 4X12s side by side and runs the sap into one, through a joining pipe to the other and out as syrup – all continuously non-stop. Our evaporator now is 16ft long and 4ft wide and I usually boil an eight hour day during which time we go through a cord of wood - 4'x4'x8' (128 cubic ft) - and make about 10 gallons of syrup. I refuse to boil at night and purposely have not run electricity out to the sugar house so if there is more sap, I put it off till tomorrow and the next day till it's boiled out. These are approximate figures and they vary considerably according to the sugar content of the sap and the wind direction and barometric pressure which greatly influence the rate of burn. The fire might be sluggish and reluctant to reach the back pan during a low-pressured warm and misty day and then leap forward when the weather turns high and cool. But if we play with the mathematics of it, we see that the fire eats 16 cu ft per hour and the firewood is 4ft long and approximately 4"x4" square so that gives us 36 pieces per hour to throw into the inferno. However we know that a real wood pile of split 4ft pieces doesn't stack tight and tidy like a bunch of 4x4s, so let's put in a fudge factor and call it 30 pieces per hour. Multiply everything by more or less 15 days of boiling and the result is – a lot of sugar wood.

Where does all that wood come from? The quick answer is – wherever you can get it. The long answer starts with the land clearing operation which occupied us for the first several years.

Opening things up back to the original fence lines and stone walls yielded vast quantities of small diameter poles which kept us in maple syrup for a while. A local saw mill which no longer operates, but which we used extensively, produced huge quantities of slabs that they were happy to give away to sugar makers. As the slabs came off the saw, they were bundled and then secured with steel bands. These bundles were piled by the dozens in the yard and the sawyer would load them into Two-Ton Tony such that one time coming steeply out of the yard, Tony sat back on his tail gate and hung there with his front wheels in the air, but usually we managed to get home with the load and slice into the bundles with the chain saw like cutting bread to accumulate our sugar wood for the season. That was neat and easy and satisfying to utilize a byproduct of one operation to accomplish another. However, easy things have a way of not lasting forever so we moved on to the next and long term stage of working up full sized trees into sugar wood.

I have already mentioned that sugar wood is almost exclusively softwood because you are looking for flame and minimal ash, not a mountain of glowing coals that you would get burning hardwood for hours at a time. An exception to that rule would be for trees such as popple and bass which are very light weight. We burned a lot of popple over the seasons which I searched out especially because I knew their time clock was ticking down and they were starting to die off. Popple maxes out at about 20" diameter and is extraordinarily heavy when green. This explains, when sawn for lumber, why it splits and checks so badly while drying. It has to lose more water than most other woods while drying. I had given up splitting sugar wood to size with axe and maul and wedge when the sheer quantity requirements overwhelmed and had turned to a tractor mounted hydraulic splitter for salvation. I was able to barter syrup every year for the use of both the tractor and the splitter. If the trees were already skidded out, cut to length and piled, I could finish with that splitter in two days. But when it came to those big, bad popple monsters, those were two days of hell. Those were days of swearing and heaving and wrassling those popple sweat-hogs onto the splitter. I cursed them interminably in pig Latin calling them porci persperati and porcus miseratus, feeling much better about things the sillier I latinized them. But even the worst of the popple monsters only offered a limited number of sweat-hogs and as I moved up the trunk to split the many limbs and branches, I would already begin to sing triumphant victory songs about the Battle of the Persperati.

Popple always contributed to the sugar wood stack but the bulk of it was provided by the white pines and balsam firs. First choice every year went to the dead and dying – there are always some to be cleaned up – and then there would be blowdowns and storm damaged that could be cut and split. It happens that within a tight stand of conifers like balsam fir, if one tree keels over in a storm, it will start a chain reaction taking down others with it. And then in following years, that hole in the stand will grow as neighboring trees also give way either snapping off or keeling over having lost their mutual support society. The hole in this case, once opened in the thick Balsam along the gingerbrook, did not regrow the same but gave way to maple, beech and ash rushing skyward competing for the newly offered sunlight. Balsam fir is also not a strong tree and not very long lived, so adding all these factors together, it was always the mainstay providing fuel for the sap fire.

In the early days, we were always running out of wood while the sap was still coming in. We would keep the buckets out there until, and sometimes after, the spring peepers opened up. Some time around April 20, it is called the Frog Run. That syrup often came out like molasses and smelled like slightly old fish while boiling, but we would be scrounging for more wood long before that. Sometimes a call to the sawmill would bring the big truck out through the mud to dump a pile of slabs down by the road. These required M&M and a sled to get to the sugar house. One season, the two boys, Ben and Will, saved the day dragging in dead stuff with M&M while I boiled. In between syrup draw-offs, I would run out with the saw, knock down a few dead hop-hornbeams and run back to stoke the fire while the boys and the mules went to drag them in. The boys were just old enough to pull this off and they acted like they had never had so much fun. For the hop-hornbeam, this was a one-time affair because they have a habit of dying tall and skinny and remaining standing for years before toppling. We cleaned out the inventory within range of the sugar house that season.

Given the steepness of the western hillside and the preponderance of maples there, it was inevitable that we would get around to installing pipeline. Anything is possible I suppose, but the thought of dealing with sap buckets in such terrain sends the Misery Factor gauge off the scale. Gathering sap from buckets is hard work anyway but the year we quit doing that was after the help had grown up and disappeared and the snow was deep and had been subjected to two separate serious thaws. A 'serious' thaw melts the top layer of the snow pack which then refreezes into a crust which is sometimes strong enough to support your walking on it. If you are wading through this snow that has two of these crusts buried somewhere underneath, and you are carrying two pails of sap, at some point you will crash through perhaps one crust and then maybe the other. This gets exceedingly wearisome so after that season, we decided to end our relationship with sap buckets and collect sap with pipeline.

Gravity. There's a word with some weight to it. Isaac Newton used it to describe the attraction that two bodies exert on each other. Like, for instance, the attraction the Earth has for you which, if it were somehow switched off, would leave you to fly into space. We like to use the word to describe why things prefer to move downhill. Farmers who till the soil have always coveted flat land but homesteading in hill country has many advantages that we could call gravitational. Many things here go or go easier because they are gravity assisted. Our water comes off the hill gravity flow. Our firewood comes downhill to the house site and down off the bank into the woodshed. This is much appreciated by the resident equines. Manure goes downhill from the barn to the garden. This is appreciated by me. The haybarn is situated on the highest point so that bales are carried or rolled down to their destination. Apples come in at the top at the cider mill and cider flows out the bottom. The pomace cart rolls downhill full and pulls back easy. We could and have put Buster in neutral at the top of the driveway and ended up in Chelsea four miles downhill without turning the key. This was an irresponsibly entertaining thing to do with children to see how far we could get along the main street before being stopped once again by Isaac Newton. There was always the potential thrill of setting a new long distance record. However the biggest boost we get from gravity comes down the sap lines. Sap lines can be strung in several different patterns but as long as they are pointing downhill and strung relatively tight, the sap will end up in your holding tank. There are days when sap is coming out of the pipeline system and not dripping into the buckets and vice-versa. There is a certain inscrutability at play here. Here are the basic rules put into a ditty long before plastic even existed: "Wind from the north, sap comes forth. Wind from the West, sap flows best. Wind from the south, sap in drouth. Wind from the east, sap is least." Natural systems refuse to always follow man-made rules but usually the above criteria hold true. However wind is not the only factor in play. Air pressure changes influence sap flow. The osmotic pressure within the tree which moves the sap responds to the outside air pressure so that when a high pressure system moves in (wind from the north), wind or not, the sap will begin to flow. But somehow the plastic tube system maintains its own interior pressure disconnected from the exterior. Put a vacuum pump at the end of the pipeline and that changes everything but without that there are those times when you notice the entire system is loaded with sap and it's not moving anywhere – it's like holding your finger on the end of a water-filled straw. With a weather change, the sap is suddenly released and it rushes downhill. It's a closed system so the only explanation is that the maple trees are supplying the pressure pushing the sap out and down.

Really nothing about the flow of maple sap can be predicted or quantified with absolute certainty. You can pontificate all you want with a half-century of experience behind you and the next sap run or lack thereof will prove you wrong. There are 1000 maple trees on our hillside and in the middle of a good run, the sap comes out of the pipe into the tank blasting like a fire hose and there have been occasions when I've gone to bed knowing for certain that the run was over only to find the tank overflowing in the morning, the sap having run all night in temperatures hovering on the freezing mark. There have been other times in the middle of a 'sugar snow' when there was nothing northerly or westerly about it and non-stop sap overflowed again while I was inside reading a book. It's a constant topic of conversation with people predicting how the sap season will go based on criteria of their own devising like for instance: deep snow makes for a good season; or a wet, warm summer has allowed the trees to accumulate plenty of sugar and that will give us a good season; or, the thrips were bad this summer so there won't be any syrup to speak of . . . etc. I'm sure that all and every explanation has its unknowable effect, however it appears to me that the overwhelming determining factor is the day to day local weather in March and April. It's simple – if the weather conditions come on right, the sap will flow and syrup will be made. Of course, the only beings who know what this particular 'right' entails are the maple trees.

The majority of pipeline systems, once installed, are left in place year round. The larger the system, the more likely this is to be true. It's a tradeoff between the amount of work required to maintain the lines versus the work required to put them up and take them down each year. The systems form spiderwebs through the woods and they are susceptible to being knocked down or pulled apart or chewed upon or sun-damaged. One moose that decides to sashay through your sugar bush will create an incredible mess. Deer and squirrels can do their part and falling branches or whole trees going over will create some havoc.

We coil each line which may have 15 to 20 taps on it, attach a number tag to it and put it with its fellows in a pile to wait for the next season in the sugarhouse. The saves the plastic from deteriorating and opens the woods to the chainsaw and sled the following winter. There are still some sugar makers that insist on using only buckets. They aren't necessarily crusty old-timers – let's just call them purists. They are often known for specially making 'fancy' syrup. Despite the wide spread adoption of plastic sap lines, there are several drawbacks inherent in their usage. One big one is that it's almost impossible to keep them clean. You can run water through them at the end of the season. You can add cleansers to the water. You can buy a specialized machine to pump them clean with high pressure. Try as you will, the lines resist ever again being factory clean. This doesn't actually matter for most syrup because the sap is boiled for so long but if you are set on making fancy, your sap has to be pristine. Sap buckets do scrub clean and you can be assured of fancy quality sap, all other factors being right. Another drawback isn't so much with the lines but with the reverse osmosis procedure attached to the lines. With an RO it is theoretically possible to make syrup as clear as water just by successively concentrating the sap until it reaches the density of syrup. That product wouldn't taste anything but sweet. The unique maple flavor and color come from prolonged exposure to heat. ROed syrup hasn't been exposed to the fire as long so the carmelization isn't as intense. It has been known to change color in storage.

There are homestead possibilities for lowering the expense of setting up an evaporator. Making your own pans is a theoretical possibility but one best left to the professionals. Used pans are always available, however you could make your own arch, stack base and stack. A good used arch, not even considering a new one, would cost you several thousand dollars. So to make your own, the most unusual possibility would be an arch made of stone, concrete and fire brick Made to fit your pans, it couldn't get any better than this. I have seen one of these deep in the woods surrounded by 100 years of trees but as solid as ever. I did not do this because of the damp soil next to the Gingerbrook wanting to lift and move when freezing. The next possibility is to put one together starting with the cast iron pieces scavenged off an old one. That would include the front, the back and the doors. The body can be put together with angle iron, tin roofing and a torch.

Homestead Solutions #9

Syrup Stack

We have discussed the economics of getting started making maple syrup – how it's possible to sink uncountable thousands into a brand new setup and how it's also possible through judicious searching or just plain luck, to cobble something together that will work for you and not destroy your bank account. There are not many sugaring items that you can actually make for yourself but one that I have done and saved $800 in today's prices (that is if you are not buying stainless) is the stack, the stack base and the stack cover.

In order to draw well, the stack needs to be as high as or higher than the arch is long. In this case, that would be 16+ ft and that can be accomplished by stacking five 30 gallon syrup drums measuring 18" diameter by 3ft long on top of a 5ft stack base. To do this, you'll need to make a 15ft four-sided scaffold to sit on the sugar house roof and be guyed off in four directions. That can be done with slim poles. The drums are held together with levered barrel clamps and the whole thing is kept from falling over by wiring it to the scaffold. The barrel clamps allow you to easily replace a rusted out drum – a difficult proposition if they are welded together. The stack base can be fabricated with 4 pieces of metal roofing, tin snips and some screws. The stretcher is needed the force the base into the right shape and size to slip over the lips of the cast iron arch end piece. The cover which is necessary for keeping out the snow and rain to prevent the bottom of the arch from rusting out, is then made from the end removed from a 50 gallon drum and brazed to a hinge at the top of the stack and controlled with two lengths of hanging wire.

Stack Made from Barrels

Stack Base

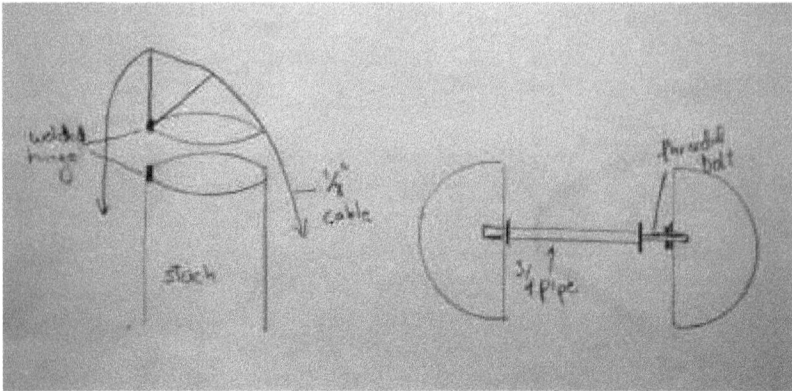

Stack Cover and Stretcher

Isn't it cruel, drilling holes into maple trees? Someone once asked me that and I replied: how does it compare on the cruelness scale to plucking leaves off a lettuce plant and eating them? I feel that plants are sentient beings on some level but knowing that about other beings more obviously sentient doesn't stop us from doing all sorts of 'cruel' things with them. Throughout the history of Europeans making maple syrup, the level of damage and the size of the holes have slowly but surely diminished as people have become more aware of the cumulative damage a tree might absorb and as new technologies have appeared. Originally the colonists followed the example of the Indians, took a hatchet and chopped a cavity into the side of the tree where the sap could accumulate and be scooped out. After a while, some unknown genius came up with the idea of using spouts and buckets. Both were originally made of wood. I came upon a hand carved wooden spout which requires a 1" hole drilled to accommodate it. More time passed and metal buckets became available along with steel spouts and the hole size standardized at 7/16" for many years. Even with the arrival of plastic lines and spouts, the hole size remained the same until recently when 5/16" and even ¼" are the recommended bits. The other factor which concerns the trees is the number of tap holes drilled. As a rule of thumb, it was recommended that you hang one bucket for every foot of diameter, however there are very few four foot wide maple trees and I used to see plenty of trees with four buckets on them. Quite a number of those big old maples have been tapped repeatedly for generations. That would calculate to perhaps hundreds of tap holes hidden inside a tree like that.

The question is: do these tap holes harm the maple trees? Well, a tree like the one above is still alive and apparently well after being drilled out four times a year for 50 to 100 years. As you have seen in the photo of the maple disc shown earlier, each hole leaves a streak of dead wood at least 5 inches above and below within the tree just the width and depth of the hole. You can see this if you split a chunk of tapped maple right through the tap hole.

This old maple is in a good spot with plenty of calcium in the soil otherwise it would be showing some signs of stress from all that dead wood. Within ten years it has closed over the hole and laid on perhaps an inch of new wood leaving a pucker of a scar in the bark. You look for the puckers when selecting where to drill but after maybe 15 years, you might not see it anymore and if you are tapping 3 inches deep, you will drill into dead wood as evidenced by the color change of the shavings. So the problem multiplies but trees in a fortunate spot can handle it. I was shown a small group of 30 trees located between outbuildings on a farm with history which has been tapped for 40 years by the nephew and another 40 years before that by the great uncle and they are now obviously still thriving. However the current sugar maker is now hanging two buckets instead of three and tapping 2 inches deep instead of three. I have cut into smaller maples that have died and seen the dark wood of the taphole scar merge into a dark core of deadwood at the center. That seemed ominous to me so I started varying the depth of hole according to the diameter of the maple – only an inch into the smallest and no more than two and a half for the very biggest. Beyond that, we put only one tap in any tree no matter how big and we move the taps all around and up and down the trunk. In a deep snow year, you can put taps 8ft up and conversely, in a dry year, you can get pretty close to the ground. This is one advantage that pipeline has over buckets – buckets are limited as to how high and how low they can go. It does, however, become an athletic event extracting those high taps after the snow has gone.

Maple syrup is graded by color and only secondarily by taste. If it tastes strange for whatever reason, it is automatically designated as cooking syrup – ie grade C - no matter what the color. Why it would taste strange could be because it was stored improperly and began to ferment; or it was put into an unclean can; or that it was made from sap that had started to ferment and turn cloudy while in the holding tank; or that it was genuine grade C by color and was made from that sap that I mentioned before from the very end of the season which smelled like fish boiling in the pan. Sap is the lifeblood of the tree and is a powerhouse of creative force containing many substances beyond sugar all which make it a desirable target for invisible critters borne on the wind. It needs to be kept cold, clean and boiled soon or it quickly will begin to become lunch. However not to worry because most syrup does not fall into this category and there is plenty that is graded C because of color alone which tastes just fine. The color gradient for syrup is a pretty good indicator of taste but not always. I have bought syrup over the years from different producers so I've had the opportunity to taste and reject syrup that was dark and was indistinguishable from sugar water and syrup that was light and tasted like some unnamed tropical fruit. There is a wide variation of tastes which I attribute to something similar to the French wine concept of 'terroir'. History and tradition figure in to the way syrup is priced. It has always been that lighter syrup is worth more. Why is this? Probably because there was always less of it due to the limiting conditions necessary to make it. Fancy syrup is usually only made from the earliest sap runs of the season when the sugar content is high and the mineral content is at its lowest. As the season progresses, the syrup generally colors darker as the sap comes in with more enzymes and minerals. It is these additions to the sap which give dark syrup its more robust maple flavor. From the very beginning when we began to sell our extra syrup, we decided to sell all grades for the same price. The traditional pricing system didn't make any sense to us. Some people prefer lighter and some darker – why should one be charged any more than the other? In the intervening years, the whole industry has been slowly coming around to the same idea. Dark syrup has become more desirable for its intense flavor and consequently the price differential has narrowed to very little. One more factor is probably at work and that is the prevalence of space age syrup operations has made for the production of a higher percentage of fancy. With sap that has been RO'd, it would spend less time over the fire and therefore likely to syrup out a lighter color.

The question might arise as to why syrup makers are called sugar makers and why is the syrup season known as 'sugar time'. Cultural tradition dies hard because back before industrial systems began supplying cans and jugs tailor-made for packaging maple syrup, the available alternative was to turn it into bricks of hard sugar. These could be stored forever and shipped easily and historically were in great demand before sugar cane production in the Caribbean islands overwhelmed the market with cheap white sugar. Of course, plenty of maple sugar is still produced but not in bricks and just hard enough to melt in your mouth. To get to sugar, you just keep boiling the syrup, driving off the remaining water until all you have left is crystal. The longer you boil it, the harder the sugar, until it solidifies onto the bottom of your pot and starts to smoke. You keep track of the consistency by way of a thermometer. At our altitude of 1500ft, water boils at 209° so syrup boils at 216° and in order to make those melt-in-your-mouth maple leaves which I do up every Christmas, you watch the thermometer as the temperature rockets up to 235° then off the stove with it, whip it briskly and spoon it into the rubber molds before it solidifies. If you are looking for candy on which to break a tooth, you can take it up to 260°o or so before it would start to burn.

Besides drowning your pancakes in it, maple syrup can be used as a sugar substitute in many different situations which I will not bother you with here except to say that it can't be beat poured over your bowl of vanilla ice cream. One particular though which I like is hot cocoa with syrup and without milk. Put however much cocoa you wish into a cup and mix just enough syrup into it with a fork until you have a uniform paste, then pour in boiling water and continue to whisk with the fork and you will end up with something that tastes terrific and froths and feels like cappuccino.

If you get to the point where you are making enough syrup to supply a store, things begin to get fussy. One of the joys of homesteading is that you do not have to keep any customers satisfied. So branching out into the world of retail shenanigans requires a bit of compromising. One customer might come looking for grade B in a pint plastic jug, while another wants medium amber in a half gallon jar. If you are going to supply one, you've got to supply them all. That requires putting out three color grades in three different sizes in two different containers. We put all our own syrup into glass canning jars and also sell it that way believing that glass makes the most righteous container but most tourists prefer those handsome plastic Vermont jugs. So its grades B, Dark, and Medium in pints, quarts and half-gallons in glass and plastic – that adds up to 18 different containers to hot-pack with syrup

Maple syrup is pure carbohydrate and carbohydrates are fuel to burn either in your body or in other hot situations such as when your syrup is separated from a raging fire by a mere 1/8 inch of steel. The temperature beneath that steel may reach 2000oF and things can go awry very quickly if systems break down. I have heard tell of an entire front pan bursting into flame as the incoming sap flow slowed. The temperature rocketed up, the syrup boiled down past sugar and the whole thing ignited – all within minutes. This has not happened to me but I have come close to meltdowns when high spots on the pans have started to smoke and scorched leaving a carbonized circle behind. Every time a pan is overheated, it will rumple and dimple making it even more susceptible to being overheated again. We have had mad panic attacks in the sugar house running for water from the brook in order to avert a disaster. You can see also why the pans have to be perfectly and completely level. The back 12ft of the arch is set on heavy bolts that can be threaded up and down and adjusted to level before each day's boil. However we have seen how fast syrup can ignite several times by failing to supervise five gallon pots of syrup heating on the cook stove. They will sneak up on you and suddenly erupt, boil over, sizzle across the hot steel surface and burst into flame. In this case, you lift a lid and with a metal spatula, scrape the flaming gobs into the fire box and open a vent in the dome to evacuate the smoke. Stuff happens. We know this because we read it on bumper stickers. But really is doesn't happen all that often. There are thousands of people making syrup every year and the potential for disaster always lurks close by but beautiful syrup keeps pouring with hardly a hint of trouble.

What time is it, Bob?

It's sugar time.

But I thought …

Yep, it's mud time

Now what time is it?

Its frog time

What time is it, Bob?

It's the trilling of the toads

And now?

Its dandy flower time

What time is it now?

Its black fly time

But it was just …

Now it's spring time

How about now?

Its apple blossom time

Now?

It's planting time

What time is it, Bob?

Its deer fly time

Now it must be ..?

It's summer time

What…?

Don't ask. Its hoe down time.

What time is it, Bob?

It's cider time.

Already?

It's fall.

What time is …?

It's leaf peeper time

Who …?

They're gone. It's harvest time.

But …?

Its November – its the monkey's raincoat.

Now, Bob?

It's snow time.

What time is it, Bob?

It's winter time

Once Upon a Dream

Invariably at high school graduation ceremonies, the featured speaker will say – "You can be whatever you want to be." The audience absorbs this stoically as one of those given American truths but realistically we all know that this statement is patently not true. However we also know that the ideas of having hope and following your dreams have power and that even though these teenagers are not likely to be nuclear physicists or professional athletes or multimillionaire stock traders, that power can carry them beyond themselves. The age-old virtues of hard work, tenacity and luck can still propel a dream but many a dream gets hamstrung by lack of finance. If one wanted to farm, a life style that wouldn't seem to require a college degree in higher mathematics, she or he would either have to inherit the whole thing, or have a fortune set aside to buy into it, or have a blood-brother relationship with a generous bank that would finance the whole show up front with a high power mortgage. That is if the farming were to be done on the industrial/commercial model in which just to get started you would need a couple of tractors, mowing machines, tedders, rakes, or combines, plows, discs, silage choppers etc. The list is long and the expense, even if you buy used, is very high. It has been done before and will continue to be done by some but the toll is high financially and psychologically. Of course just merely living takes its own toll and any life takes energy and gives back satisfaction in varying proportions but the life style portrayed in these pages is at least one which can be embarked upon without selling your soul to a bank. How does one get started then? You need to buy land and that takes money. You need to keep buying stuff all along until you get built up to the point when you're seeing some income, and that takes money. You can't put down roots and build a life without owning your own property. The ethics of private property are not debated in America and the beauty of it is that you can do whatever you wish to that piece of land and the beast is exactly the same. We were determined not to carry a mortgage – not to have to produce money on schedule. We knew that this would inevitably pull one of us away from the homestead in order to come up with that payment. It's obvious that you can't materialize a homestead at a promising location out of nothing, so if you were to keep out of the clutches of the banks, you would either be fueled by savings or family money or a combination of both or for a long shot chance, you might get help from a land trust which likes to marry vacant farmland with prospective farmers.

However you might manage the beginning, once you are on the spot, you'd want to follow the dictates of the Homesteaders Bible, some of which have been discussed herein, and attempt to divorce yourself from the money economy. This would not be impossible but highly unlikely. We don't claim to have done that completely ourselves but just always keeping it in mind helps to influence you to try to do things for yourself. It's the homesteader's mantra – do it yourself. It's the joy of your existence and the bane. It leads to the best of times and the worst. The challenges are infinite – from baking bread with home-milled flour to chopping mortises in spruce poles – and the more you learn, the more you don't know and knowing what you don't know is the spice of life. If you are satisfied with mere competence and don't need to attain mastery in every farm, garden or household skill, then you can take care of this one and roll on to the next.

How to do things is the mainspring that drives the homesteading life. Starting from scratch your life parallels that of a newborn. Her existence is all about learning to do things – use a spoon, tie shoelaces, read and write, make a bed, drive a car – but by the time most have reached adulthood, the necessaries have been covered and for anything else you might need, you hire and buy. But if you're not hiring or buying and you've got an entire world to create, then you're bound to keep learning to do things. Things you don't learn from your neighbors or from 'how-to' books, you just have to figure out yourself. And figuring it out for yourself is where the real fun lives. Some expert might drop in while you are in the middle of your version, check it out and burst out laughing: "What the hell are you doing" and then tell you how this problem is usually solved but you're enjoying yourself and years later when this problem reoccurs, you won't remember what he said and do it again as if for the first time. Country people are happy to pass time talking and a lot of time talking about 'how to do things'. Advice, good, bad and ugly, is readily available. Do want to know what kind of file is best for sharpening an ax; or the best fertilizer for blueberries; or when to harvest your potatoes? Bring up the subject and the answer will be forthcoming and perhaps years later you will have improved upon that suggestion and come back to inform your informant that, for instance, aluminum sulfate is not really the best fertilizer for blueberries.

Because there is always something to do, doing things becomes your religion and how to actually do those things your obsession. They are the strategies and challenges of everyday living. However not to forget that this living takes place in a realm of beauty. Your time is your own. There is no boss directing your day. You can dream and dawdle and watch the clouds. There is a lot to learn and admire watching clouds. The tree-clad hills defining our horizons are forever changing colors following the sun shadows and the seasons. There is always a raven croaking through the sky in the distance. The wind is your constant companion even when it's not there creating an internalized baseline to your background awareness. The rustling of leaves is one of those things you don't notice and don't miss until you're out there on one of those days in mid-August and you stand up to wipe off the sweat and realize the world has gone completely silent – not a sound in the entire universe and you feel like you might feel walking into Chartes cathedral. You are doing things but doing them in a cathedral, that is unless you have ignored the Misery Factor or unless you find yourself under an old truck cursing with a transmission on your chest.

Automobiles are arguably the curse of the homesteader. Unless you have somehow staked out an urban homestead cultivating gardens in empty city lots, you are going to need an automobile – in fact several automobiles. In a very rural state like Vermont interlaced with dirt roads, there is no bus, taxi or any other semblance of mass transit for anybody living out of the city. You need a car. You need two cars or a car and a truck or better yet, a car, a pickup and a heavy truck. Automobiles represent a serious drain on your resources and an unwanted interface with governmental bureaucracy. You've got to pay for your driver's license, for your vehicles plates, for compulsory insurance and that's on top of buying the vehicle plus fuel, oil, tires and maintenance costs. Just contemplating the weight of this curse causes me to admire the Amish lifestyle even more. Getting around with horses, buggies, wagons and sleighs was what everybody used to do less than 100 years ago but it's a lot easier and safer to do on the flatlands and rolling hill country of Pennsylvania and Ohio.

The most irritating aspect to running automobiles on the homestead is that you can't carve a carburetor out of maple – or a piston, or valve or a distributor cap. You have no choice if you are going to keep vehicles running but to buy these parts and join in on the global economy. However there are things to do to limit the pain. First, get a set of mechanics wrenches. Second, buy a shop manual for your vehicle of choice. And third, have an oxy-acetylene torch on hand. Yep – its do it yourself maintenance and repair and the rule is – the older the vehicle, the more you will be able to do with it. For instance, if you could possibly find a truck like Buster (54), after a bit of study and knuckle busting, you would be able to fix just about anything including rebuilding an engine. But any automobile younger than a 70s model that is run by a computer would limit your possibilities considerably. However you would be surprised at how much you can do to keep your hard-earned cash out of the hands of the local mechanic. You can do things like body work and paint – your automobile will look just dandy if you paint it with rustoleum and a brush. Or exhaust systems that can be replaced with the help of a torch. Or broken glass – buy the window and put it in yourself. Or helpless door locks or window cranks – tear the door apart, peer in there, figure out what's gone off and replace it.

Unless you love grease and skinned knuckles, messing with automobiles falls under the heading of 'onerous chore'. If you sensibly refuse to do anything except add anti-freeze and check the oil, then disregard the 'old truck' rule and buy the newest car that you can afford. There is a good chance that it will run for years without you having to think about it. Otherwise you place yourself in the hands of the god of luck when you plunk down $200 like I did for Two Ton Tony (52) who during 30 years of neglect proceeded to disintegrate into an uninspectable shambles ignored by the police but ever the faithful carrier of a thousand loads who always made it home with his cargo.

There will always be unpleasant tasks to procrastinate around and ultimately take care of. But even when walking from one chore to the next or headed back to the shop for a forgotten tool, there are sights and sounds to marvel at. You might stop to watch a bumblebee pushing into a blueberry flower. Or you might wander off track to count the flower buds on the plum trees; or wander a bit farther to check on a couple of newly grafted apple treelings; or pause to wonder is that really the catbird I hear that is newly arrived. Then a flock of geese go over flying low and honking madly to whirl into a nearby pond and by then you have no idea where you were actually going or for what.

We have made a life here on this homestead. We came to this place with an idea and we stayed here. We haven't taken a 'vacation' since we've been here. There is no place we would rather be. We have put a lifetime of labor into this small piece of landscape but not so that a time-traveler would not recognize it. There are a few buildings here that weren't. There are a few more fruit trees and perennial plants. The pastures and other spaces that were cleared originally have been reopened back to their stone walls and fence lines and the only scars on the land are the tilled garden plots. But the forest seems untouched even though several hundred cords of firewood and many a saw log have come out behind mule and horse. And the springs and seeps on the hillside that give birth to the gingerbrook haven't paid any attention to our presence. And though I shoveled a course for the gingerbrook to run freely through the marsh, the wet peat continues to act like a marsh to the delight of the cattails and the red wing blackbirds.

When we came, we had the idea that this land could provide for us. It was 50 acres of abandoned and neglected sidehill. Although that time-traveler might notice some changes in the landscape, he also might miss the most profound transformation and that is in the fertility of the soil. The pastures, orchard and gardens have absorbed uncountable tons of mule, horse, cow, goat, pig, chicken and human manure; thousands of imported bales of hay; a couple of hundred cords worth of wood ash, yearly Buster loads of sawdust and yearly compost piles. We've learned that even the most depleted, leached out soils can be brought back to life and made fertile. And fertility yields wealth. On our scale, this is not wealth as most of America would calibrate it but it has been wealth to feed us and wealth to sell and wealth to build a house and wealth to build a farm and wealth to keep warm and wealth to tell stories.

www.ingramcontent.com/pod-product-compliance
Lightning Source LLC
Chambersburg PA
CBHW051212090426
42742CB00021B/3418